"A superb treatment of important gospel. Carefully researched and the book is also an easy and enjoyable read that laypersons can engage with great profit. That is a remarkable feat, and Charles Quarles has accomplished it with excellence!"

  —**Daniel L. Akin**, President, Southeastern Baptist Theological Seminary

"Here is a work that focuses well on Matthew's presentation of Jesus. It is a biblical theology seen through christological glasses that sees in Jesus' shadow Moses, David, Abraham, Israel, and the creation. It shows well how Jesus' story is ultimately important to all of us. That is well worth reflection in the directions Quarles points us, filling a need that those who study Matthew can be grateful now has been filled."

  —**Darrell L. Bock**, Executive Director of Cultural Engagement, Howard G. Hendricks Center for Christian Leadership and Cultural Engagement; Senior Research Professor of New Testament Studies, Dallas Theological Seminary

"Quarles has authored a wonderful introduction to the theology of Matthew. It is accurate, yet accessible; thorough, yet succinct; true to the text, yet with excellent suggestions for contemporary significance. Abreast of the best of recent scholarship, Quarles wears his academic garb lightly. Highly recommended."

  —**Craig L. Blomberg**, Distinguished Professor of New Testament, Denver Seminary

"This is biblical theology at its finest. Dr. Quarles is closely tethered to the text, attentive to allusions from the Old Testament, and unrelenting in his emphasis on the one-of-a-kind glory of Jesus as God. I commend this book very highly. It will stoke a fire in your heart and create a burning desire to herald the glories of Jesus from the treasures, new and old, in the Gospel of Matthew."

  —**Jason Meyer**, Pastor for Preaching and Vision, Bethlehem Baptist Church

"Using key Old Testament figures and themes as his framework, Charles Quarles summarizes very nicely Matthew's main theological ideas. The book is marked by an admirable combination of biblical exposition and practical application."

—**Douglas J. Moo**, Wessner Chair of Biblical Studies, Chair of the Committee on Bible Translation, Wheaton College

A Theology of Matthew

Explorations in Biblical Theology

Robert A. Peterson, series editor

A Theology
of Matthew

Jesus Revealed as Deliverer, King, and Incarnate Creator

Charles L. Quarles

P U B L I S H I N G

P.O. BOX 817 • PHILLIPSBURG • NEW JERSEY 08865-0817

Printed in the United States of America

ISBN: 978-1-59638-167-4 (pbk)
ISBN: 978-1-59638-653-2 (ePub)
ISBN: 978-1-59638-654-9 (Mobi)

Library of Congress Cataloging-in-Publication Data

Quarles, Charles L. (Charles Leland)
 A theology of Matthew : Jesus revealed as deliverer, king, and incarnate creator / Charles L. Quarles. -- 1st ed.
    pages cm. -- (Explorations in biblical theology)
 Includes bibliographical references and index.
 ISBN 978-1-59638-167-4 (pbk.)
 1. Bible. Matthew--Theology. 2. Bible. Matthew--Criticism, interpretation, etc. I. Title.
 BS2575.52.Q37 2013
 226.2'06--dc23
                                     2013030453

In memory and honor of my precious grandparents

Dr. Chester L. Quarles (1908–68) and Virginia E. Quarles (1915–)

Contents

CONTENTS

Series Introduction

BELIEVERS TODAY need high-quality literature that attracts them to good theology and builds them up in their faith. Currently, readers may find several sets of lengthy—and rather technical—books on Reformed theology, as well as some that are helpful and semipopular. Explorations in Biblical Theology takes a more midrange approach, seeking to offer readers the substantial content of the more lengthy books, while striving for the readability of the semipopular books.

The series includes two types of books: (1) some treating biblical themes and (2) others treating the theology of specific biblical books. The volumes dealing with biblical themes seek to cover the whole range of Christian theology, from the doctrine of God to last things. Representative early offerings in the series focus on the empowering of the Holy Spirit, justification, the presence of God, and preservation and apostasy. Examples of works dealing with the theology of specific biblical books include volumes on the theology of the Psalms and Isaiah in the Old Testament, and books on the theology of Mark and James in the New Testament.

Explorations in Biblical Theology is written for college seniors, seminarians, pastors, and thoughtful lay readers. These volumes are intended to be accessible and not obscured by excessive references to Hebrew, Greek, or theological jargon.

Each book seeks to be solidly Reformed in orientation, because the writers love the Reformed faith. The various theological themes and biblical books are treated from the perspective of biblical theology. Writers either trace doctrines through the Bible or open up the theology of the specific books they treat.

Writers desire not merely to dispense the Bible's good information, but also to apply that information to real needs today.

Explorations in Biblical Theology is committed to being
warm and winsome, with a focus on applying God's truth to
life. Authors aim to treat those with whom they disagree as they
themselves would want to be treated. The motives for the rejection
of error are not to fight, hurt, or wound, but to protect, help, and
heal. The authors of this series are godly, capable scholars with
a commitment to Reformed theology and a burden to minister
that theology clearly to God's people.

Robert A. Peterson
Series Editor

Foreword

AS I READ Chuck Quarles's book on the theology of Matthew, one thought kept returning to my mind: How easily we fail to see what is right in front of our eyes. Nothing captures this idea better than Quarles's story near the end of the book about sitting down with the young man who asserted that all religions were the same. Quarles patiently showed him from the Scriptures that Jesus was truly God. How astonishing it was to learn that this young man was the son of a pastor. Perhaps his father didn't faithfully teach the Scriptures, or perhaps the son didn't listen, but in either case the truth about Jesus was staring them in the face every Sunday.

We can read the Gospel of Matthew for many different reasons, and our motives might be entirely justified and our conclusions eminently reasonable. We might study Matthew to learn about what it means to live a virtuous life, or to discover his perspective on discipleship, or to explore his teachings about eschatology. If those studies don't lead us to Jesus Christ, if we learn about these matters and don't see Jesus more clearly, our study has veered off course. In the same way, there is a lot of talk about the kingdom of God in the Gospels today—and rightly so, for the Gospels feature that topic. Still, we must beware lest the kingdom become more important than the King. We don't rightly understand the kingdom if our study of it doesn't lead us to worship the King.

Quarles's book reminds me of the story in John's gospel of some Greeks who came to Philip and said, "Sir, we wish to see Jesus" (John 12:21), for that should be the goal of every Christian. Or remember the story of Zacchaeus, who wanted to see Jesus so desperately that he forgot about his dignity as a respected and wealthy man (Luke 19:1–10). He ran ahead and climbed into a sycamore tree to see Jesus. Grown men didn't run in the ancient world, and they certainly didn't climb trees! But Zacchaeus didn't care about his reputation; he cared about seeing Jesus.

We see a similar phenomenon in the story of the transfiguration. Peter, James, and John were overcome with what they saw on the mountain. How amazing it was for the disciples to see Moses and Elijah, two of the most prominent and godly men from the Old Testament. Many Israelites would have given virtually anything to see Moses and Elijah. Peter was naturally overcome by the occasion. And as he often did, he blurted out some incoherent nonsense—about building a tent for Moses, a tent for Elijah, and a tent for Jesus. What Peter said was completely wrongheaded, for Moses and Elijah aren't on the same plane as Jesus. Moses and Elijah point us to Jesus; they had prophesied about him. So the divine voice spoke from the cloud: "This is my beloved Son . . . ; listen to him" (Matt. 17:5). The disciples were to listen to Jesus, as the One who fulfills the Law and the Prophets. He was the prophet that Moses said would succeed him (Deut. 18:15). The disciples were stunned and overwhelmed. Perhaps they even fainted. The story concludes with great significance. Matthew closes the scene with these words: "When they lifted up their eyes, they saw no one but Jesus only" (Matt. 17:8). God wanted them to see Jesus only. The focus wasn't on Moses. The focus wasn't on Elijah. The focus wasn't on all three of them together. The focus was on Jesus.

The New Testament is Christ-centered, and Quarles reminds us throughout his learned study of Matthew that the greatness of Jesus is on virtually every page. If we see Jesus and if we know Jesus, then we see God and we know God. Jesus said to Philip, "Whoever has seen me has seen the Father" (John 14:8). Indeed, the goal of all redemptive history is to see God in Jesus Christ. What makes the heavenly city heavenly is God's presence in Jesus Christ. As Revelation 22:4 promises, we "will see his face" and enjoy his presence forever.

In this work Quarles unpacks for us the identity of Jesus in the Gospel of Matthew. I was repeatedly struck with the insight and wisdom pervading this work. Quarles regularly shows us from the Old Testament the significance of what Matthew says about Jesus. We can easily fail to see the connections, since we aren't immersed in the Old Testament, but Quarles rightly demonstrates that we won't truly understand Jesus if we are ignorant of Old Testament antecedents. Quarles is a learned and expert guide, helping us to see the import of what is said about Jesus in Matthew.

We can be grateful that Quarles has given us an intellectual and theological feast. The work is written with wonderful clarity so that the message is accessible to laypeople. Still, the book's message isn't simplistic. Scholars and students will be challenged by the exegetical and theological depth of Matthew's theology. Nor does Quarles simply rehearse what Matthew teaches about Jesus. He exults in it. He leads us to worship. The book has a devotional and spiritual dimension that helps readers to see Jesus. What more could a reader ask for?

Thomas R. Schreiner

Acknowledgments

THE DEDICATION of this book to the memory and honor of my Quarles grandparents is more than perfunctory. I am deeply grateful to follow the rich Christian legacy left for me by these faithful disciples of our Lord. Dr. Chester L. Quarles was a devoted Christian servant who served as pastor, missions volunteer, and Baptist leader. In 1950, he was elected as Executive Secretary-Treasurer of the Mississippi Baptist Convention and served in that office for the next eighteen years until his untimely death. He also served as the first vice president of the Southern Baptist Convention. Grandfather was widely known as a passionate evangelist, gifted preacher, and wise Baptist statesman. Though he died nearly half a century ago, I have never preached in a church in Mississippi, large or small, in which he was not remembered by some aged saint for his powerful messages, his kind and humble character, and his longing to unite Baptists, often beleaguered by controversy, for the sake of bringing the gospel to the nations.

When I began to preach in my early teens, Grandmother recognized that I needed guidance and help so that I would be a faithful workman who correctly handled the Word of truth. She offered me some of the gifts that I count most precious among all my earthly possessions: the remnant of my grandfather's library; the plaque that adorned his pastoral desk, reminding him of the charge of 2 Timothy 4:2, "Preach the Word"; and his old, dilapidated Greek New Testament. That library helped me to discover the riches of Holy Scripture and sparked my interest in biblical scholarship. The verse on the plaque became the theme of my ministry and stirred my longing to be a faithful biblical expositor. It now serves as the motto of the divinity school that I helped to found. That old Greek Testament with its then-strange and indecipherable characters stirred a longing to study the New Testament in its original language that prompted me to major in Greek in college and focus on the New Testament and Greek in my master's and doctoral work. Teaching the Greek New Testament to eager students remains one of my life's greatest joys. I owe that opportunity to the gracious providence of God and to the legacy of my grandparents. I simply cannot thank him or them enough.

I am also deeply grateful for beloved mentors such as Richard R. Melick Jr. and Kendell H. Easley. These two men taught me how to exegete the Greek New Testament and how to construct a biblical theology. Although I never had the opportunity to meet him personally, perhaps no one has contributed more to my understanding of the Gospel of Matthew in particular than R. T. France. I am particularly indebted to France for his keen insights into the Old Testament background of many Matthean themes. France wrote with the mind of a scholar, the heart of a pastor, and the devotion of a faithful disciple. His death last year was a great loss to Matthean scholarship. Like Elisha facing the departure of Elijah, I pray that God will grant a double portion of his spirit to those of us devoted to the study of this gospel.

I am convinced that we do our best work in dialogue with a community of faithful scholars. I thank God for my little community, particularly my colleagues Michael Shepherd and Jason Hiles. Our brief discussions about Old Testament studies and biblical theology have helped open my eyes to new truths in Matthew. My students in the undergraduate program at Louisiana College and particularly in the Biblical and Theological Studies program of the Caskey School of Divinity have asked many helpful questions and offered insightful suggestions that have sharpened my thinking about the Gospel of Matthew. Lucas Moncada, Terry Isles, Wes McKay, and Ron Lindo gave feedback on an early draft of this book, and their comments have been invaluable. I am also grateful for the many ways in which JoAnne Timothy contributed to this book, especially for the tedious work of verifying all Scripture references and quotations.

I am thankful for the family of William Peterson Carter for their generous contributions to the Research Professorship I hold. This professorship ensures that I have time to devote to writing, one of my greatest loves in ministry. I am also grateful for the anonymous donors who give sacrificial financial support to the Caskey School of Divinity. Their faithfulness enables me to train the next generation of biblical expositors in our state.

I express gratitude to my beloved wife, Julie, for her love, encouragement, and support. She is especially patient when writing deadlines approach and I must burn the midnight oil to fulfill my commitments. I am grateful for her hard work in preparing the Scripture Index for the book.

Finally, I thank my editor, Robert Peterson, for his gracious and unexpected invitation to contribute this volume to the Explorations in Biblical Theology series. Throughout the entire process of producing this book, he has been Christlike, kind, encouraging, and patient. His suggestions for revision have strengthened the book significantly. His prayers for me have given me strength to persevere in writing this book in the face of numerous challenges.

Soli Deo Gloria
Charles L. Quarles
March 6, 2013

Introduction

The Doctrinal Anemia of the Contemporary Church

THE MODERN CHURCH suffers from a tragic case of doctrinal anemia. The church has become weakened and sickened by a lack of clear and firm doctrinal convictions. For over a decade, many Christian leaders have sounded the alarm regarding the problem of biblical illiteracy in contemporary Christianity. They often demonstrate this biblical illiteracy, however, by showing that today's churchgoers are unfamiliar with Bible trivia that, though important, are not vital to the soul. Although biblical illiteracy is a serious concern, and the church must take steps to address it, doctrinal anemia is a far more frightening malady. Doctrinal anemia involves ignorance of fundamental truths of the Christian faith that are essential to the salvation of individuals or necessary for the spiritual health of God's people.

For the past several years, I have administered a brief test designed to measure understanding of basic Christian doctrines to over a thousand freshmen entering an evangelical Christian college. Although over 90 percent of these students claim to be Christians, many clearly do not understand the most elementary truths of the Christian faith:

- 78% believe that all people are basically good.
- 65% cannot identify a simple definition of *new birth* in a multiple-choice question.
- 54% think that faith in Jesus is unnecessary for salvation.
- 54% affirm that Jesus forgives believers but deny that he transforms them.

1

- 42% believe that people go to heaven because of their personal morality rather than because of Jesus' sacrificial death.
- 32% do not know that Christianity affirms the deity of Jesus Christ.
- 25% do not know that Christianity claims that Jesus literally rose from the dead.

The test's instructions ask the students to indicate by their answers their perceptions of what Christianity teaches. Thus, the test does not measure the students' personal convictions but instead merely assesses their understanding (or misunderstanding) of the teachings of the Christian faith. The poor scores on the test reflect not rejection of the Christian faith, but basic ignorance of the faith. The results of the test are even more alarming than the statistics above demonstrate. For example, of the 65 percent of students who cannot identify a simple definition of *new birth*, most believe that *new birth* is a reference to reincarnation or transmigration! The data clearly demonstrate that the views of many professing Christians today are more greatly influenced by our culture than by the Holy Scriptures.

In such a spiritual climate, rediscovery of true biblical theology is crucial. No aspect of biblical theology is more important than Christology. Salvation itself is dependent on an individual's understanding of Jesus of Nazareth. Yet alarmingly, some who believe that they are Christians do not know that Jesus is God in the flesh or that he rose from the dead, even though texts such as Romans 10:9 are quite clear that only those who confess Jesus as Lord (a title of deity) and believe in their heart that God raised him from the dead will be saved!

Rediscovery of biblical theology best begins with a rediscovery of who Jesus is and why he came. The Gospel of Matthew is an excellent place to rediscover the biblical view of Jesus. Matthew clearly articulates Jesus' identity as our God, our Savior, and our King in memorable, even gripping, ways. His presentation of Jesus compels careful readers to worship him, trust him, submit to him, and proclaim him.

Part 1

Foundations for a Theology of Matthew

Introduction to the Gospel of Matthew

THIS BOOK is titled *A Theology of Matthew* rather than *A Theology of the Gospel of Matthew*. This implies that the book intends to summarize and describe the theology of an individual by a particular name who served as the author of this gospel. This is possible, of course, only if a man named Matthew actually wrote this gospel. Yet many scholars today contest the claim that this gospel was written by the apostle Matthew. Some theologians seek to evade potential problems in describing the theology reflected in this gospel by placing the name *Matthew* in quotation marks, indicating that *Matthew* refers not to the apostle by that name but to the assumed author, whoever he may have been. This book does not place the name *Matthew* in quotation marks. This book seeks to explore the theology of the apostle Matthew himself. This naturally leads to an exploration of introductory issues related to the Gospel of Matthew. Did the apostle really write this gospel? If so, when, where, and why?

Who Wrote This Gospel?

The Gospels in the New Testament are formally anonymous. Unlike Paul's letters, in which the introduction to each letter identifies Paul as the author, one never finds a statement such as

"Matthew, apostle of Jesus Christ, to the churches" in the body of the Gospels. Yet this is not as significant as it might seem at first. R. T. France has pointed out that most books even today would have to be considered formally anonymous by this standard.[1] Authors rarely identify themselves in the body of the work, unless the work is an autobiography. Instead, they identify themselves on the cover of the book and the title page.

Authors of ancient books sometimes identified themselves by name in the body of their work.[2] In many other instances, however, authors identified themselves only by titles, headings, a preface (called a *proem*), or an inscription at the end of the book called a *colophon*.[3] For the gospel writers, the most important collection of books was the Old Testament. Many of the Old Testament books identified the author and the circumstances of writing only in headings. The gospel writers followed this model. The author's name is disclosed only by the title or heading of the work.

The title *According to Matthew* appears as the heading to this gospel in the earliest manuscripts available today.[4] Later manuscripts elaborate the title to *The Gospel according to Matthew*, to *The Holy Gospel according to Matthew*, or to a similar title. No manuscript evidence suggests that the gospel ever circulated without a title. The titles are definitely very early. From the moment that multiple Gospels began to circulate among the churches, believers would have needed a way to distinguish them, and titles such as *According to Matthew* and *According to Mark* would have been useful, even necessary. If another gospel was in existence when Matthew wrote his gospel, he might have personally assigned the gospel a title to prevent confusion with the other

1. R. T. France, *Matthew: Evangelist and Teacher*, New Testament Profiles (Downers Grove, IL: InterVarsity Press, 1989), 50.

2. See, for example, Josephus, *Jewish War*, 7.11.3 § 448.

3. Josephus identified himself as author in the proem to *Jewish War*, 1.1 § 3. Interestingly, Josephus does not appear to have identified himself as the author of the *Jewish Antiquities* in the body of that work. His authorship had to be inferred by the fact that the earlier work, *Jewish War*, and his autobiography, *Life*, were appended to *Jewish Antiquities*.

4. The codices Vaticanus and Sinaiticus, dating to around A.D. 325 and 350, respectively.

gospel. Consequently, a growing number of scholars suspect that the titles of the Gospels are original.

The earliest preserved testimony regarding the authorship of Matthew's gospel is that of Papias, bishop of Hierapolis, in his *Expositions of the Lord's Sayings*. Although some scholars date Papias's work to the mid-second century, strong evidence suggests that it should be dated to the early second century.[5] Papias received his information about the Gospel's authorship directly from older Christians who had been personally taught by Jesus' disciples. Papias wrote, "Therefore, on the one hand Matthew arranged in order the sayings in the Hebrew dialect; on the other hand, each translated these as he was able."[6]

This statement describes Matthew as one who collected and arranged Jesus' sayings in Hebrew or Aramaic. Some scholars believe that these sayings are the major discourses of Matthew's gospel that are absent from Mark.[7] Others believe that the word *sayings* is used in a broader sense and refers to the gospel as a whole.

Many scholars deny that Matthew or any significant portion of his gospel was first written in Hebrew or Aramaic. They further reason that if Papias was wrong in his comment about the original language of the gospel, we can have no confidence in his statement about Matthew's authorship. This, of course, is not a necessary conclusion. One can be wrong about something, perhaps even many things, without being wrong about everything. Papias could be incorrect about a Hebrew Gospel of Matthew but still correct that Matthew wrote the gospel.

It is also possible that Papias was correct about both the original language and authorship of Matthew's gospel. Rejection of a Hebrew original of Matthew is based on the assumption that the excellent Greek of Matthew's gospel could not have been

5. See Andreas Köstenberger, Scott Kellum, and Charles Quarles, *The Cradle, the Cross, and the Crown: An Introduction to the New Testament* (Nashville: B&H Academic, 2009), 181, esp. n7.

6. Eusebius, *Ecclesiastical History*, 3.39 (my translation).

7. Donald A. Hagner, *Matthew*, Word Biblical Commentary (Dallas: Word, 1993–95), 1:xliii–xlvi.

produced by a translator. But a skilled translator would have been capable of translating an original Hebrew document into Greek of the quality that appears in Matthew's gospel. Numerous early church fathers insisted that this gospel was first written in Hebrew, and as native Greek speakers they were in a better position than modern scholars to judge whether the Greek could have been produced by a skilled translator. Furthermore, features such as the allusion to David in the number fourteen in Matthew 1:17, the comment on the significance of Jesus' name in 1:21, and the significance of Jesus' identity as a Nazarene in 2:23 are meaningful only in Hebrew. This seems to suggest that at least portions of Matthew's gospel, such as the account of Jesus' birth, were first written in Hebrew.[8] Modern scholars are wise to acknowledge that sufficient evidence is lacking to determine with absolute confidence the original language of the gospel. Thus, arguments regarding authorship based on presumptions about the gospel's original language are necessarily weak.

A few clues from the gospel itself support the claim of the title and of early church fathers that Matthew was its author. First, abundant evidence in the gospel shows that the author was a Jewish Christian. Second, only Matthew's gospel indicates that the tax collector named Levi who became one of the twelve apostles was also called Matthew (Matt. 9:9; cf. Mark 2:14; Luke 5:27). The mention of this alternative name could be a personal touch from Levi/Matthew himself. Third, although Mark and Luke use the term *denarius* to describe the payment of the imperial tax, Matthew uses the more precise expression "coin for the tax" (Matt. 22:15–22). The more precise nomenclature might express the expertise of a former tax collector.

By itself, this internal evidence would not be very persuasive. When added to the very early evidence of the title and the testimony of Papias, however, it amounts to rather impressive evidence in support of the traditional view that Matthew is the author of the gospel that bears his name. The evidence in support of Mat-

8. See "Did Matthew Write His Gospel in Hebrew?," in Köstenberger et al., *The Cradle, the Cross, and the Crown*, 182–83.

thew's authorship is sufficiently persuasive that some scholars who previously denied Matthew's authorship of this gospel have now changed their minds and affirm that Matthew had some role in the composition of the gospel.[9]

When Was the Gospel Written?

Many scholars date the composition of the Gospel of Matthew to the mid- to late 80s A.D. This late date is generally based on the assumption that Jesus was not capable of predictive prophecy. Thus, his "prediction" of the fall of Jerusalem in texts such as Matthew 22:7 must actually have been a statement created by the author of the gospel, looking back in time to the destruction of the city.

Notice that this approach to dating the gospel is not based on historical evidence but rather on a modernist worldview that denies the possibility of supernatural revelation. For Christians who believe that Jesus was capable of predicting the future, a date of composition before the fall of Jerusalem in A.D. 70 is entirely plausible. The historical evidence strongly suggests that the gospel was written considerably earlier than these skeptics claim.

Early Christian documents such as the letters of Ignatius (c. 35–110), the Didache (second half of first century or early second century), and the letters of Polycarp (c. 69–155) quote from the Gospel of Matthew. Around A.D. 135, the epistle of Pseudo-Barnabas quotes the gospel as inspired Scripture. The quotation of Matthew by such early sources is best explained if the gospel was written well before the late 80s.

Several features of Matthew's gospel also support a date of composition before the fall of Jerusalem. Matthew is the only gospel to record Jesus' teaching about swearing by the temple or its gold (Matt. 23:16–22). A vow that meant "May the temple be destroyed if I break my promise" would be ridiculous if the

9. Craig Keener, *A Commentary on the Gospel of Matthew* (Grand Rapids: Eerdmans, 1999), 40.

temple had already been destroyed. Similarly, 17:24–27 contains Jesus' instruction that his disciples should pay the temple tax to avoid offending fellow Jews. After the destruction of the temple, however, the Romans continued to collect this tax to support their own pagan temple of Jupiter Capitolinus in Rome.[10] It is hard to imagine that Matthew would have recorded this instruction in a historical context in which paying the tax supported idolatry and was thus a great offense to the Jews. Jesus' instruction about the proper manner in which to offer sacrifice (5:23–24) would also have been most meaningful to Matthew's readers while the temple still stood and sacrifice was still being offered.

Thus, the historical evidence best supports a date of composition before the climactic events leading to the fall of Jerusalem, probably in the late 50s or early to mid-60s. This early date fits within the early church's claim that the apostle Matthew wrote the gospel. The date is also consistent with the earliest specific testimony regarding the date of Matthew, given by Irenaeus, who said that Matthew wrote this gospel while Peter and Paul were preaching the gospel and founding the church in Rome.[11]

Where Was the Gospel Written?

Scholars have proposed many different sites as the likely place of origin for the Gospel of Matthew. Since B. H. Streeter argued that the gospel was written in Syria, most modern scholars have embraced that view. Streeter pointed out that Ignatius, bishop of Antioch, referred to the Gospel of Matthew more frequently than any other gospel. He also detected a reference to Antioch in Matthew 17:24–27, which equates a *stater* with two *didrachmae*, claiming that such an equation was true only in Antioch and Damascus.[12]

Although the majority of scholars have embraced Streeter's view, good reasons exist for abandoning it. The fact that Ignatius

10. See Köstenberger et al., *The Cradle, the Cross, and the Crown*, 188n27.
11. Irenaeus, *Against Heresies*, 3.1.1.
12. B. H. Streeter, *The Four Gospels* (London: Macmillan, 1951), 500–523.

quotes more frequently from Matthew than the other Gospels is not surprising, since Matthew was clearly the favorite gospel of the early church. Streeter did not document his claim regarding the value of the ancient coins, and it now appears that he was mistaken. Nevertheless, for other reasons, Syria remains a possible provenance. It had both a large Jewish community and a thriving Christian church and thus would form a suitable background for Matthew's gospel.

The early church fathers generally believed that the Gospel of Matthew was composed in Palestine. Irenaeus wrote that the gospel was written "among the Hebrews."[13] The *Anti-Marcionite Prologue* and Jerome both claim that the gospel was written in Judea. Jerome even claimed that the Hebrew original of the Gospel of Matthew was still preserved "to this day" in the library in Caesarea.[14] Some early church leaders might have just assumed that the gospel was written from Palestine based on the interests of the gospel in matters of concern to Jewish Christians and their relationships to their fellow Jews, as well as the widely held view that the gospel was first written in Hebrew. But some, such as Jerome, seem to have more specific knowledge. Given the fact that the content of the gospel fits well with a Palestinian provenance and that Palestine is the only location for the composition of the gospel suggested by the early church, the balance of evidence tips slightly in favor of Palestine.

The evidence is insufficient to inspire total confidence in either view. Fortunately, the location of composition does not significantly affect one's interpretation of the book.

To Whom Was the Gospel Written?

Conclusions about the destination and the original audience for whom the gospel was intended are closely related to the question of where the gospel was written. Those who accept Palestine

13. Irenaeus, *Against Heresies*, 3.1.1.
14. Jerome, *De viris illustribus*, 3.

11

as the place of origin generally see the church in Palestine as the primary audience. Those who accept Syria as the place of origin generally see the church in Syria as the primary audience.

Although Matthew probably wrote his gospel primarily for a particular group in a particular setting, he likely intended it to enjoy wider circulation. Paul's letters were already being widely circulated beyond the churches to which they were specifically addressed. Matthew must have realized that his gospel would be useful to the church at large as well. The fact that Matthew's gospel was soon quoted in sources from all over the ancient world shows the gospel was widely circulated. By the middle of the second century, Matthew was quoted by Ignatius (Antioch), Polycarp (Smyrna), Pseudo-Barnabas (Alexandria?), Clement (Alexandria), and Justin Martyr (Ephesus).

Matthew clearly expected his original readers to be familiar with the Old Testament. He anticipated that they would understand the broader context of the Old Testament passages that he quoted and would recognize even subtle allusions to familiar Old Testament texts. Thus, Matthew plainly wrote his gospel primarily for Jewish Christians familiar with the Old Testament from instruction received in the synagogue.

What Is the Structure of the Gospel?

Scholars still debate the intended structure of Matthew's gospel. Two major theories vie for consideration. B. W. Bacon suggested that Matthew intended to divide his gospel into five major sections, plus an introduction and a conclusion. For Bacon, the key to the gospel's organization was the statement "And when Jesus finished . . . ," followed by some reference to Jesus' teaching. This kind of construction appears in Matthew 7:28–29; 11:1; 13:53; 19:1; and 26:1. Each of the major sections demarcated by this construction has a similar makeup: a narrative segment followed by one of Jesus' major discourses.[15] The major weakness

15. B. W. Bacon, *Studies in Matthew* (New York: Holt, 1930), 82, 265–335.

of this proposed structure is that it reduces the account of Jesus' birth and childhood to a mere prologue and the narrative of Jesus' arrest, trial, crucifixion, and resurrection to a mere epilogue.

Jack Kingsbury saw another phrase as the key to the structure of the gospel. He pointed out that the phrase "from that time Jesus began to . . ." appeared twice in the gospel (Matt. 4:17; 16:21). He argued that this construction is the primary structural marker and demarcates three major sections of the gospel: The Person of Jesus Messiah (1:1–4:16); The Proclamation of Jesus Messiah (4:17–16:20); and The Suffering, Death, and Resurrection of Jesus Messiah (16:21–28:20).[16] This proposal also has its problems. It is difficult to label the middle section the "proclamation" of Jesus Messiah when two of the five major discourses appear in the final section of the gospel. The inclusion of these two major discourses in the final section shows that the label "suffering, death, and resurrection" does not quite capture the content of that section either.

Although more scholars seem persuaded by Bacon's proposal than Kingsbury's, neither schema has approached consensus. Perhaps the best view is the one recently proposed by Craig Evans. Evans points out that Matthew is essentially a "retelling" of Mark's gospel. Matthew repeats approximately 90 percent of Mark's account of Jesus' life and teaching and hardly ever deviates from Mark's sequence. Thus, Matthew essentially adopts the structure of Mark's gospel. Mark's gospel, in turn, follows a fairly simple outline based on Jesus' geographical movement: his ministry in Galilee, a journey south to Judea and Jerusalem, and at last the passion in Jerusalem.[17]

Matthew's structure is complex and involves a combination of several different strategies operating at once. The five major discourses are clearly important, but chronology (birth, infancy, ministry, death, resurrection) and geography (Galilee, Judea, Jerusalem) drive the progress of the gospel as well. Kingsbury was

16. Jack D. Kingsbury, *Matthew: Structure, Christology, Kingdom*, 2nd ed. (Minneapolis: Fortress, 1989), 1–39.
17. Craig A. Evans, *Matthew*, New Cambridge Bible Commentary (New York: Cambridge University Press, 2012), 9.

correct that Matthew 4:17 and 16:21 mark important transitions in the narrative. But 4:17 primarily serves a chronological function by marking the beginning of Jesus' adult ministry. The marker in 4:17 does not denote geographical movement, since Jesus was already stationed in Galilee (first Nazareth, then Capernaum) and the ministry described following 4:17 is likewise in Galilee. On the other hand, 16:21 marks a geographical transition (Jesus says that "he must go to Jerusalem") as well as a chronological function (Jesus' ministry is drawing to a close and he must "suffer many things from the elders and chief priests and scribes, and be killed, and on the third day be raised"). These transitions point to the chronological and geographical progression of Mark's gospel. At the same time, the construction "and when Jesus finished" marks the conclusion of each of the five major discourses with content largely absent from Mark. These features suggest a broad outline:

1. Introduction (1:1–4:16)
   a. Genealogy, Birth, and Childhood of Jesus (1:1–2:23)
   b. Preparation for Jesus' Ministry (3:1–4:16)[18]

2. Galilean Ministry (4:17–16:20)
   a. First Stage of Jesus' Galilean Ministry (4:17–25)
   b. First Discourse: Sermon on the Mount (5:1–7:29)[19]
   c. Second Stage of Jesus' Galilean Ministry (8:1–9:38)
   d. Second Discourse: Instruction of the Twelve (10:1–11:1)[20]
   e. Third Stage of Jesus' Galilean Ministry (11:2–12:50)
   f. Third Discourse: Parables about the Kingdom (13:1–53)[21]
   g. Rejection and Withdrawal to the North (13:54–16:20)[22]

3. Journey to Jerusalem (16:21–20:34)[23]
   a. Return to Galilee (16:21–17:27)

18. "From that time Jesus began to . . ." (4:17).
19. "And when Jesus finished these sayings . . ." (7:28).
20. "When Jesus had finished . . ." (11:1).
21. "And when Jesus had finished . . ." (13:53).
22. "Jesus . . . withdrew" (14:13; 15:21). Jesus travels to Gennesaret (14:34), the district of Tyre and Sidon (15:21), and the district of Caesarea Philippi (16:13).
23. "From that time Jesus began . . ." and "he must go to Jerusalem" (16:21).

    b. Fourth Discourse: Parables of the Kingdom (18:1–35)
    c. Journey through Judea (19:1–20:34)[24]

4. Jerusalem Ministry (21:1–28:20)
    a. Final Ministry in Jerusalem (21:1–22:46)
    b. Rebuke of the Pharisees and Abandonment of the Temple (23:1–39)
    c. Fifth Discourse: The Fall of Jerusalem and the Coming Kingdom (24:1–25:46)
    d. Jesus' Passion (26:1–27:66)
    e. Jesus' Resurrection (28:1–20)

What Is the Purpose of the Gospel?

Some recent works on Matthew have tended to emphasize ecclesiology more heavily than Christology. Robert Gundry gave the second edition of his commentary on Matthew the subtitle *A Commentary on His Handbook for a Mixed Church under Persecution*. In his section on "The Theology of Matthew," he argues that Matthew's primary concern behind his gospel was the mixture of true disciples and false disciples in the church of his day. Consequently, Matthew wrote to emphasize the characteristics of true Christian discipleship. Gundry claims that the emphasis on Christ in Matthew merely supported Matthew's greater ecclesiological concerns: "To accentuate the authority of Christ's law Matthew paints an awe-inspiring portrait of Jesus."[25] Gundry apparently regards Matthew's ecclesiological concerns as primary and his Christological concerns as secondary.

Far better is the approach of Frederick Dale Bruner, who titled the first volume of his Matthew commentary *Christbook* and the second volume *Churchbook*.[26] But even this approach falls short of properly expressing Matthew's purpose. From the first

---

24. "Now when Jesus had finished these sayings, he went away from Galilee and entered the region of Judea beyond the Jordan" (19:1).

25. Robert Gundry, *Matthew*, 2nd ed. (Grand Rapids: Eerdmans, 1994), 9.

26. Frederick Dale Bruner, *The Christbook: Matthew 1–12*, rev. ed. (Grand Rapids: Eerdmans, 2007); Bruner, *The Churchbook: Matthew 13–28*, rev. ed. (Grand Rapids: Eerdmans, 2007).

line of Matthew's gospel, it is apparent that Matthew intends to focus his gospel on Jesus Christ. The description of Jesus as the Son of David and Son of Abraham indicates that Matthew intends to explain multiple facets of Jesus' identity. Thus, Matthew's gospel is Christocentric, and any responsible treatment of the theology of his gospel must emphasize Matthew's Christology.[27]

Some readers might object that the present work is wrongly titled, since the book focuses largely on Matthew's Christology rather than his broader theology. Yet this focus is intentional and necessary. Matthew's primary concern is to reveal Jesus Christ, Son of David, Son of Abraham, Savior, Son of God, and Immanuel, to his readers. Matthew has other concerns—theological, soteriological, ecclesiological, and so forth—but these are subordinate to his focus on Jesus. This book will focus on Matthew's portrait of Jesus, even if this means that some theological stones are left unturned and room remains for detailed treatment of some aspects of Matthew's theology elsewhere.

On the other hand, this book is more than a mere Christology of Matthew. Many other theological themes are so tightly integrated with Matthew's Christology that separating them is practically impossible. For example, Matthew's presentation of Jesus as the new Moses is closely related to his doctrine of salvation, his teaching about the new covenant, Jesus' identity as the Servant of Yahweh who will die for the sins of God's people, and Matthew's call to repent of sin and believe in Jesus. *A Theology of Matthew* attempts to preserve Matthew's integrative approach. The list below shows important titles and theological themes that are treated in each section.

- New Moses
  - liberation from slavery to sin
  - new covenant
  - Jesus' identity as the Servant of the Lord who dies for the sins of his people
  - the necessity of repentance and faith

27. Jack D. Kingsbury, *Matthew: Structure, Christology, Kingdom* (Philadelphia: Fortress, 1975), 36; France, "The Ecclesiastical Gospel?," in *Matthew: Evangelist and Teacher*, 242–44.

- New David
  - the Davidic covenant
  - the kingdom of heaven
  - the Son of Man
  - Jesus as eschatological Judge
  - the necessity of submitting to Jesus' authority
- New Abraham
  - God's rejection of unrepentant Israel
  - the church as the new Israel
  - gracious election
  - the inclusion of Gentiles in God's redemptive plan
  - the holiness of God's people
  - the necessity of evangelism and missions
- New Creator
  - Jesus' deity
  - Jesus' supremacy
  - Jesus' virginal conception
  - Son of Man
  - personified Wisdom
  - Lord
  - Son of God
  - Immanuel
  - the miracle of new creation

Introduction to
the Theological Study
of Matthew

IN THE PAST, some scholars have approached the Christology of Matthew as if a simple survey of the titles of Jesus, such as *Immanuel* and *Son of God*, were sufficient to uncover Matthew's comprehensive view of Jesus. Most scholars today recognize that although such a survey is a necessary component of discovering Matthew's Christology, a robust understanding of that Christology involves a much more careful and detailed analysis of the gospel. A few simple word searches on a computer are not enough. Instead, one must work through the entirety of Matthew's gospel phrase by phrase and line by line, seeking to mine the depths of Matthew's portrayal of Jesus.

To a certain extent, this painstaking study is the goal of a lifetime. On the other hand, one's understanding of Matthew's theology, and particularly his Christology, may be greatly facilitated through a few simple steps.

Discovering the Central Message

The New Testament authors often express the primary thesis of their work in a single verse or paragraph known as the *programmatic statement* of the book. Much as modern readers can facilitate their reading of a book by first reading the introduction and conclusion and glancing over the table of contents, students of the Gospel of Matthew can glean much insight into its contents and purpose by a careful study of its programmatic statement.

Most scholars regard Matthew 1:21 as the programmatic statement of the gospel. The verse expresses the angel's command to Joseph to name Mary's baby boy *Jesus*. This name is both historically and etymologically significant. Historically, the name recalls the Old Testament Joshua, the successor to Moses. As will later be shown, the name hints at Jesus' identity as the new Moses, the prophet like Moses, foretold in the Old Testament. Etymologically, the name in Hebrew means "Yahweh saves." The name implies that through the coming of Jesus, Yahweh himself is acting to save his people. The use of the name meaning "Yahweh saves" in combination with the statement that "he [Jesus] will save" serves to equate Jesus with Yahweh. This equation is confirmed by the parallel reference to Jesus' naming in verse 23 that identifies Jesus as Immanuel, God with us.

The verse not only implies Jesus' deity, but also describes his identity as Savior. Jesus is One who will save or rescue people from their sins. This description implies that Jesus will do more than merely provide forgiveness. He will also accomplish redemption. That is, he will liberate his people from their slavery to sin.

Finally, the reference to "his [Jesus'] people" implies that Jesus came to create and gather a people belonging to himself. At first, one might assume that "his people" simply refers to the Jewish nation. But the promise that Jesus "will save" (not "may save") indicates that Jesus' true people are those whom he saves. This implies that the people who belong to Jesus cannot simply be equated with national Israel.

We will later see that this programmatic statement encompasses three of the four major Christological emphases of Matthew's gospel: Jesus' identity as the new Creator, the new Moses, and the new Abraham. We are already well on our way to understanding the heart of Matthew's Christology.

20

Understanding First-Century Judaism

Matthew presents his theology to his readers in a variety of ways. Sometimes he speaks very plainly and simply. Sometimes he communicates his message very subtly and ingeniously. Sometimes Matthew shouts his message. At other times, he barely whispers it. Sometimes a whisper is more powerful than a shout because it causes the hearer to lean forward and strain his ears so that he does not miss a single word.

The modern reader's understanding of Matthew's gospel is often impoverished because he hears the shouts and misses the whispers. He lacks the familiarity with the Old Testament and understanding of Jewish expectations of the Messiah to pick up on some of Matthew's more subtle nuances. The modern reader fails to understand the gospel as Matthew's original readers would have understood it. He is trying to read with the lights off.

Some of Matthew's ways of communicating seem strange to modern readers, who might even question their legitimacy. Would Matthew really communicate through a numeric code such as gematria?[1] Would he use titles, characteristic expressions, and characteristic actions to show that Jesus is the new Moses, new David, new Abraham, and new Creator?

Only a little thought will convince that people do communicate in such subtle ways even today. After all, modern Americans have their codes like gematria, too. Just about every American teenager knows what codes such as *OMG*, *LOL*, and *XOXO* mean. They might seem strange and foreign to senior adults. My teenage kids thought it was hilarious when I recently interpreted *LOL* as "lots of laughs," because *"everybody* knows that *LOL* means 'laugh out loud.'" Those who know the code need no time to pause and reflect to understand what it represents. Modern readers miss the point of features such as gematria because twenty-first-century readers of Matthew's gospel are very much like senior adults reading a teenager's text messages. They do not know the codes

---

1. *Gematria* is the numeric code that is the key to the arrangement of Matthew's genealogy.

familiar to first-century Jewish Christians and thus do not understand the message.

Modern readers might also wonder whether titles such as *Wisdom*, association with Bethlehem, characteristic expressions such as "I AM," or characteristic actions such as "stretching out the hand" would really have prompted ancient readers to better understand Jesus' identity. Yet modern people communicate like this, too. Most Americans, especially those over forty in the South, know that the title *The King of Rock and Roll* belongs to none other than Elvis Presley. Certain distinctives, such as a lip curl, a particular gyration, wearing long black sideburns, or donning a white jumpsuit with a cape, will inevitably remind most Southerners of Elvis. Certain expressions, such as "Thank you very much" and "he *has left the building*," will be recognized by many as a clear allusion to the boy from Tupelo, Mississippi. Association with a particular place, such as Graceland, is more than enough to tip off many audiences that an allusion to Elvis is in play.

Of course, not everyone will pick up on these allusions. People from another culture and another time will probably completely miss the point of these subtle references. They might even accuse those who see a reference to Elvis in such titles, expressions, actions, and references to origin of having an overly vivid imagination. But to people of the proper background, these allusions are as loud as the color of the carpet in the Jungle Room.

Modern readers of the Gospel of Matthew need to step into Matthew's world and read his gospel as his original readers would have understood it. Such an exercise greatly enriches our understanding of the gospel.

Matthew's original readers were likely Jewish Christians who had studied the Old Testament in depth in the Jewish synagogue. Matthew's first readers were likely much more familiar with the Old Testament than many Christians today are. Thus, modern readers miss important allusions to Old Testament texts that highlight the significance of Jesus. Carefully reading the Old Testament texts that Matthew quotes in their original context sheds an enormous amount of light on the gospel. Generally speaking, the better one knows and understands the Old Testament, the better he will know and understand the Gospel of Matthew. When we give attention to its Old Testament allusions, we discover that Matthew has a theological depth that rivals even that of the Gospel of John.

Although Christians should certainly prioritize becoming more familiar with the Old Testament, some knowledge of other Jewish literature written around the time of Christ is also very helpful. Writings such as 1 Enoch, the Dead Sea Scrolls, and the Babylonian Talmud are not inspired Scripture and do not serve as authorities for Christian faith and conduct. Nevertheless, they help us to understand how the Jews of Matthew's day understood the Old Testament, expected the Messiah, and understood important theological concepts.

First Enoch, for example, teaches many things that Christians should dismiss. But the book uses the title *Son of Man* in clear reference to Daniel 7 and describes him as a figure worthy of worship who bears the divine name *Yahweh*. Thus, it demonstrates how some of Jesus' hearers and many of Matthew's readers would have understood Jesus' favorite title for himself. Jesus spoke to be understood. Unless he very carefully clarified his use of a particular title, he probably used that title in the manner to which most of his readers were accustomed. Ancient sources such as 1 Enoch can help modern readers to understand the "mental dictionary" that the original readers used to define words and concepts.

Vertical Reading of the Gospel

The practice of *vertical reading* of the Gospels refers to the process of reading a gospel from start to finish, preferably in a single sitting. This practice gives the reader a good idea of the movement, flow, and major emphases of each gospel. Readers should pay special attention to the introduction and conclusion of a gospel because these are likely to contain the major themes of the gospel. For example, the very first verse of Matthew identifies Jesus as the "son of David." This title is given special emphasis in the gematria. Furthermore, the title *Son of David* is frequently applied to Jesus in the gospel narrative. The theme of Jesus' kingship—the essence of the title's meaning—reaches its climax in the final words of the gospel as the resurrected Jesus claims to possess "all authority in heaven and on earth" (Matt. 28:18). These themes might be missed without careful and perhaps multiple vertical readings.

Because of Matthew's emphasis on Jesus as the fulfillment of the prophecies given in the Old Testament Scriptures, it is particularly important to examine Old Testament quotations and allusions in the second or third vertical reading. For example, a careful investigation of the Old Testament background of Jesus' identity as a Nazarene (Matt. 2:23) points to an important series of prophecies about the Davidic Messiah that dovetail perfectly with the description of Jesus as the Son of David. As one examines the Old Testament quotations and allusions, he should carefully explore the larger contexts of these Old Testament passages. He will discover that Matthew does not snatch Old Testament verses from their original context and use them without sensitivity to their original meaning. Instead, he handles the Old Testament very carefully and often assumes familiarity with the broader context of a quoted passage.

Horizontal Reading of the Gospel

Horizontal reading refers to reading the Gospel of Matthew in a synopsis or harmony that places the three Synoptic Gospels—Matthew, Mark, and Luke—in parallel columns. In horizontal reading, one should give special attention to comparing the readings in Matthew and Mark. Most scholars today are convinced that Matthew used Mark in writing his own gospel. Thus, differences between Matthew and Mark are often clues to Matthew's theological emphases.

One example of the helpfulness of this approach should suffice. Matthew's account of Jesus' healing of the daughter of the Canaanite woman (Matt. 15:21–28) is paralleled in Mark 7:24–30. Matthew appears to have made a number of changes in his retelling of the account that highlight important emphases. For example, only Matthew contains the woman's plea to Jesus, "Have mercy on me, O Lord, Son of David." We will later see that several elements of this plea relate to Matthew's favorite portrayals of Jesus. In light of the emphasis on Jesus as the Son of David in the genealogy, however, this title practically leaps off the page. This slight difference between Matthew and Mark hints at a description of Jesus that is very important to Matthew. This hypothesis is confirmed by a comparison of the accounts of Jesus' triumphal entry (Matt. 21:1–9; Mark 11:1–10; Luke 19:28–40; John 12:12–19). All four accounts record the exclamation of the crowds, "Hosanna! Blessed is he who comes in the name of the Lord!" Only Matthew's account adds the phrase "to the Son of David" to the exclamation "Hosanna!" It is probably no coincidence that Matthew's gospel includes the title on multiple occasions when the parallel accounts lack it. Matthew includes detail that the other Gospels omit because this title is particularly important to his portrayal of Jesus as the Messiah.

Recognizing these subtle differences between Matthew's gospel and the parallel accounts will open the interpreter's eyes to new and important details of Matthew's theology. Normally, these cohere nicely with elements of Matthew's gospel already recognized by applying the other approaches.

Matthew's Vision for His Theological Work

Matthew 13:52 records an important parable of Jesus that is preserved only in the Gospel of Matthew: "Therefore every scribe who has been trained for the kingdom of heaven is like a master of a house, who brings out of his treasure what is new and what is old." This somewhat enigmatic statement has long puzzled commentators. Many interpreters have suspected that the parable is partly autobiographical. Although the adjective *every* implies that both Jesus and Matthew regarded many as scribes trained for the kingdom, Matthew almost certainly understood himself as one who fulfilled this role.[2]

The word *scribe* is used throughout the Gospel of Matthew to describe experts in the study of the Hebrew Scriptures.[3] The scribes first appear in Matthew in 2:4 as experts in messianic prophecy who explain to Herod that Micah 5:2 identifies Bethlehem of Judea as the Messiah's birthplace. Similarly, in Matthew 17:10, the scribes are said to explain that the Messiah could not come to Israel until Elijah appeared again. Their view is clearly based on careful exegesis of Malachi 4:5. In addition to being experts in the Hebrew Bible and its promises about the coming Messiah, the scribes were trained scholars who specialized in the traditions of the rabbis and the demands of the law on every detail of conduct for faithful Jews. Jesus' rebuke of the scribes in Matthew 23 shows that the scribes acted as interpreters of the Scriptures, teachers of the Scriptures, and missionaries for Judaism.

On two occasions in Matthew, Jesus uses the term *scribes* in a positive sense to describe a particular group among his own disciples. In Matthew 23:34, Jesus promises to send to the Jews "prophets and wise men and scribes" but warns that the Jews would severely persecute these servants of Jesus and would suffer the consequences that their actions deserved. Matthew 13:52 contains a more extensive description of these Christian scribes. The Christian scribe "has been trained for the kingdom of heaven." Although the Jewish scribes "shut the kingdom of heaven in people's faces" because they did not enter themselves or permit oth-

2. Ulrich Luz, *Matthew*, Hermeneia (Minneapolis: Augsburg Fortress, 2001–7), 2:287. Luz affirms this view and lists Joseph Hoh, Jacob Kremer, Simon Légasse, Michael Goulder, Hubert Frankemölle, W. D. Davies, and F. W. Beare in support.

3. See "γραμματεύς," in *A Greek-English Lexicon of the New Testament and Other Early Christian Literature*, ed. Frederick W. Danker, 3rd ed. (Chicago: University of Chicago Press, 2000), 206. See esp. definition 2a. See also the detailed description of the scribes of Jerusalem in Joachim Jeremias, *Jerusalem in the Time of Jesus* (Philadelphia: Fortress, 1969), 233–45.

ers to enter (23:13), the Christian scribes' study of Scripture led them to a proper understanding of the kingdom and the way in which it was entered. The correct understanding of the kingdom naturally required a correct understanding of the messianic King.

The reference to the scribe's "treasure" clearly recalls the parable of the hidden treasure that appears only a few verses earlier (Matt. 13:44). The parable of the treasure emphasizes two aspects of the messianic kingdom. First, it is "hidden." Many were unable to see and understand this kingdom, but Jesus had clearly revealed it to his disciples (11:25–30; 13:10–17, 34–35). Second, the kingdom is precious, completely worthy of any sacrifice necessary to obtain it.

Jesus teaches that the scribe's treasure, his kingdom teaching, consists of things "old" and "new." Since interpreting Scripture was the scribe's fundamental task, the old content of the treasure is likely the teachings of the Hebrew Scriptures, including both demands and promises, particularly the promises related to the coming King and kingdom. The new content of the treasure is Jesus and his gospel of the kingdom. Jesus, and his disciple Matthew, saw a clear connection between the new and the old. This is especially clear in Matthew's frequent claim that Jesus fulfilled the Law and the Prophets.[4]

In his well-known "fulfillment formula" (Matt. 1:22; 2:15, 17, 23; 4:14; 8:17; 12:17; 13:35; 21:4; 26:54, 56; 27:9), Matthew clearly expresses his view of Scripture. First, statements such as "what the Lord had spoken by the prophet" (1:22; 2:15) show that Matthew clearly regards the Scriptures as the Word of God. Although God had operated through the agency of the prophets in the composition of the Bible, God himself was the ultimate Author of all that it contained. Even the shortened construction "what was spoken by the prophet" (2:17, 23; 4:14; 8:17; 12:17; 13:35; 21:4; 27:9) uses the divine passive, plus a construction expressing intermediate agency, to identify God as the true source and Author of Scripture who had spoken through his prophets.

4. See Luz, *Matthew*, 2:287.

Second, Matthew regards the Scriptures, the Word of God, as the message about Jesus. Jesus was the focus and fulfillment of the Old Testament message. Jesus taught that he was the fulfillment of the Law and the Prophets (Matt. 5:17–20; 26:54, 56).[5] Based on these statements, Matthew's gospel stresses the many ways in which Jesus fulfilled Old Testament messianic prophecies and types. Most scholars regard Jesus' fulfillment of Old Testament promises as one of Matthew's most prominent themes. Matthew presents Jesus as the fulfillment of the following Old Testament prophecies:

1. Isaiah 7:14 (Matt. 1:22–23) foretold that the Messiah would be born of a virgin.
2. Micah 5:2 (Matt. 2:6) foretold that the Messiah would be born in Bethlehem.
3. Hosea 11:1 (Matt. 2:15) foretold that the Messiah would be called out of Egypt.
4. Jeremiah 31:15 (Matt. 2:18) foretold the slaughter of the infants.
5. Isaiah 40:3 (Matt. 3:3) foretold that a prophet in the wilderness would prepare for the Lord's coming.
6. Isaiah 9:1–2 (Matt. 4:14–16) foretold that the Messiah would come to Galilee of the Gentiles.
7. Isaiah 53:4 (Matt. 8:17) foretold that the Messiah would take our sicknesses and carry our infirmities like a sacrificial lamb.
8. Micah 7:6 (Matt. 10:35–36) foretold that the Messiah would turn family members against one another.
9. Isaiah 26:19; 29:18; 35:5; 42:18; and 61:1 (Matt. 11:5; 15:31) foretold that the Messiah would give sight to the blind, cause the lame to walk, cause the deaf to hear, raise the dead, and preach good news to the poor.

5. For an extensive discussion and a defense of the view that "fulfill" here refers to prophetic fulfillment, see Charles L. Quarles, *The Sermon on the Mount: Restoring Christ's Message to the Modern Church* (Nashville: B&H Academic, 2011), 89–104.

10. Exodus 23:20 and Malachi 3:1 (Matt. 11:10) foretold that a messenger would precede the coming of the Messiah.
11. Isaiah 42:1–4 (Matt. 12:18–21) predicted that the Messiah would not be loud or pretentious.
12. Isaiah 6:9–10 (Matt. 13:14–15) predicted that the Messiah's teaching would be misunderstood.
13. Psalm 78:2 (Matt. 13:35) predicted that the Messiah would teach in parables.
14. Isaiah 29:13 (Matt. 15:8–9) foretold that God's people would rebel against him and teach false things.
15. Malachi 4:5 (Matt. 17:10–13) predicted that the coming of the Messiah would be preceded by the arrival of an Elijah-like figure.
16. Isaiah 62:11 and Zechariah 9:9 (Matt. 21:5) predicted the Messiah's triumphal entry into Jerusalem.
17. Zechariah 13:7 (Matt. 26:31) predicted that the Messiah's disciples would abandon him.
18. Zechariah 11:13 (Matt. 27:9) predicted that the Messiah would be betrayed for thirty pieces of silver.
19. Psalm 22:1–2, 6–8, 18 (Matt. 27:35, 43, 46) foretold that people would gamble for the Messiah's garments and mock him, and that the Father would forsake him during his suffering on the cross.[6]

Jesus taught that all the Scriptures said about the Messiah had to be fulfilled. The failure of these prophecies was inconceivable, since they were divinely inspired. Furthermore, all they said about the Messiah would be fulfilled perfectly. The Scriptures did not need to be revised or adapted to accommodate the details of the Messiah's life. On the contrary, not so much as an iota or dot (Matt. 5:18) needed to be changed to force the "prediction" to fit the "fulfillment." The scriptural predictions perfectly matched the events that they foretold without the slightest modification.[7]

6. Ibid., 91–93.
7. Ibid., 93–95.

29

Although scholars struggle to identify precisely the new and old treasures that are displayed and shared by the Christian scribe,[8] most identify the old treasures as the Old Testament and the new treasures as the new revelation in Jesus. These new treasures include the understanding of "how Jesus' arrival has fulfilled the promises of the coming of the Messiah and the messianic kingdom (e.g., 1:22; 2:5, 15, 17, 23; 3:15; 4:14–17) and how Jesus truly fulfills the Law and the Prophets (5:17–20)."[9]

When Matthew wrote his gospel, he sought to fulfill the role of scribe of the kingdom. He pointed to old treasures in the Hebrew Scriptures, new treasures in the life and teaching of Jesus, and the amazing correspondence between the two. The titles of the next four parts of this book attempt to express Matthew's theological strategy by highlighting the relationship between the new and the old. Jesus is the new Moses who corresponds in many ways to the Moses of the Old Testament; he is the new David who corresponds in many ways to the David of the Old Testament; and so forth.

A Theology of Matthew seeks to highlight Matthew's role as a Christian scribe by placing these treasures on display. Influenced by Matthew's reference to new and old treasures, it summarizes Matthew's Christology by pointing to Matthew's description of Jesus as the new Moses, the new David, the new Abraham, and the new Creator. These Christological themes emphasize Jesus' identity as the Deliverer who rescues God's people from their sins, the King who rules over God's kingdom, the Founder of a new chosen people, and God with us acting to make his people new.

The scribe Matthew has stepped into his storeroom and is dragging out a massive treasure chest filled with wonders that defy description. So draw close, fix your gaze on the chest, and prepare to be amazed.

8. For a list of options, see W. D. Davies and Dale Allison Jr., *The Gospel according to Matthew*, 3 vols., International Critical Commentary (Edinburgh: T & T Clark, 1988–1997), 2:447.

9. Michael J. Wilkins, *Matthew*, NIV Application Commentary (Grand Rapids: Zondervan, 2004), 490, citing David E. Orton, *The Understanding Scribe: Matthew and the Apocalyptic Ideal* (Sheffield, UK: JSOT Press, 1989), esp. 140–53.

Part 2

The New Moses:
Jesus, Our Savior

Matthew's Development of the *New Moses* Theme

AS MATTHEW REACHES into his treasure chest and draws out treasures that are both new and old, he dazzles onlookers by displaying one of his most beautiful and precious gems—the new Moses. The beauty of a gem is seldom fully appreciated unless it is displayed in the proper manner. The color and texture of the fabric on which the gem is placed and the light that is focused on the jewel highlight the brilliance, fire, and hue of the stone. Similarly, Matthew recognizes the importance of presenting Christ against the proper background. He intentionally compares Jesus to the descriptions of the Old Testament's greatest redeemer so that readers can more fully appreciate the glory and greatness of the Messiah.

Matthew does not wait long to develop this background. He begins his work of comparing Jesus to Moses even in the introduction to his gospel. Insightful readers familiar with the Old Testament and ancient Jewish literature quickly and easily pick up on this theme. In fact, those who already know about Jesus' claims to be the Messiah may have already been expecting a comparison of Jesus to Moses. They know that God had promised the coming of a prophet like Moses a millennium and a half earlier (Deut. 18:15–19).

The New Testament shows that Jews in the first century regarded Deuteronomy 18:15–19 as a prophecy about the coming of the Messiah. They frequently referred to the Messiah as "the Prophet" (John 1:21, 25; 7:40), that is, the coming prophet whom God had promised through Moses. Peter explicitly quotes the Deuteronomy 18 prophecy in his sermon at the temple in Jerusalem after the healing of the lame man (Acts 3:22–23) and presents Jesus as the fulfillment of this promise. Although Stephen is martyred by the angry mob before he can finish his last sermon, the primary theme of his message is that Jesus is the prophet like Moses (7:37), since both were redeemers who were rejected by the very ones they came to save.

Matthew's presentation of Jesus as the new Moses is not a theological idiosyncrasy. It was a view of the Messiah shared by many Jews and Christians. Yet no New Testament writer develops this portrait as fully as the apostle Matthew.

Jesus Is Like Moses in Many Important Ways

A later rabbinic tradition shows that expectation of a Messiah like Moses persisted among the Jews for nearly a millennium after the time of Jesus:

> R. Berekiah said in the name of R. Isaac: As the first redeemer [Moses] was, so shall the latter Redeemer [Messiah] be. What is stated of the former redeemer? "And Moses took his wife and his sons, and set them upon an ass" (Exod 4:20). Similarly it will be with the latter Redeemer, as it is stated, "Lowly and riding upon an ass" (Zech 9:9). As the former redeemer caused manna to descend, as it is stated, "Behold, I will cause to rain bread from heaven for you" (Exod 16:4), so will the latter Redeemer cause manna to descend, as it is stated, "May he be as rich as a cornfield in the land" (Ps 72:16). As the former redeemer made a well to rise (Num 21:17–18), so the latter Redeemer brings up water, as it is stated, "And a fountain shall come forth of the house of the Lord, and shall water the valley of Shittim" (Joel 4:18 [3:18 in English Bible]).[1]

1. *Qoheleth Rabbah* 1:9 (references are to the Hebrew Old Testament). This midrash on Ecclesiastes dates to the first half of the ninth century. Thus, one cannot automati-

Thus, the rabbis recognized that the Messiah would reenact important deeds associated with the ministry of Moses. Matthew writes his gospel primarily to a Jewish Christian audience that affirms the principle "as the first redeemer was, so shall the latter Redeemer be." Consequently, Matthew highlights important similarities between Jesus and Moses to present Jesus as the fulfillment of God's promise to send his people a prophet like Moses. Matthew shows that Jesus is like Moses in his infancy, his teaching ministry, his fasting, his miracles, and his transfiguration.[2]

Jesus Is Like Moses in His Infancy

Matthew's account of Jesus' birth and infancy is rich with theological significance. The conception of Jesus by the Virgin Mary through the activity of the Holy Spirit highlights Jesus' identity as incarnate Deity, the Immanuel. The appearance of magi from the East to worship Jesus in his infancy is a jaw-dropping display of Jesus' intention to save Gentiles as well as Jews, and of his power to summon even the worst of sinners to repentance and faith. Herod's plot to kill the infant Messiah by slaughtering the male infants and toddlers of Bethlehem might seem theologically insignificant in comparison to these other episodes. On the contrary, through his description of Herod's attempt to assassinate Jesus, Matthew demonstrates that Jesus is the fulfillment of the prophecy about a prophet like Moses.

The early Jewish Christian readers of this gospel would have pored over Matthew 2 with a sense of déjà vu. The account would have a strange and even disturbing familiarity, causing the reader to ask, *Where have I heard this before?* The answer would come when the reader recalled the account of Moses' birth in Exodus 1 and 2.

Matthew's account of the circumstances surrounding Jesus' birth in Matthew 1–2 resonates with echoes from the Exodus

---

cally infer that the views contained in it are representative of Second Temple Judaism.

2. These similarities and many others are discussed in greater detail in Dale C. Allison Jr., *The New Moses: A Matthean Typology* (Minneapolis: Fortress, 1993).

account of Moses' birth. After Jesus' birth, magi from the east, seeking the newborn Messiah, are guided by a heavenly light to Jerusalem. Herod the Great, king of Judea, is deeply disturbed by the announcement of the Messiah's birth, for he fears that the Messiah poses a threat to his own rule. When Herod interrogates the chief priests and Jewish scribes, he discovers that an ancient prophecy in Micah 5:2 foretold that the Messiah would be born in Bethlehem. The wicked king dispatches his soldiers to slay the male children in Bethlehem and the surrounding region.

The parallels between the accounts of Jesus' birth and of Moses' birth are obvious. Herod the Great was an evil, paranoid ruler very much like Pharaoh. His slaughter of male Hebrew infants is strongly reminiscent of Pharaoh's murder of male Hebrew infants hundreds of years earlier. Popular Jewish traditions about the birth of Moses even more closely parallel Matthew's account of the circumstances surrounding Jesus' birth. One important example is the account of Moses' birth in the *Antiquities of the Jews*, an account of Jewish history completed by Flavius Josephus in A.D. 93. According to Josephus, Pharaoh did not murder the male Hebrew children merely because he feared their rapidly growing numbers. Rather, a sacred scribe in Pharaoh's court foretold that an Israelite boy would be born and would bring down Egyptian dominion, liberate the Israelites, be more righteous than any other man, and obtain a glory that would be remembered through all ages. The terrified king ordered the execution of the male Hebrew children specifically in order to terminate this promised deliverer. In both Josephus's account of Moses' birth and Matthew's account of Jesus' birth, a wicked pagan king ordered the slaughter of male Israelite infants because he feared the rise of a deliverer whose coming had been foretold by scribes.

Any notion that these parallels are a mere coincidence is dispelled by the remarkable allusion to Moses in the angel's words to Joseph in Matthew 2:20. The angel appears to Joseph to inform him of Herod the Great's death and to announce that it is now safe for the holy family to return to Palestine from Egypt, where they had sought refuge during Herod's slaughter of the innocents. The angel's words "those who sought the child's life are dead" in the original Greek version of Matthew are a clear and direct quotation of the Greek version of Exodus 4:19.[3] Only a few minor adjustments have been made to adapt the Old Testament statement to a new context. The angel of the Lord seems to apply words originally spoken to and about Moses to Jesus Christ in order to signal that Jesus will somehow be like Moses.

Jesus Is Like Moses in His Teaching Ministry

Although Matthew refers briefly to Jesus' preaching and teaching ministry earlier in his gospel (Matt. 4:17, 23), his first extended report of Jesus' teaching is given in chapters 5–7, a summary of Jesus' teaching known as the Sermon on the Mount. The specific wording of the introduction to the sermon makes Jesus' ascent of a mountain to deliver his authoritative interpretation and application of the law of Moses to his disciples strangely reminiscent of Moses' ascent of Mount Sinai to receive and deliver the law.

Three details show that Matthew wishes to highlight this parallel. First, the words "he went up on the mountain" in Matthew 5:1 are a verbatim quotation of Exodus 19:3, a description of Moses' ascending Sinai to receive the law from God. This particular phrase appears only three times in the Greek Old Testament. All three of the occurrences are descriptions of Moses' ascent of Sinai (Ex. 19:3; 24:18; 34:4). Second, the use of the definite article in the phrase "*the* mountain" seems to suggest that Matthew is inviting comparison of this mountain to the most prominent mountain in the Old Testament. Except in instances in which Matthew uses the definite article to show that he is referring to a mountain mentioned in the preceding context (Matt. 8:1; 17:9), Matthew does not normally use the definite article to refer to unnamed mountains (4:8; 17:1). Of the normal uses of the definite article in Greek grammar, the most likely here is the

---

3. The Greek translation of the Old Testament is known as the Septuagint.

definite article par excellence, which identifies an object as the best of its kind.[4] When Matthew referred to "the mountain," his readers would likely have wondered about the identification and location of this unnamed mountain, just as modern readers do. Matthew's grammar would probably have triggered recollection of the most famous mountain of the Old Testament, Mount Horeb, also known as Sinai.

Finally, the description of Jesus' sitting to teach may recall Moses' stance when he received God's law on Mount Sinai. Although the Hebrew verb in Deuteronomy 9:9 may be translated "remain" or "dwell," references in the Talmud show that Jewish interpreters regarded the Hebrew text of Deuteronomy 9:9 to mean that Moses sat on the mountain. Matthew 23:2 shows that the scribes and Pharisees seated themselves "on Moses' seat" when they preached and taught. Thus, the posture of Jesus when he taught was likely a conscious imitation of the posture of Moses as well.

Many scholars are convinced that Matthew structures Jesus' teaching in his gospel in such a way as to highlight Jesus' similarity to Moses. As we saw in chapter 1, B. W. Bacon may have been the first scholar in modern times to observe clues suggesting that Matthew intended to divide his gospel into five major sections, plus a prologue (chaps. 1–2) and an epilogue (26:3–28:20). Each major section concludes with a statement such as "And when Jesus finished," followed by some reference to Jesus' sayings, instruction, or parables (7:28–29; 11:1; 13:53; 19:1; 26:1; cf. Deut. 32:45). These major sections share a similar design, containing narrative segments followed by major discourses.[5]

Bacon argued that the organization of Matthew into five major sections is a part of Matthew's attempt to present his gospel as a new Pentateuch. The five sections mirror the five books of Moses in the Old Testament. Matthew's structure is a conscious imitation of the structure of the five books of Moses. Bacon's theory has much to commend it. Other Jewish literature con-

4. Daniel Wallace, *Greek Grammar: Beyond the Basics* (Grand Rapids: Zondervan, 1997), 222.
5. B. W. Bacon, *Studies in Matthew* (New York: Holt, 1930), 82, 265–335.

sciously imitates the Pentateuch's five-book structure,[6] and this structure closely matches the parallels that Matthew establishes between Jesus and Moses in his narrative details and Old Testament quotations.

Jesus Is Like Moses in His Fasting

All three of the Synoptic Gospels describe Jesus' temptation by the devil in the wilderness (Matt. 4:1–11; Mark 1:12–13; Luke 4:1–13). All three mention that Jesus fasts for forty days. Only Matthew, however, adds the phrase "and forty nights" to describe Jesus' fast. The phrase "forty days and forty nights" appears ten times in the Old Testament. Six of these ten occurrences relate to Moses (Ex. 24:18; 34:28; Deut. 9:9, 18, 25; 10:10). Three of these occurrences refer specifically to the duration of Moses' fasts. Two describe his fast related to the reception of the law (Ex. 34:28; Deut. 9:9). Another refers to Moses' fast during which he begged God to spare his people after they provoked God's wrath through their idolatry (Deut. 9:18).

Thus, when the early Jewish Christian readers of Matthew's gospel read of Jesus' fast lasting forty days and forty nights, they would likely have thought of his remarkable similarities with Moses.[7] This would have prompted recognition that Jesus was indeed "the Prophet," the prophet like Moses whose coming was foretold in Deuteronomy 18:15–22.

Jesus Is Like Moses in the Miracles That Are Associated with His Ministry

Matthew refers to Jesus' activity as a miracle-worker in general terms early in his gospel (Matt. 4:23–24). The first miracle

6. Robert Gundry, *Matthew*, 2nd ed. (Grand Rapids: Eerdmans, 1994), 10–11.
7. Allison has shown that the detail that Moses' fast lasted forty days and forty nights was both celebrated and well remembered in Judaism contemporary with Jesus. *New Moses*, 167.

that he describes in detail, however, is the cleansing of a man afflicted by leprosy in 8:1–4. It is probably no coincidence that the first miracles associated with Moses' ministry were the transformation of a rod into a snake and the affliction and healing of leprosy (Ex. 4:1–9).

God miraculously heals someone of leprosy only three times in the Old Testament. Two of these instances are associated with Moses. In Exodus 4:6–7, God commands Moses to place his hand inside his cloak. When he withdraws it, it is "leprous like snow." Then God commands him to place his hand inside his cloak again. When he withdraws it a second time, his hand is cleansed of any trace of leprosy and the flesh of his arm is as healthy as the rest of his skin. In Numbers 12:1–16, when Miriam is struck with leprosy for speaking against Moses, Moses prays, "O God, please heal her—please." Healing someone afflicted with leprosy is thus primarily associated with Moses in the minds of Jews who knew the Old Testament well.

All three of the gospel writers who record this miracle (Matthew, Mark, and Luke) use an important expression to explain the means by which Jesus performs it: Jesus "stretched out his hand" (Matt. 8:3; Mark 1:41; Luke 5:13).[8] This expression occurs over a hundred times in the Old Testament. More instances of the expression occur in Exodus by far than in any other book. In fact, nineteen of the instances, nearly a fifth of the total number of occurrences in the Old Testament, appear in Exodus 3–14. Although a few of these examples refer to Yahweh's or Aaron's stretching out his hand to perform miracles or swear an oath, most refer to Moses' stretching out his hand to perform the miracles associated with the exodus. Moses stretches out his hand to transform the snake back into a rod (Ex. 4:4); to call down the plagues of thunder and hail (9:22–23), locusts (10:12), and darkness (10:21–22); to part the waters of the Red Sea (14:16, 21); and to close the waters of the sea over the Egyptians (14:26–27).

8. This expression occurs thirteen times in the New Testament. Only in the account of the healing of the leper does the expression describe Jesus as stretching out his hand to perform a miracle.

Consequently, by healing a leper and by imitating a characteristic gesture of Moses when performing a miracle, Jesus closely associated himself with Moses. This initial miracle in the gospel prepares one to understand subtle allusions to the ministry of Moses in later miracles as well. Jesus' miraculous crossing of the sea in Matthew 14:22–33 reminds readers of the miraculous crossing of the Red Sea associated with the ministry of Moses. This is especially true since this account contains the same expression "he went up on the mountain" (14:23) that was used in 5:1–2 to associate Jesus with Moses. The fact that Jesus goes up the mountain "by himself" and "to pray" makes the expression even more reminiscent of Moses, who ascended Mount Sinai alone to converse with God.

Furthermore, Jesus' miraculous provision of food in Matthew 15:32–38 certainly reminds readers of the miraculous provision of the manna during Israel's journey in the wilderness (Ex. 16). The provision of the manna in the "wilderness" (vv. 3, 14; cf. John 6:41, 49) and the multiplication of the loaves and fish in a "desolate place" (Matt. 14:15—literally "wilderness," the same word as in the Septuagint) heighten the connection between the two events. In the dialogue surrounding the account of the miracle in John 6, Jewish observers expressly comment on the connection between the two events. Interestingly, this miracle is also introduced by the now-familiar phrase "[he] went up on the mountain," which consistently associates Jesus' words and deeds with those of Moses. Jews familiar with the "prophet like Moses" prophecy apparently expected the Messiah to reenact the miracles of Moses. *Qoheleth Rabbah* 1:9 says:

> As the former redeemer caused manna to descend, as it is stated, "Behold, I will cause it to rain bread from heaven for you" (Exod 16:4), so will the latter Redeemer cause manna to descend, as it is stated, "May he be as rich as a cornfield in the land" (Ps 72:16).

Ancient Christians recognized the similarities between the miracles of Moses and Jesus. Ancient writers such as the author of the *Clementine Recognitions*, the author of the *Acts of Pilate*, and Eusebius compared the miracles of the two figures.[9] *Clementine Recognitions* 1.57 reads:

> As Moses did signs and miracles, so also did Jesus. And there is no doubt but that the likeness of the signs proves him [Jesus] to be that prophet of whom he [Moses] said that he should come "like myself."

Jesus Is Like Moses in His Transfiguration

All three of the Synoptic Gospels (Matt. 17:1–9; Mark 9:2–10; Luke 9:28–36) describe Jesus' transfiguration in terms that are clearly reminiscent of Moses' experience on Sinai recorded in Exodus 24 and 34. The following parallels exist between the gospel accounts and the Exodus narrative:

- The events occur after a period of six days (Ex. 24:16; Matt. 17:1).
- The events occur on a high mountain (Ex. 24:12, 15–18; 34:3; Matt. 17:1).
- A cloud descends and covers the mountain (Ex. 24:15–18; 34:5; Matt. 17:5).
- A voice speaks from the cloud (Ex. 24:16; Matt. 17:5).
- The central figure reflects or radiates the divine glory (Ex. 34:29–30, 35; Matt. 17:2).
- Three individuals are given special mention (Ex. 24:1; Matt. 17:1).
- The witnesses are struck with fear (Ex. 34:29–30; Matt. 17:6).

Some of these parallels would likely have escaped the attention of the casual reader. On the other hand, some of them practically leap off the page. Eusebius of Caesarea, a Christian of the early fourth century who is famous for his *History of the Christian*

9. Allison, *New Moses*, 207.

Church, noticed some of the parallels between Moses and Jesus in Matthew's account of the transfiguration. He wrote:

> When Moses descended from the mountain, his face was seen to be full of glory; for it is written: "And Moses descending from the mountain did not know that the appearance of the skin of his face was glorified while he spoke to him. And Aaron and all the elders of Israel saw Moses, and the appearance of the skin of his face was glorified" (Ex. 34:29). In the same way, only more grandly, our savior led his disciples "to a very high mountain, and he was transfigured before them, and his face shone as the sun, and his garments were white like the light" (Matt. 17:2).[10]

It is probably no accident that Eusebius chose to quote Matthew's account of the transfiguration. Although the major parallels between Jesus and Moses are present in Mark and Luke, Matthew contains a few additional descriptions that are designed to heighten the parallel. For example, while Mark's account places more emphasis on Elijah ("And there appeared to them Elijah with Moses," Mark 9:4), Matthew's account names Moses first, thereby placing greater emphasis on him (Matt. 17:3). Only Matthew's account mentions that Jesus' "face shone like the sun" (v. 2). Although this detail is not mentioned in the Old Testament accounts of Moses' encounter with Yahweh, it is emphasized in later Jewish traditions about Moses' experience. Paul mentions that Moses' face reflected the divine glory (2 Cor. 3:7). When Philo, a contemporary of Jesus, described the event, he mentioned that "those who saw him [Moses] wondered and were amazed, and could no longer endure to look upon him with their eyes, inasmuch as his countenance shone like the light of the sun."[11] Similarly, a passage in the Babylonian Talmud distinguishes the glory of Moses from that of Joshua by saying, "The face of Moses glows like the face of the sun, the face of Joshua like the face of the moon."[12]

10. Eusebius, *Demonstration of the Gospel*, 3.2.
11. Philo, *Moses*, 2.70.
12. *b. Baba Batra* 75a. See also *L.A.B.* 12; *Sipre Numbers* 140; *Deuteronomy Rabbah* 11 (207c).

Perhaps most importantly, the divine utterance at the transfiguration alludes to the prophecy about the prophet like Moses in Deuteronomy 18:15. The utterance is identical to the one given at Jesus' baptism, except for the addition of the words, "Listen to him" (Matt. 17:5; Mark 9:7; Luke 9:35). Deuteronomy 18:15 says that when the prophet like Moses comes, "it is to him you shall listen." The two phrases are identical in Greek except for the grammatical forms of the verbs. The Septuagint uses the imperatival future, while the Gospels use the normal imperative rather than the more archaic form.

Many other features of Matthew's gospel confirm his intention to demonstrate Jesus' similarity to Moses. But those mentioned above should be sufficient to show that the portrayal of Jesus as the prophet like Moses is an important part of Matthew's theological purpose.

These Similarities Are Highlighted by Matthew but Not Invented by Him

The prevalence of the *prophet like Moses* motif in Matthew's description of Jesus has prompted some scholars to suggest that Matthew made up the events that show Jesus' similarity to Moses. Did Matthew use his imagination to create details such as the slaughter of the innocents or Jesus' transfiguration? Absolutely not! The evidence shows that one must not drive a wedge between Matthew's theological purpose and his historical reliability. Matthew's gospel is both theological *and* historical.

This is clear from a comparison of Matthew with the other Gospels. Almost all the details that highlight Jesus' similarity to Moses in the transfiguration narratives are present in the Gospel of Mark (which, as we have noted, most scholars believe was a source for Matthew), and some additional similarities are shared with the Gospel of Luke. For example, Matthew and Luke add to Mark an emphasis on the radiance of Jesus' face (Matt. 17:2; Luke 9:29). This echoes the description of the radiance of the skin of Moses' face in Exodus 34:30. Furthermore, both Matthew and Luke add to Mark an emphasis on the fearful reaction of the disciples, corresponding to the fear of the Israelites in Exodus 34:30.

FEATURES REMINISCENT OF MOSES IN THE ACCOUNTS OF JESUS' TRANSFIGURATION			
Exodus	Matthew	Mark	Luke
after six days (24:16)	17:1	9:2	
on a high mountain (24:12, 15–18; 34:3)	17:1	9:2	9:28
a cloud descends and covers the mountain (24:15–18; 34:5)	17:5	9:7	9:34
a voice speaks from the cloud (24:16)	17:5	9:7	9:35
central figure reflects or radiates the divine glory (34:29–30, 35)	17:2	9:3	9:29
three individuals are given special mention (24:1)	17:1	9:2	9:28
bystanders react with fear (34:29–30)	17:6	9:6	9:34

This shows that Matthew did not invent this episode in order to portray Jesus as the new Moses. He did not have to do so. The Father providentially directs the events of Jesus' life so that his life parallels some of the most important features of Moses' life. Jesus' miraculous feeding of the multitude in the wilderness, his miraculous crossing of the sea, and other events similar to those that Moses experienced are also recorded in the other Gospels. These parallel accounts show that similarities between Jesus and Moses are a by-product of prophetic fulfillment, not theological invention. We can now proceed to the critical question: What does this imply about Jesus' identity and role?

The Theological Significance of the *New Moses* Theme

Jesus Will Lead His Followers on a New Exodus

Modern readers are likely to miss the theological significance of Jesus' identity as the new Moses. This is because modern readers tend to think of Moses quite differently from the way Matthew's original readers viewed him. Modern readers tend to think of Moses primarily as a lawgiver. They might even see Moses in a negative light because of their low view of the Old Testament law. Matthew's original readers, however, viewed Moses much more positively. For them, Moses was not primarily a lawgiver. He was a savior, a redeemer, and a deliverer.

Stephen's sermon in Acts 7 gives a clear example of this positive view of Moses. Stephen's sermon is designed to show that Jesus is the fulfillment of the prophecy about the coming of a prophet like Moses. He attempts to demonstrate Jesus' identity as the new Moses by highlighting similarities between these two important figures. Most importantly, Jesus, like Moses, was a misunderstood and persecuted savior, a redeemer rejected by the very people he longed to save. Acts 7:25 says, "He [Moses] supposed that his brothers would understand that God was giving them salvation by his [Moses'] hand." Acts 7:35 is even more explicit: "This Moses, whom they rejected . . . this man God sent as both ruler and redeemer by the hand of the angel who appeared to him in the bush." Stephen's sermon (and his life) is cut short by the angry mob before he can make his point that Jesus was also a misunderstood Savior and rejected Redeemer. Still, his positive view of Moses is clear, and this sheds enormous light on the significance of Jesus' identity as the new Moses.

This positive view of Moses surfaces also in the writings of Josephus, who, as we have seen, was a Jewish writer from later in the first century. He describes the deliverance of the Hebrews from their slavery in Egypt as Moses' "first and greatest work."[1]

This positive view of Moses also appears in the rabbinic maxim that we became acquainted with in the previous chapter: "As the first redeemer [Moses] was, so shall the latter Redeemer [Messiah] be."[2] Moses and Messiah are similar, primarily because they are both redeemers. The word *redeem* means "to rescue someone from an oppressive situation."[3] Moses is described as a redeemer because of the role that he plays in Israel's exodus.

Leviticus 26:13 and Exodus 1:11 aptly describe the condition of God's people under the pharaoh of Egypt. The Israelites have become Pharaoh's slaves, wearing yokes like beasts of burden, their backs bowed by the crushing weight of oppression and cowering beneath the taskmaster's lash. God speaks to Moses from the burning bush on Mount Horeb and appoints him to lead the Hebrews out of bondage:

> And now, behold, the cry of the people of Israel has come to me, and I have also seen the oppression with which the Egyptians oppress them. Come, I will send you to Pharaoh that you may bring my people, the children of Israel, out of Egypt. (Ex. 3:9–10)

The Israelites recognize that it is God who accomplishes their deliverance (Ex. 3:19–20; 14:30; Ps. 106:10). Yet God's people never forget the fact that God chose to save them through his servant Moses.

1. Josephus, *Against Apion*, 2.17 § 157.
2. *Qoheleth Rabbah* 1:9.
3. "λύτρωσις," in *A Greek-English Lexicon of the New Testament and Other Early Christian Literature*, ed. Frederick W. Danker, 3rd ed. (Chicago: University of Chicago Press, 2000), 606.

Matthew's presentation of Jesus as the new Moses identifies him as a Savior and Redeemer as well. That is, the new Moses will lead God's people on a new exodus. He, too, will rescue slaves from their captivity. But the slavery from which Jesus will deliver captives is not a political one; it is a spiritual one. Jesus will rescue his people from slavery to sin.

Matthew introduces this important truth at the beginning of his gospel. When the angel of the Lord appears to Joseph in a dream to assure him that the child that Mary carries has been conceived by the miraculous work of the Holy Spirit, the angel adds these instructions: "You shall call his name Jesus, for he will save his people from their sins" (Matt. 1:21). Jesus' name is significant for two reasons. First, the etymology of the name is important. The name *Jesus* is the New Testament equivalent of the Old Testament name *Joshua*, which in Hebrew means "Yahweh saves." The angel explains that this name is appropriate, since "he [Jesus] will save his people from their sins."

The name assigned by the angel and the accompanying explanation clearly show that Jesus is the Savior. Unfortunately, most readers interpret the explanation of the name as if it said that "he will save his people from the punishment their sins deserve." In fact, the statement insists that Jesus will rescue his people from sins themselves. The statement personifies the concept of sin, portraying sins as cruel masters who enslave mankind and force it into a harsh bondage. The verb *to save* typically means to rescue someone from a fate from which he cannot deliver himself. The verb implies that sinners are helpless, completely unable to free themselves from slavery to sins. The sinner's only hope is the One named *Yahweh saves*. He wields Yahweh's saving power to crush the shackles of sin and set its captives free.

The name *Jesus* is also significant because it is the name of Moses' first successor. Thus, the name serves to confirm Jesus' identity as the true and ultimate successor of Moses, the promised prophet like Moses. While Moses was primarily associated with Israel's exodus, Joshua was associated with Israel's conquest. Joshua led Israel to conquer and vanquish the pagan tribes that

49

inhabited the land that God had promised to his people so that they could occupy this land flowing with milk and honey. Jesus is likewise a divine warrior who conquers and vanquishes the enemies of God's people so that they can see the fulfillment of his promises. Jesus implies his identity as Moses' true successor by promising that his disciples "shall inherit the earth [lit. *land*]" (Matt. 5:5). The phrase "inherit the land" was frequently used to express God's promise that the Israelites would inhabit Canaan, the Promised Land, after their enemies were conquered (e.g., Ex. 23:30; Lev. 20:24; Deut. 4:38).

Other features of Matthew's gospel demonstrate that Jesus will lead his people on a new spiritual exodus. Some modern readers heavily criticize Matthew's use of a couple of Old Testament texts in his account of Jesus' infancy. After Matthew describes the flight of the holy family to Egypt, he adds, "This was to fulfill what the Lord had spoken by the prophet, 'Out of Egypt I called my son'" (Matt. 2:15). Some scholars argue that Matthew's quotation terribly distorts Hosea 11:1, since in its original context the passage apparently referred to the exodus of Israel, God's spiritual son, from Egypt rather than to the residence of the Messiah in the land of the pharaohs. Nevertheless, careful examination of Matthew's use of Hosea shows that Matthew is sensitive to the original context of Hosea 11:1. He quotes a text describing the exodus and applies it to Jesus because he wants to demonstrate that Jesus is the Moses-like Redeemer who will lead a new exodus.

Some modern interpreters think Matthew botches his reference to Hosea in portraying Jesus as the "son" who was called out of Egypt. This view misunderstands Matthew's purpose entirely. The original immediate context of Matthew's quotation makes it clear that "son" is a reference to Israel. Hosea 11:2 confirms this by referring to this son using the third-person-plural pronoun ("they"). The Septuagint highlights this interpretation by replacing "son" with "his children." Although Matthew's Greek translation follows the Hebrew Bible rather than the Septuagint, no evidence suggests that Matthew rejects the implications of the context by attempting to portray the "son" as the Messiah. Instead,

Matthew's appeal to Hosea 11:1 is intended to show that Jesus' departure from Egypt signals that Israel's promised deliverance from Egypt has begun. The portrayal of Israel's restoration as a new exodus in Hosea 11 and the reference to the prophecy of a prophet like Moses in Hosea 12:13, coupled with the promise of the Messiah in Hosea 3:4–5, may have stirred Israel's hope for a new Moses. Matthew does not interpret Hosea allegorically. Rather, he picks up on Hosea's own cues that point to a time of messianic deliverance.

The theme of Jesus as the new Moses fits perfectly with the powerful description of Jesus as One who will save his people from their sins in Matthew 1:21. Just as Moses was used by God to set Israel free from its slavery to Pharaoh, Jesus will set his people free from their slavery to sin. The new Moses will lead God's people on a new exodus, a spiritual exodus.

Other New Testament texts confirm that Jesus is a liberator who frees his people from bondage to sin (John 8:32, 34, 36; Rom. 6:16–18). John and Paul affirm with Matthew that though we were once slaves, we have been set free. The new Moses breaks the will of our spiritual Pharaoh with his mighty power and shouts his forceful command, "Let my people go!" When our spiritual Pharaoh pursues us, determined to enslave us again, Christ sends the torrents of the Red Sea crashing down on him and his minions. Our liberation is final. We have been set free, never to be enslaved again. The new Moses still liberates sinners from their spiritual slavery today. He can break the bondage to sinful habits and destructive addictions. Glory to God!

Jesus Will Initiate a New Covenant

Although Moses was primarily regarded by the ancient Jews as a redeemer, deliverer, or savior, he was recognized as a lawgiver as well. Yet the Jews viewed the law as far more than an oppressive list of commands and prohibitions. The law was God's covenant with Israel and an expression of his special love for them. The

Jews recognized that through the covenant, God declares Israel to be "his treasured possession" (Deut. 26:18–19).

The covenant offers enormous blessing to those who obey God's commands (Deut. 28:1–6). God promises Israel a victory over her enemies that will cause the Jews to be feared by all the peoples of the earth. He promises that all they do will prosper and that "the LORD will make you the head and not the tail, and you shall only go up and not down" (v. 13).

This covenant is an expression of God's grace toward Israel. The Jews do not deserve this special relationship with Yahweh in any way (Deut. 7:7–8). In particular, Deuteronomy 9 explains that God did not choose Israel for a unique relationship with him because of Israel's supposed righteousness (vv. 4, 6). Israel is a sinful people; the covenant is an expression of God's grace.

The covenant that God establishes with Israel on Sinai (Ex. 19:1–6) is given to God's people through the mediation of Moses (vv. 7–8, 18–21; cf. Gal. 3:19). Not only does Moses deliver the covenant to God's people, he also encourages Israel to commit to the covenant, reads the covenant to the people, and initiates the covenant by sprinkling sacrificial blood on the altar and on the people while shouting, "Behold the blood of the covenant that the LORD has made with you in accordance with all these words" (Ex. 24:1–8).

The covenant is so closely associated with Moses that the Old Testament frequently refers to the covenant as the "law of Moses." The covenant is described as the "law of God" five times and "the law of the LORD" ten times, but it is described as the "law of Moses" thirteen times. Jewish literature written between the time of the Old and New Testaments equates "the book of the covenant of the Most High God" with "the law that Moses commanded us"[4] and praises Moses for his role in establishing God's covenant with Israel:

> He gave him commandments for his people, and revealed to him
> his glory. For his faithfulness and meekness he consecrated him,

4. Sir. 24:23.

choosing him out of all humankind. He allowed him to hear his voice, and led him into the dark cloud, and gave him the commandments face to face, the law of life and knowledge, so that he might teach Jacob the covenant, and Israel his decrees.[5]

In light of Moses' role as the mediator of the covenant, those who looked for the coming of the prophet like Moses might have expected him to be the mediator of a covenant as well.

Matthew demonstrates that Jesus, the new Moses, is the Mediator of a covenant, much like his predecessor. But the covenant that Jesus establishes with God's people is vastly superior to the law of Moses. This new covenant is anticipated by Moses himself. Moses foretells that God's people will abandon the covenant he mediated and that all the curses of the covenant will befall them. Yet he promises that after the people repent, the Lord will graciously restore them. To ensure that God's people do not abandon him again, God will transform the hearts of his people. Deuteronomy 30:6–8 promises:

> And the LORD your God will circumcise your heart and the heart of your offspring, so that you will love the LORD your God with all your heart and with all your soul, that you may live. . . . And you shall again obey the voice of the LORD and keep all his commandments that I command you today.

Deuteronomy 10:16 is helpful for understanding the nature of this promise. God commands: "Circumcise therefore the foreskin of your heart, and be no longer stubborn." The command "be no longer stubborn" translates the Hebrew idiom *stiffen the neck*. The idiom refers to an ox or donkey that refuses to be guided by its master. It resists the tug of the reins that seeks to turn it to the right or left by locking the muscles in its neck and stubbornly insisting on going its own way. The circumcised heart is the very opposite of the stiff neck. Rather than obstinately resisting the will of the master, the circumcised heart joyfully complies with the

5. Sir. 45:3–5.

master's will. The circumcised heart eagerly awaits the master's commands and finds great joy in fulfilling those commands. The circumcised heart prompts a person "to fear the LORD your God, to walk in all his ways, to love him, to serve the LORD your God with all your heart and with all your soul, and to keep the commandments and statutes of the LORD" (Deut. 10:12–13).

The people of Israel fail to circumcise their own hearts. Thus, God promises that one day he will circumcise their hearts for them. This circumcision of the heart will ensure that God's people love him deeply and express that love through obedience to his commands. The shift from the command "circumcise your heart" to the promise "the LORD your God will circumcise your heart" demonstrates that in the restoration of his people, God will do for them the very thing that they have proved incapable of doing for themselves.

The Old Testament prophets further develop the promise that God will transform the hearts of his people. Jeremiah 29:10–14 looks back to the promise of Israel's restoration given in Deuteronomy 30. Jeremiah 31:31–34 elaborates God's promise to circumcise the hearts of his people. Although every word of Jeremiah's prophecy is significant, space permits only a brief discussion of the highlights of this important passage. The introduction, "Behold, the days are coming," signals that the fulfillment of this promise will occur in the messianic age.[6] The old covenant is explicitly identified as "the covenant that I made with their fathers on the day when I took them by the hand to bring them out of the land of Egypt." This is the Mosaic covenant, the law of Moses, associated with the events of the exodus. This covenant requires obedience from God's people, but they consistently fail to live obediently. "I

6. Carl F. Keil correctly observes that the expression "the days are coming" probably owes its origin to the idea expressed in the phrase "at the end of days" (ESV: "in the latter days") in texts such as Jeremiah 23:20. The phrase in Jeremiah 23:20 refers to the messianic era, in which God brings his entire redemptive plan to completion. See Carl F. Keil and Franz Delitzsch, *Biblical Commentary on the Old Testament* (Grand Rapids: Eerdmans, 1986), 1:360, 2:38. Some commentators argue that the phrase in Jeremiah 23:20 merely means "afterward" and bears no eschatological sense. Yet Jeremiah is surely aware of the use of the phrase to refer to the messianic era in texts such as Genesis 49:1 and Numbers 24:14 and appears to mimic the usage in the Pentateuch.

took them by the hand" shows that the exodus is an expression of Yahweh's compassion to Israel by introducing the concept of a loving covenant similar to the marital covenant to which Jeremiah later alludes: "I was their husband." The contrast between the old and new covenants demonstrates that they differ in their efficacy. Although the old covenant is broken by God's people despite the grace that he lavishes on them in claiming Israel as his bride, the new covenant will be effective in making God's people faithful to him. The difference in the efficacy of the covenants is directly related to the difference in the nature of the covenants. The old covenant consists of external standards written on tablets of stone that the Israelites are unable to satisfy, while the new covenant will ensure that God's righteous demands are engraved on the hearts of his people. God will transform his people internally so that they naturally and spontaneously live the righteous lives he desires. The new covenant will result in new intimacy with God. The knowledge of God will no longer be mediated through others, for each person will know God personally and relate to him directly. The new covenant will also entail forgiveness of sin as God wipes the very memory of his people's transgressions from his mind and chooses to relate to them as if they had never sinned at all.

The prophet Ezekiel also promises the new covenant. Ezekiel refers to this covenant as the "covenant of peace" and an "everlasting covenant" (Ezek. 37:26). He also clarifies that this covenant will be initiated by the Messiah (vv. 24–25). Like Jeremiah, Ezekiel stresses that the covenant will be transformational (36:26–27). The "new heart" described by Ezekiel is the equivalent of the circumcised heart of Deuteronomy 30:6 and the heart inscribed with God's law of Jeremiah 31:31–34. The "heart of stone" is a hard heart that rebels against the will of God. The "heart of flesh" is a heart sensitive to God and compliant to his will. This change of heart is wrought by the indwelling Spirit, who powerfully prompts God's people to obey his commands willingly and gladly. "Walk in my statutes and be careful to obey my rules" closely parallels "walk in my rules and be careful to obey my statutes" in Ezekiel 37:24, thus closely associating the transformation of the heart and giving of the Spirit with the reign of the Messiah.

Matthew alludes to the new covenant at both the beginning and end of Jesus' ministry. These allusions form an *inclusio*, a pair of allusions that serve as brackets for literary unit, and demonstrate that the new covenant is an important theme of Jesus' ministry.

The first allusion to the new covenant appears in Matthew 1:21, which most scholars regard as the programmatic statement for the gospel. The angel explains to Joseph the significance of the name *Jesus*: "he will save his people from their sins." Interpreters still debate the Old Testament background for this statement. Most argue for Psalm 130:8 ("he will redeem Israel from all his iniquities"), although a few opt for Judges 13:5 ("Behold, you shall conceive and bear a son . . . and he shall begin to save Israel"). Nevertheless, Matthew 1:21 seems to have a tighter connection to Ezekiel 36–37, both semantically and thematically.[7] Ezekiel 36:29 says, "I will deliver you from all your uncleannesses." Although the parallels with Matthew 1:21 initially seem modest, they are heightened when one observes that "you" is identified with "my people" in Ezekiel 36:28. Furthermore, when the promise is repeated in Ezekiel 37:23, Israel's lawless deeds are described as acts in which the people "sinned." Thus, the promises in Ezekiel share three critical terms—*save, people*, and *sin*—with Matthew 1:21.

The implications of this are enormous. Ezekiel 36 and 37 express the promise of the new covenant, which Ezekiel identifies as the "covenant of peace." If the programmatic statement of Matthew is drawn from Ezekiel's promise, interpreters can no longer treat the new covenant as a minor or peripheral theme in Matthew's gospel. This theme is not merely associated with the identity of Jesus as the prophet like Moses. As will later be

7. R. T. France, *The Gospel of Matthew*, New International Commentary on the New Testament (Grand Rapids: Eerdmans, 2007), 54; Nicholas Piotrowski, "'I Will Save My People from Their Sins': The Influence of Ezekiel 36:28b–29a; 37:23b on Matthew 1:21" (paper presented to the Midwest Region of the Society of Biblical Literature, Olivet Nazarene University, Bourbonnais, IL, February 12, 2011).

demonstrated, the allusion to Ezekiel's covenant of peace also confirms Jesus' identity as the new David.

A second allusion to the new covenant comes in Matthew's quotation of Jeremiah 31:15 in Matthew 2:17–18. Jeremiah 31:15 precedes the promise of the new covenant by only a few verses. The quotation thus strategically signals that God is on the brink of fulfilling the promise of Jeremiah 31:31–34. The era of the new covenant has dawned with the coming of Messiah Jesus. Admittedly, this reference to the new covenant is subtle, but Matthew communicates some of his most important messages in subtle ways. Sometimes a whisper can communicate more powerfully than a shout, for it causes the listener to lean forward and strain to listen more intently. Matthew's whispers have the same effect.

The truth implied by the quotation of Jeremiah 31 is made abundantly clear by the content of John the Baptist's message to Israel. John preaches, "I baptize you with water for repentance. . . . He will baptize you with the Holy Spirit and fire" (Matt. 3:11). The reference to the Messiah's baptizing with the Holy Spirit most likely alludes to prophetic references to the eschatological outpouring of the Spirit of God (Isa. 32:15; 44:3; Ezek. 36:26–27; 39:29; Joel 2:28–29).[8] John's coupling of references to water and the Spirit recall references to "pouring out" the Spirit in Ezekiel 39:29 and the combination of references to water and Spirit in Ezekiel 36. With the promise of the new covenant, God assures his people that he will "sprinkle clean water on you, and you shall be clean from all your uncleannesses" and that he will "put my Spirit within you" (vv. 25, 27).

Finally, Jesus directly refers to the new covenant toward the close of his ministry. During the Last Supper, Jesus gives thanks for the cup and passes it to his disciples with the words, "This is my blood of the covenant, which is poured out for many for the forgiveness of sins" (Matt. 26:28). The statement alludes to the fact that God's

8. D. A. Carson, "Matthew," in *Matthew, Mark, Luke*, Expositor's Bible Commentary (Grand Rapids: Zondervan, 1984), 104–5; R. T. France, *The Gospel of Matthew*, New International Commentary on the New Testament (Grand Rapids: Eerdmans, 2007), 114–15; John Nolland, *Matthew*, New International Greek Testament Commentary (Grand Rapids: Eerdmans, 2005), 145–47.

earlier covenants with Israel were generally established through an act of sacrifice. God's covenant with Abraham was initiated by the sacrifice of a heifer, a she-goat, a ram, a turtledove, and a pigeon (Gen. 15:1–20). The Mosaic covenant was initiated by the sacrifice of oxen. Moses collected the blood of the slain oxen and threw half of it against the altar. Then he read the book of the covenant to the people and threw the other half of the sacrificial blood on them, shouting, "Behold the blood of the covenant that the LORD has made with you in accordance with all these words" (Ex. 24:8). The words "blood of the covenant" appear only twice in the Old Testament: in Exodus 24:8 and in an allusion to that passage in Zechariah 9:11. Consequently, Jesus' words indicate that by his death he will initiate a covenant that will replace the Mosaic covenant. This covenant is none other than the new covenant that was promised by Moses, Jeremiah, and Ezekiel, as the parallel in Luke 22:20 explicitly states.

Many of Jesus' teachings in the Gospel of Matthew are dependent on the promise of the new covenant. Jesus' description of his disciples as the "pure in heart" (Matt. 5:8) points back to the giving of the new covenant. Jesus teaches that man's heart in its natural state is thoroughly corrupt and sinful. All of man's wicked words and deeds issue from his wicked heart. Jesus corrects the Pharisees' notion that eating with unwashed hands defiles a man. He insists, "For out of the heart come evil thoughts, murder, adultery, sexual immorality, theft, false witness, slander" (15:19). The disciples' hearts can be described as "pure" only because Jesus radically changes the hearts of his followers. The "pure in heart" are those who experience the fulfillment of Moses' promise that God will circumcise the heart (Deut. 30:6), Ezekiel's prophecy that God will "give you a new heart" (Ezek. 36:26), and Jeremiah's prophecy that God will "put my law within them, and . . . will write it on their hearts" (Jer. 31:33).

The fact that Jesus' disciples participate in the new exodus and are beneficiaries of the new covenant ensures that they are characterized by an extraordinary righteousness. Because they are set free from slavery to sin and have God's law written on their hearts, Jesus expects his disciples to be increasingly characterized by the righteousness that he describes in the Sermon on the Mount.[9] Through the new exodus and the new covenant, Jesus' disciples receive a righteousness that exceeds that of the scribes and Pharisees, generally recognized as the most righteous people of the time (Matt. 5:20). They have an extraordinary righteousness that exhibits God's own holy character (5:43–48). Jesus' disciples are "healthy trees" that produce the "good fruit" of righteous words and actions (7:17).[10]

Other New Testament writers rightly see the new covenant promises fulfilled through the saving work of Jesus Christ. Paul teaches that the Spirit circumcises the hearts of Jesus' followers (Rom. 2:29; Col. 2:11). Paul also interprets the words of Deuteronomy 30:11–14 as referring to the gospel (Rom. 10:6–11). He comes to this understanding by recognizing that the promise of the circumcised heart is fulfilled only by Christ through the gospel.

Paul refers to the law written on the heart through the Spirit's work in fulfillment of the new covenant as "the law of the Spirit of life" (Rom. 8:2). Paul's most extensive discussion of the new covenant appears in 2 Corinthians 3:1–18. Here he teaches that through this covenant, God's law is "written not with ink but with the Spirit of the living God, not on tablets of stone but on tablets of human hearts" (v. 3). Paul insists that although the old covenant resulted in death, the new covenant results in life. Although the old covenant resulted in the condemnation of God's people, the new covenant results in the righteousness of God's people. Although the old covenant had passed away, the new covenant is permanent. Consequently, this new covenant is of far greater glory than the old covenant. Paul teaches that Jesus' own words confirm that the new covenant was initiated through Jesus' sacrificial death (1 Cor. 11:25).

As the new Moses, Jesus thus replicates the ministry of Moses and at the same time greatly exceeds Moses' ministry. He leads God's people on a new and greater exodus that liberates them from slavery to sin. He also offers the sacrifice that initiates a new covenant, a

---

9. See Charles L. Quarles, *The Sermon on the Mount: Restoring Christ's Message to the Modern Church* (Nashville: B&H Academic, 2011).

10. For other references to the extraordinary righteousness that characterizes Jesus' disciples, see the section "The New Israel Will Be Holy" in chapter 8.

covenant vastly superior to the Mosaic law. Through this new covenant, God grants forgiveness to his people and radically transforms them so that they long to obey God as an expression of love for him and are empowered by God's Spirit to obey his commandments.

Jesus Will Be the Servant of Yahweh

One important extension of Matthew's portrayal of Jesus as the new Moses is his presentation of Jesus as the Servant of the Lord. Although Matthew could conclude that Jesus was the fulfillment of two unrelated prophecies, the prophecy of the coming of a prophet like Moses and the prophecy of a Suffering Servant, it is more likely that Matthew sees the two prophecies as interrelated. As will soon be demonstrated, the prophet of Deuteronomy 18 and the Servant of Isaiah share much in common.

Isaiah's prophecies are rich with references to a figure known as the *Servant of Yahweh*. Isaiah's writings contain four sections typically referred to as *Servant Songs* because a figure identified as a Servant is prominent in the texts. These four Servant Songs appear in Isaiah 42:1–7; 49:1–6; 50:4–11; and 52:13–53:12. Matthew quotes from these songs in Matthew 12:18–21 (Isa. 42:1–4) and 8:17 (Isa. 53:4). His quotations present Jesus as the Servant of Isaiah's prophecies.

The term *servant* is used of various persons and groups in Isaiah, including Isaiah himself (Isa. 20:3), David (37:35), and the nation of Israel (41:8–9). But the subject of the Servant Songs cannot be identified with any of these persons or groups. In the Servant Songs, Isaiah distinguishes the Servant from Israel. He describes the Servant as messenger of a new covenant to Israel (42:6), One who acts on Yahweh's behalf to redeem and restore Israel (49:5–6), and most importantly, the atoning sacrifice for the sins of Israel (chap. 53). These descriptions of the Servant also go far beyond the Old Testament descriptions of the ordinary prophet. This makes it highly unlikely that a prophetic figure such as Isaiah is the Servant. Ancient Jewish interpretation preserved in the Targums—Aramaic paraphrases of the Hebrew Old Testament—identifies the figure as the Messiah. The New Testament writers interpret the Servant Songs as prophecies about the Messiah as well (Matt. 8:17; 12:18–21; John 12:37–41; Acts 8:30–35; 13:47; 1 Peter 2:22–25). Thus, readers should recognize the Servant Songs as prophecies about the coming Messiah.

Isaiah appears to have drawn the title *the Servant* from descriptions of Moses in the Pentateuch. Moses is frequently described as Yahweh's "servant" in the five books of Moses[11] as well as in later Old Testament books[12] and the New Testament.[13]

Based on the numerous descriptions of Moses as the Lord's servant in the Old Testament, Gerhard von Rad suggests that the Servant of the Lord who dies vicariously in Isaiah 53 is the prophet like Moses promised in the Pentateuch (Deut. 18:15, 18–19).[14] This view seems to be supported by the verbal parallels between descriptions of Moses in the Pentateuch and descriptions of the Servant in Isaiah 52 and 53. For example, Numbers 12:7 describes Moses as a "faithful" servant: "Not so with my servant Moses. He is faithful in all my house." Isaiah 52:13 describes the Servant as One who acts "wisely."[15] Numbers 12:13 shows that Moses sought healing for his sister Miriam, who was struck by God with leprosy because of her sin: "And Moses cried to the LORD, 'O God, please heal her—please.'" Similarly, Isaiah 53:5 shows that the Servant provides healing for others:

> But he was wounded for our transgressions;
>   he was crushed for our iniquities;
> upon him was the chastisement that brought us peace,
>   and with his stripes we are healed.

11. E.g., Ex. 4:10; 14:31; Num. 11:11; 12:7–8; Deut. 3:24; 34:5.
12. Josh. 1:1–2, 7, 13, 15; 8:31, 33; 9:24; 11:12, 15; 12:6; 13:8; 14:7; 18:7; 22:2, 4–5; 1 Kings 8:53, 56; 2 Kings 18:12; 21:8; 1 Chron. 6:49; 2 Chron. 1:3; 24:6, 9; Neh. 1:7–8; 9:14; 10:29; Ps. 105:26; Dan. 9:11; Mal. 4:4.
13. Heb. 3:5; Rev. 15:3.
14. Gerhard von Rad, *The Message of the Prophets*, trans. D. G. M. Stalker (New York: Harper & Row, 1965), 227–28.
15. Hebrews 3:5–6 stresses that both Moses and Jesus were "faithful over God's house," the former as a servant, but the latter as a son.

There are other parallels between descriptions of Moses and descriptions of the Servant. Isaiah 53:12 says that the Servant "makes intercession for the transgressors." The description is reminiscent of Moses, who intercedes for Miriam (Num. 12:13) and for the entire nation (Ex. 32:11–14, 31–32) when they transgress. Psalm 106:23 and Jeremiah 15:1 show that Moses was famous for this act of intercession. Moses is described as a prophet (Deut. 18:15–18; 34:10; Hos. 12:13). Although the Servant is not assigned the title *prophet*, he is unmistakably portrayed as one.[16] God's Spirit rests on both Moses and the Servant (Num. 11:17; Isa. 42:1). Both are characterized by unmatched meekness (Num 12:3; Isa. 42:2–3; 50:5–6; 53:3–4). The Servant will sprinkle people with blood (Isa. 52:15), much as Moses throws the blood of the covenant on the people of Israel (Ex. 24:8).

Ancient Jewish interpreters of Isaiah spotted some of the parallels between the Servant of the Lord and Moses. The Babylonian Talmud discusses Isaiah 53:12 in connection with Moses.[17] Even earlier, Peter's sermon in Acts 3 presents Jesus as both One like Moses and the Servant of the Lord.[18] Matthew also appears to have been aware of the connections between Moses and the Servant of the Lord. His emphasis on Jesus' identity as the new Moses is coupled with an insistence that Jesus is the fulfillment of the Suffering Servant prophecies of Isaiah.

Matthew twice quotes Isaiah's Servant Songs. The longest quotation of the Old Testament in Matthew's entire gospel (Matt. 12:15–21) is drawn from the prophet's description of the Servant in Isaiah 42:1–4. Two features of Matthew 12:15–16 apparently serve as the fulfillment of Isaiah's promise.[19] First, Jesus' withdrawal from an area where the Pharisees seek to debate him and conspire to destroy him serves to evade, for the moment at least,

16. Sigmund Mowinckel, *He That Cometh: The Messiah Concept in the Old Testament and Later Judaism* (Grand Rapids: Eerdmans, 2005), 213–33.

17. *b. Sotah* 14a.

18. R. F. Zehnle, *Peter's Pentecost Discourse: Tradition and Lukan Reinterpretation in Peter's Speeches of Acts 2 and 3* (Nashville: Abingdon, 1971), 48–49, 75–89.

19. France, *Matthew*, 122–24.

a quarrel with them.[20] Second, Jesus orders the man
him not to make him known. This demonstrates the
of Jesus' ministry and shows that he is One who wi
or cry aloud, nor will anyone hear his voice in the streets (v. _

Matthew quotes the passage at length, not merely the portion
that was being fulfilled at the moment, because he sees Jesus as
the fulfillment of the entire description of the Servant in Isaiah.
Jesus is chosen by God, beloved by the Lord, and pleasing to
the Father, as God's own statement at Jesus' baptism confirms
(Matt. 3:17). The Father's description of the Son "with whom I am
well pleased" is itself an echo of Isaiah 42:1. Furthermore, God's
Spirit rests on Jesus, and Jesus is endowed with the power and
authority to baptize others with the Holy Spirit. Matthew probably
also sees special significance in the concluding promise: "in his
name the Gentiles will hope" (Matt. 12:21).[21] By skipping the first
clause of Isaiah 42:4 and leaping to a reference to the hope of the
Gentiles, fitting one of his most prominent theological themes,
Matthew is particularly eager to show from Isaiah's prophecy
that Messiah Jesus will bring hope to those previously excluded
from God's chosen people.

Matthew also quotes Isaiah's Servant Songs to present Jesus
as the Savior who will die a sacrificial death in order to provide
salvation for his people. Matthew 8:17 explains that Jesus' healing ministry is a fulfillment of Isaiah 53:4: "He took our illnesses
and bore our diseases." When Matthew quotes an Old Testament
prophecy, he intends to appeal to the entire original context of
the passage and not merely the brief portion quoted. Matthew no
doubt recognizes all of Isaiah 52:13–53:12 as a description of Jesus.
The prophecy foretells the following truths about the Messiah:

- He is a wise servant who will be exalted.
- The beatings that he suffers are so severe that he is hardly
  recognizable as a human being.
- He purifies many nations by sprinkling his blood on them.

20. Ibid., 472.
21. See the Septuagint of Isa. 42:4.

- He reduces kings to silence.
- He is rejected by humanity in general and becomes an object of reproach.
- He is wounded (lit. *pierced*) for the transgressions of his people.
- Yahweh transfers our sin guilt to him.
- He suffers silently and without protest and then dies, even though completely innocent.
- The dead, righteous sufferer is raised back to life, even after dying as an offering for sin, since "he shall see his offspring; he shall prolong his days" (Isa. 53:10).
- The One who bears the iniquities of God's people enjoys the spoils of victory.

Matthew recognizes Jesus as the human sacrificial lamb who dies in the place of sinners so that they can escape the wrath their sins rightly deserve.

Matthew appears to allude to the prophecy of the Suffering Servant on other occasions. Matthew quotes Jesus' declaration that he will "give his life as a ransom for many" (Matt. 20:28; Mark 10:45). With the exception of "ransom," all the terminology of the phrase appears to be drawn directly from Isaiah 53:12. With only minor differences, the Septuagint refers to the Servant's "giving his life for many."[22] Furthermore, Jesus' statement refers to his coming to serve, not to be served, and this fits well with the descriptions of the righteous Servant in Isaiah. France rightly notes, "It would be hard to compose a better brief summary of the central thrust of Isa 53 than 'to give his life as a ransom in place of many.'"[23]

At the Last Supper, Jesus refers to the cup as "my blood of the covenant, which is poured out for many for the forgiveness

22. A dependence on Isaiah 53 is affirmed in W. J. Moulder, "The Old Testament Background and the Interpretation of Mark x.45," *New Testament Studies* 24 (1977): 120–27; Dale C. Allison Jr., *The New Moses: A Matthean Typology* (Minneapolis: Fortress, 1993), 234; France, *Jesus and the OT*, 110–32; R. T. France, "The Servant of the Lord in the Teaching of Jesus," *Tyndale Bulletin* 19 (1968): 26–52.

23. France, *Matthew*, 762.

of sins" (Matt. 26:28). Some scholars find an allusion to the Suffering Servant prophecy here as well.[24] The primary reference in Jesus' statement is clearly the new covenant promises of Jeremiah and Ezekiel discussed earlier. Although there is only one verbal parallel between Jesus' statement here and Isaiah 52–53 in the Septuagint—the shared occurrence of the adjective *many*—an allusion to the Suffering Servant prophecy is supported by the fact that Matthew's words "poured out" could be his own translation of the Hebrew verb used in Isaiah 53:12: "he poured out his soul to death."

These texts demonstrate that the prophecy of the Suffering Servant is a key element in Jesus' understanding of his identity and mission. Jesus' statements in Matthew 20:28 and 26:28 and his frequent teaching that he "must suffer" (16:21; see also 17:22; 20:18–19; 26:2) show his own careful reflection on the prophecy of the Suffering Servant.

Although the Servant prophecies of Isaiah show the influence of the prophecy of a prophet like Moses, Isaiah's prophecies also show that the new Moses will go far beyond Moses to save and redeem his people. Although Moses passionately intercedes for his people (Ex. 32:11–14), and even asks to have his own name blotted out of God's book if Israel is not forgiven, God refuses his offer with the retort, "Whoever has sinned against me, I will blot out of my book" (vv. 31–33). Although God graciously responds to Moses' intercession by refraining from destroying the entire nation (v. 14), Moses' intercession is not always effective. Jeremiah 15:1 warns, "Though Moses and Samuel stood before me, yet my heart would not turn toward this people. Send them out of my sight, and let them go!" Jesus, the new Moses and Suffering Servant, is always effective in his intercession for sinners. He actually suffers the punishment that his people deserve, in their place. God accepts his offering as a worthy sacrifice (Isa. 53:10–11). Thus, although Jesus is like Moses, he is vastly superior to Moses. He leads his people on a greater

24. Allison, *New Moses*, 234. See also Donald A. Hagner, *Matthew*, Word Biblical Commentary (Dallas: Word, 1993–95), 2:773.

exodus. He serves as Mediator of a greater covenant. He offers his people salvation through a greater sacrifice.

Conclusion: Repent and Believe

Matthew's presentation of Jesus as the new Moses, the Savior and Deliverer of sinners, drives his readers to a critical decision. The only proper response to the Savior is to repent of sin and to trust Jesus as the One who will save his people from their sins.

The Gospel of Matthew stresses the importance of repentance and faith. John the Baptist's preaching could be summed up in one command: "Repent, for the kingdom of heaven is at hand" (Matt. 3:2). Shockingly, he demands this repentance not only of Israel's notorious sinners, but even of those that many considered to be among the most righteous of Jews. John orders even the Pharisees and Sadducees to "bear fruit in keeping with repentance" (v. 8). Jesus' preaching echoes these emphases: "Repent, for the kingdom of heaven is at hand" (4:17). Repentance is necessary to prepare for the coming kingdom and for the judgment that will accompany the Messiah's arrival. Repentance is the only means possible for escaping the coming wrath (3:7–8). Those who truly repent are expected to demonstrate the sincerity of their repentance by receiving baptism and by producing fruits of repentance in the form of deeds of righteousness (vv. 8, 11).

Jesus gives a stern rebuke to the cities at the focus of his Galilean ministry and warns that they will find the day of judgment unbearable and be brought down to Hades (Matt. 11:20–21). Just as the people of Nineveh repented in response to the preaching of Jonah, so the people of Israel should repent in response to Jesus' resurrection (12:41). Tragically, most refuse to repent, and thus the men of Nineveh will rise up at the judgment and condemn them for their inexcusable evil. Jesus laments Israel's rejection of his gracious offer of salvation, demonstrated by their refusal to repent: "O Jerusalem, Jerusalem, the city that kills the prophets and stones those who are sent to it! How often would I have gathered your children together as a hen gathers her brood under her wings, and you would not!" (23:37).

Repent and *repentance* refer to a change of mind and heart in which a person realizes the heinousness of his sin, shudders in the face of God's coming judgment, renounces his sin, and determines, by God's power, to live as God desires. Matthew's gospel does not offer a precise definition of the terms *repent* and *repentance*—the vocabulary was already well known to its readers because of their familiarity with the Old Testament. Jesus nevertheless described his disciples as those who are "poor in spirit" (Matt. 5:3). Jesus' disciples recognize themselves as spiritual beggars who have nothing to offer God, totally dependent on his grace. Furthermore, Jesus' disciples are those who "mourn" (5:4), and this description compares a disciple's sorrow over his sins to a person's grief over the death of a loved one. Jesus' disciples also "hunger and thirst for righteousness" (v. 6). They crave righteousness more than a starving man craves his next morsel of bread or a man with parched tongue longs for his next sip of water. These descriptions of Jesus' disciples serve as a graphic depiction of genuine repentance, characterized by abandonment of notions of one's personal goodness, deep remorse over one's sins, and a longing for true righteousness.[25]

Jesus also offers a clear illustration of repentance in the parable of the two sons, a parable that appears only in Matthew's gospel. Repentance is illustrated by a rebellious son who initially rejects his father's command to work in his vineyard but later changes his mind and obediently serves the father (Matt. 21:28–32). Jesus uses the parable to illustrate the humble repentance of tax collectors and prostitutes.

Matthew's gospel clearly teaches that sinners who wish to escape the coming wrath and receive God's gracious pardon must repent. And they should do so without delay. They should then express the repentance of their hearts through actions such as confessing sin, receiving baptism, and living righteously.

---

25. For a detailed explanation of the interpretation of the Beatitudes that is assumed here, see Quarles, *Sermon on the Mount*, 42–62.

True repentance is accompanied by faith in Jesus. Matthew's gospel emphasizes the necessity of faith's accompanying repentance. In Matthew 8:5–13, Jesus commends the centurion for his faith in Jesus, a faith unparalleled among the Israelites. He also heals the man's son in accordance with the centurion's faith. In 9:2, Jesus pronounces forgiveness and grants healing to the paralytic in response to his and his companions' faith. In verse 28, Jesus demands faith of the two blind men before miraculously giving them sight. Matthew 13:58 shows that Jesus refuses to perform miracles in Nazareth because of the people's unbelief. The context shows that their unbelief consists of dismissing Jesus as merely a carpenter's son despite his astonishing teaching and mighty works. In 15:28, Jesus commends the Canaanite woman for her great faith. In the parable of the two sons, Jesus speaks of the importance of believing the message of John (21:28–32).

Matthew clearly expresses the necessity of faith in Jesus in Matthew 18:6, where Jesus refers to his disciples as "these little ones who believe in me." Perhaps the most important statement with regard to faith in the Gospel of Matthew appears in 9:22: "Take heart, daughter; your faith has made you well." The Greek text could literally be translated, "Your faith has saved you." This statement employs the verb *to save* used in the programmatic verse of the gospel, "he will save his people from their sins" (1:21). The verb clearly functions as a double entendre—the woman's physical healing, involving rescue from a condition that leaves her ritually defiled and thus estranged from God, pictures spiritual salvation. The statement reinforces the truth implied in other healing miracles in which Jesus requires faith: faith in Jesus is necessary for salvation.[26]

Although faith in Jesus is necessary for salvation, it could not be clearer that the disciple's faith in Jesus never merits his deliverance. Sadly, the believer's faith always seems weak and unworthy

---

26. See also Matthew 23:23, in which the noun translated "faithfulness" may refer to "faith" as one of the weightier matters of the law. Although the context suggests that the word means "faithfulness" (since it is linked with justice and mercy and described as something that one does), elsewhere in Matthew the noun always refers to faith as an act of believing or trusting.

of the Savior. In the Gospel of Matthew, Jesus frequently chides his disciples for their weakness and smallness of faith (Matt. 6:30; 8:26; 14:31; 16:8; 17:17, 20). Shockingly, even after Jesus' resurrection, even after the disciples behold the risen Savior with their own eyes, their faith is still mingled with doubt (28:17). Thus, Jesus' disciples are often compelled to cry out, like the father of the demon-possessed boy, "I believe; help my unbelief!" (Mark 9:24). Fortunately, Jesus teaches that what ultimately matters is the greatness of the object of our faith, not the greatness of our faith. Even the tiniest faith is sufficient because of the great power of Jesus to perform the impossible (Matt. 17:20).

Those who desire deliverance through the new Moses, those who seek to be saved from their sins, must both repent and believe. Matthew would heartily agree with the apostle Paul, who summarizes the proper response to the gospel as "repentance toward God" and "faith in our Lord Jesus Christ" (Acts 20:21).

Part 3

The New David: Jesus, Our King

Matthew's Development of the *New David* Theme

MUCH AS MATTHEW COMPARES Jesus to Moses, he associates Jesus with King David in a number of striking ways as well. Matthew points to a special connection that Jesus shares with David in his genealogy, his titles, the circumstances of his birth, his fulfillment of prophecy, and his actions. Jesus' similarity to David is one of Matthew's favorite Christological themes.

Jesus Is Associated with David in His Genealogy

Matthew emphasizes the special relationship of Jesus to King David from the opening lines of his gospel. Matthew begins his gospel with a genealogy of Jesus, introduced with these words: "The book of the genealogy of Jesus Christ, the son of David, the son of Abraham" (Matt. 1:1). This introduction stresses Jesus' Davidic lineage. The genealogy itself is presented in chronological order. It begins with Jesus' early ancestors, the patriarchs Abraham, Isaac, and Jacob, and concludes with Jesus' most recent ancestors. One would expect the title of the genealogy to follow this same chronological order. Thus, one would expect the title: "The book of the genealogy of Jesus Christ, the son of Abraham, the son of David." Instead, Matthew lists David *before* the patriarch Abraham. This unexpected order places special emphasis on the person of David in Jesus' family line.

The arrangement of the genealogy fulfills a similar purpose. In Matthew 1:17, the evangelist arranges the genealogy into three sets of fourteen generations. This arrangement is artistic. Matthew omits four members of the dynastic succession from David to the Babylonian exile to achieve three groups of fourteen. This shows that the arrangement of three groups of fourteen generations was not demanded by the genealogical data, but was imposed on the genealogy for some other reason.

Most scholars are convinced that Matthew's emphasis on the number fourteen is an example of *gematria*.[1] Gematria is a form of biblical interpretation using numerical values of letters of the Hebrew alphabet to decipher words.[2] In gematria, the first letter of the alphabet equals the number one; the second, the number two; and so forth.[3]

In Hebrew gematria, the name *David* consists of three letters and has the numeric value of fourteen (*dalet* [4] + *waw* [6] + *dalet* [4]). This fits well with the pattern of three sets of fourteen generations in Matthew's version of Jesus' genealogy. Furthermore, the name *David* appears as the fourteenth name in the genealogy. The number fourteen most naturally points to King David. Thus, the repetition of the number fourteen in the summary of Jesus' genealogy reinforces the emphatic description of Jesus as "son of David" in the introduction to this genealogy. These features combine to show that the primary purpose of the genealogy is to show that Jesus belongs to David's legal line.

The genealogy itself offers a clue to why Matthew emphasizes Jesus' descent in the line of David. In Matthew 1:6, David is explicitly identified as "David the king." The noun *king* bears the

1. See W. D. Davies and Dale Allison Jr., *The Gospel according to Matthew*, 3 vols., International Critical Commentary (Edinburgh: T & T Clark, 1988–1997), 1:161–65. Scholars who affirm the presence of gematria here include A. W. Argyle, W. D. Davies, Robert Gundry, Samuel T. Lachs, Ralph Martin, John P. Meier, David Turner, and Michael Wilkins. Donald A. Hagner rejects this interpretation based on his conclusion that Matthew was first written in Greek, but he acknowledges, "We are unable to conclusively discern Matthew's intent in the 3X14 structure." *Matthew*, Word Biblical Commentary (Dallas: Word, 1993–95), 1:7.

2. See R. J. Werblowsky and G. Wigoder, eds., "Gematria," in *Encyclopedia of the Jewish Religion* (New York: Holt, Rinehart, Winston, 1965), 154.

3. For examples, see *m. Uqtzin* 2:12; *Sibylline Oracles* 5:12–42; *Barnabas* 9:7–8.

definite article. David was not merely *a* king; he was *the* king. This is likely the use of the definite article par excellence, identifying the noun it modifies as the best of its class.[4] This classification is supported by the fact that numerous kings are listed in the genealogy, but only David is honored with the title *king*. This reminds the reader that David was the ideal king and "serves to strengthen the link between David and Jesus as the Davidic, messianic king, an important motif in Matthew."[5]

Jesus' Davidic lineage is also emphasized in the narrative of his birth that immediately follows the genealogy. When the angel of the Lord appears to Joseph in a dream to alleviate his concerns about Mary's suspected unfaithfulness, the angel addresses him as "son of David" (Matt. 1:20). This form of address serves to remind the reader of Joseph's Davidic lineage and thus Jesus' identity as a legal descendant of David through his relationship to Joseph.

Jesus Is Associated with David by His Title

Matthew repeatedly stresses Jesus' identity as a descendant of David later in his gospel. Matthew 9:27–31 records Jesus' healing of two blind men. This account is unique to Matthew's gospel. This unparalleled account contains Matthew's second explicit description of Jesus as the "Son of David" (v. 27). It is significant that Jesus as Son of David heals the blind. The Old Testament promises that when the Messiah arrives, he will preserve the sight of those who see and grant sight to the blind (Isa. 32:1–3; 33:17). Isaiah 35:5–6 promises that in the day on which the glory of the Lord is revealed, "the eyes of the blind shall be opened, and the ears of the deaf unstopped; then shall the lame man leap like a deer, and the tongue of the mute sing for joy." Matthew's description of Jesus' miracle specifically recalls this prophecy. In Matthew 20:34 and its parallels, Jesus touches the blind men's eyes as they

4. Daniel Wallace, *Greek Grammar: Beyond the Basics* (Grand Rapids: Zondervan, 1997), 222–23.
5. Hagner, *Matthew*, 1:11.

"recovered their sight," while 9:30 says instead that "their eyes were opened," a clear allusion to Isaiah's promise that "the eyes of the blind shall be opened." Thus, the pericope both assigns to Jesus the messianic title "Son of David" and ascribes to him a distinctively messianic activity. As we will soon discuss, Isaiah explicitly identifies the coming King as a descendant of David.

In Matthew 12:22–23, Jesus heals a demon-oppressed man who is both blind and unable to speak. A parallel to the account appears in Luke 11:14. In both accounts, the crowd that witnesses the miracle marvels. Matthew's account, however, contains one important detail that is missing from Luke's version. The shocked crowd raises the question, "Can this be the Son of David?" The crowd likely raises this question, in part, because the demon-possessed man suffers two of the four conditions that Isaiah 35 promises will be healed in the messianic era—inability to see and inability to speak.

By this time, Jesus has already appealed to Isaiah's promise to confirm his identity as the Messiah. When John the Baptist wrestles with doubts over Jesus' messiahship while languishing in prison, Jesus assures him, "The blind receive their sight and the lame walk, lepers are cleansed and the deaf hear, and the dead are raised up, and the poor have good news preached to them" (Matt. 11:4–5). Jesus' reply to John blends elements of Isaiah 35:5–6 with elements of Isaiah 61:1. Readers who might have overlooked the messianic significance of the healing of the blind in Matthew 9 cannot overlook the messianic significance of the healing of the demon-oppressed blind-mute. Jesus himself supplies the key to interpreting this miracle. That which the awed crowd questions, the disciple will adamantly affirm: Jesus is the Son of David.

In Matthew 15:21–28, a Canaanite woman approaches Jesus, begging him to cast out a demon tormenting her daughter. Although the account is also preserved in Mark 7:24–30, several important features of Matthew's account are unique to his gospel. Although Mark gives only a brief summarizing indirect quotation of the woman's appeal, Matthew quotes her plea, "Have mercy on me, O Lord, Son of David" (Matt. 15:22). Jesus responds, "I was sent only to the lost sheep of the house of Israel" (v. 24). Jesus' reference to the "lost sheep" appears to be directly related to the woman's use of the title *Son of David*. Reference to the lost sheep of the house of Israel is reminiscent of Ezekiel 34:1–16. The passage is a prophecy against the spiritual shepherds of the people of Israel who have neglected their duties to the flock. The prophet describes the sheep of Israel as "lost" and "scattered" (Ezek. 34:4–6).

God warns that he will judge the wicked shepherds. He promises that he himself will come and shepherd his people. Finally, he promises that he will send the Messiah to shepherd them:

> And I will set up over them one shepherd, my servant David, and he shall feed them: he shall feed them and be their shepherd. And I, the LORD, will be their God, and my servant David shall be prince among them. I am the LORD; I have spoken. (Ezek. 34:23–24)

Thus, it is no coincidence that Jesus replies to the address *Son of David* with reference to his ministry to the lost sheep of the house of Israel. Jesus appeals to the prophecy of Ezekiel 34 to demonstrate that the Davidic Messiah is charged with the responsibility of shepherding the people of Israel specifically. The account confirms that Jesus recognizes himself as the Davidic Messiah and that he interprets the Messiah's role, at least in part, in light of the Ezekiel 34 prophecy.[6]

Matthew 20:29–34 (paralleled by Mark 10:46–52 and Luke 18:35–43) records Jesus' being approached by two blind men crying out to him: "Have mercy on us, Son of David!" In the parallels in Mark and Luke, Jesus is addressed as "Son of David, Jesus" and "Jesus, Son of David," respectively.[7] Matthew's gospel drops

---

6. For others who also see the phrase "lost sheep of the house of Israel" as referring in particular to Ezekiel 34, see R. T. France, *The Gospel of Matthew*, New International Commentary on the New Testament (Grand Rapids: Eerdmans, 2007), 372; Hagner, *Matthew*, 1:260; and David L. Turner, *Matthew*, Baker Exegetical Commentary on the New Testament (Grand Rapids: Baker, 2008), 387.

7. Although the ESV translates the titles in Mark and Luke identically, this translation highlights the different word order in the Greek texts.

the name *Jesus* in order to place greater emphasis on the title *Son of David*.

During Jesus' triumphal entry into the city of Jerusalem, the crowds exclaim, "Hosanna to the Son of David! Blessed is he who comes in the name of the Lord! Hosanna in the highest!" (Matt. 21:9). The exclamation is paralleled in Mark 11:9; Luke 19:38; and John 12:13. Although allusions to Jesus' kingship appear in the exclamations of all four Gospels, only Matthew addresses the exclamation to "the Son of David."

After the triumphal entry, Jesus proceeds to the temple. He cleanses it by driving out the merchants and money changers. The temple cleansing is described by Matthew, Mark (11:15–17), and Luke (19:45–46). Matthew's gospel (21:14–15) adds details omitted by the other Synoptic Gospels. Matthew alone mentions that children in the temple praise Jesus by shouting, "Hosanna to the Son of David!" Interestingly, the children offer this praise in response to Jesus' healing of the blind and lame in the temple. Once again, the title *Son of David* is associated with Jesus' healing miracles that fulfill the prophecy of Isaiah 35:5–6, in which "the eyes of the blind shall be opened" and "the lame . . . leap like a deer."

The climax of the *Son of David* theme in Matthew appears in a discussion in Matthew 22:41–46 (cf. Mark 12:35–37; Luke 20:41–44). After being frequently interrogated by the Pharisees, Jesus poses an important question to them: "What do you think about the Christ? Whose son is he?" The reply of the Pharisees, "The son of David," confirms that the *Son of David* title is to be interpreted as a reference to the Messiah. Jesus urges the Pharisees to broaden their thinking about the Messiah by appealing to Psalm 110:1, where the psalmist—King David himself—writing under the inspiration of the Holy Spirit, describes the Messiah as "my Lord," seated at Yahweh's right hand and enthroned with absolute authority over all his enemies. Then Jesus asks, "If then David calls him Lord, how is he his son?" Jesus' argument is not intended to undermine notions that the Messiah is a descendant of David. Rather, his argument demonstrates that the Messiah is far more than a mere descendant of David. The Messiah is both Davidic and divine.

Jesus Is Associated with David by the Circumstances of His Birth

The circumstances surrounding Jesus' birth also associate Jesus with David. Jesus and David share the same place of origin, the little village of Bethlehem. The Old Testament stresses that Bethlehem was David's family home (1 Sam. 16:1, 4, 18; 17:58).

Jesus is also from Bethlehem (Matt. 2:5–6, 8, 16). The chief priest and scribes inform Herod the Great that the prophet Micah had long ago announced that the Messiah would be born in Bethlehem of Judea: "And you, O Bethlehem, in the land of Judah, are by no means least among the rulers of Judah; for from you shall come a ruler who will shepherd my people Israel" (Matt. 2:6). This King from Bethlehem would clearly be the Davidic Messiah. First-century Jews recognized that Micah 5:2 refers to the Messiah and thus assumed that the Messiah would be born in Bethlehem. This was confirmed in both Matthew 2:5–6 and John 7:42. Admittedly, David is not explicitly mentioned in Micah's prophecy. But the description of the Ruler as One who will "shepherd" Israel stirs memories of David, the shepherd-king, and is reminiscent of Ezekiel's promise:

And I will set up over them one shepherd, my servant David, and he shall feed them: he shall feed them and be their shepherd. And I, the LORD, will be their God, and my servant David shall be prince among them. I am the LORD; I have spoken. (Ezek. 34:23–24)

Micah 4:8 also implies that the Ruler who comes from Bethlehem will be the Davidic Messiah: "And you, O tower of the flock, hill of the daughter of Zion, to you shall it come, the former dominion shall come, kingship for the daughter of Jerusalem." The "tower of the flock" refers to the capital city of

David, and the "former dominion" refers to the kingdom of David that the Messiah will restore. Verse 6 introduces this prophecy with the phrase "in that day," a temporal marker indicating that the prophecy will be fulfilled in the messianic era. Jewish and Christian interpreters both regard Micah's prophecy as eschatological and messianic.[8]

Absence of an explicit mention of David in Micah is not troubling. By the time of Christ, the Minor Prophets were treated as a single book, the Book of the Twelve.[9] Consequently, the references in Micah would be read in light of statements such as Hosea 3:5: "Afterward the children of Israel shall return and seek the LORD their God, and David their king, and they shall come in fear to the LORD and to his goodness in the latter days"; and Amos 9:11: "In that day I will raise up the booth of David that is fallen and repair its breaches, and raise up its ruins and rebuild it as in the days of old." These explicit references to David equip the reader to connect these prophecies to the promises related to David in the rest of the Old Testament.

The quotation of Jeremiah 31:15 in Matthew 2:17–18 also hints at Jesus' identity as the Davidic Messiah. Jeremiah 31:15 is a description of the grief of the nation of Israel over the Babylonian exile. Rachel weeps for her children who "are no more" because they are in exile in Babylon (chap. 29). Matthew's brief quotation assumes his reader's familiarity with the promise of deliverance that immediately follows it (31:17). Matthew recognizes that Jeremiah himself saw this deliverance as both eschatological and messianic. The eschatological and messianic nature of the deliverance is abundantly clear in Jeremiah 30:8–9:

> And it shall come to pass in that day, declares the LORD of hosts, that I will break his yoke from off your neck, and I will burst your bonds, and foreigners shall no more make a servant of

8. See *Targum Pseudo-Jonathan*, Mic. 5:2; *b. Yoma* 10a; *b. Sanhedrin* 98b.

9. Paul House, *The Unity of the Twelve* (Sheffield: Almond, 1990). For an excellent brief defense of the interpretation of the Book of the Twelve as a single composition, see Michael B. Shepherd, *The Twelve Prophets in the New Testament* (New York: Peter Lang, 2011), 1–5.

him. But they shall serve the LORD their God and David their king, whom I will raise up for them.

The passage from Jeremiah that Matthew quotes also immediately precedes Jeremiah's promise of the new covenant (Jer. 31:31–34), a covenant that Jesus initiates through his sacrificial death (Matt. 26:28). Matthew quotes this eschatological and messianic text in the context of the slaughter of the male infants of Bethlehem because that event shows how God's people are in a sense still in exile, still under the thumb of a foreign oppressor and waiting for the Lord to raise up David their king to deliver them.

Jesus Is Associated with David through His Fulfillment of Prophecy

Matthew states that the decision of the holy family to settle in Nazareth is a fulfillment of an Old Testament prophecy, "He shall be called a Nazarene" (Matt. 2:23). No specific Old Testament passage contains these words. Thus, Matthew's statement has puzzled many interpreters. One important clue to the proper interpretation of the statement is the use of "prophets" to describe the source of the prophecy. In his fulfillment citations, Matthew normally quotes a single prophet. Here, by appealing to the prophets in general, Matthew implies that the prophecy belongs to a prominent Old Testament theme rather than one specific text.

Matthew is probably alluding to the prophecies of the Old Testament that describe the Messiah as a "branch." The Branch prophecies (Isa. 4:2; 11:1; Jer. 23:5; 33:15) tell of a righteous descendant of David who will bring salvation to Judah with a wise and just rule empowered by the Spirit. The Hebrew consonants that make up the Hebrew word *branch* (Isa. 11:1)—*n*, *ts*, and *r*—are shared by the words *Nazareth* and *Nazarene*. Thus, Jesus' hometown is the "Branch place," and Jesus is a "Branch person." Matthew sees etymological significance in these names and regards Jesus' hometown as a clue to his identity as the Messiah.

Jesus Is Associated with David by His Actions

In a dispute with Pharisees who object to his disciples' plucking grain on the Sabbath in Matthew 12:1–8 (cf. Mark 2:23–28; Luke 6:1–5), Jesus appeals to 1 Samuel 21:1–6, asking:

> Have you not read what David did when he was hungry, and those who were with him: how he entered the house of God and ate the bread of the Presence, which it was not lawful for him to eat nor for those who were with him, but only for the priests? (Matt. 12:3–4)

At the most basic level, Jesus is teaching that desperate times call for desperate measures. The extenuating circumstances of his disciples' hunger in the presence of abundant grain justified eating what was normally forbidden, just as the extenuating circumstances faced by David and his men justified their eating the bread of the Presence. Yet Jesus' statement implies much more. After all, the circumstances of Jesus' disciples hardly compare to the emergency situation that David and his men faced. The argument that desperate times call for desperate measures would likely have failed to silence Jesus' critics, since Jesus' disciples faced a situation marked more by discomfort than by true desperation. Thus, Jesus probably intends to compare himself to David and his disciples to David's men, rather than merely comparing the two situations. By using the example of David and his men to justify the behavior of Jesus and his disciples, Jesus closely associates himself with David in a way that hints at his Davidic messiahship.[10]

<hr />

10. D. A. Carson, "Matthew," in *Matthew, Mark, Luke*, Expositor's Bible Commentary (Grand Rapids: Zondervan, 1984), 218; France, *Matthew*, 459.

6

The Theological Significance
of the *New David* Theme

MATTHEW'S EMPHASIS on Jesus' identity as the Son of David or new David intertwines with a rich Old Testament background. The following discussion will briefly explore the presentation of the Davidic Messiah in the Hebrew Scriptures. Although messianic promises appear in the books of Moses, the Davidic covenant closely associates the fulfillment of the promise of the Messiah with King David.

The New David Fulfills the Davidic Covenant

God's covenant with David is described in 2 Samuel 7:12–16. Several features of the passage demonstrate that much of this passage focuses on David's immediate descendant, Solomon. The phrase "when your days are fulfilled and you lie down with your fathers" implies that the prophecy foretells the reign of David's direct successor to the throne, who will replace him at death. The clause "he shall build a house for my name" refers to Solomon's construction of the temple. Most importantly, the statement "when he commits iniquity, I will discipline him" clearly refers to Solomon rather than to the sinless Messiah. Because of such features, writes Carl Keil, "it is very obvious, from all the separate details of this promise, that it related primarily to Solomon, and had a certain fulfillment in him and his reign."[1] First Kings 8:14–20; 9:1–4; and 2 Chronicles 6:1–11; 7:11–18 demonstrate that much of the prophecy points directly to Solomon.

Nevertheless, the climactic words of the prophecy relate to the coming Messiah as well. Keil notes, "The three fold repetition of the expression 'for ever,' the establishment of the kingdom and throne of David *for ever*, points incontrovertibly beyond the time of Solomon, and to the eternal continuance of the seed of David. . . . The posterity of David, therefore, could only last for ever by running out in a person who lives for ever, and of whose kingdom there is no end."[2] The Dead Sea Scrolls confirm that Jews during the time of Christ interpreted the entire oracle of Nathan as a prophecy about the Messiah. For example, 4Q174 quotes 2 Samuel 7:11–14 and explains, "He is the Branch of David who shall arise with the Interpreter of the Law [to rule] in Zion [at the end] of time. As it is written, 'I will raise up the tent of David that is fallen' (Amos 9:11). That is to say, the fallen tent of David is he who shall arise to save Israel."

When the reign of the Davidic dynasty ends after enduring for four centuries, the prophets recognize that the promise of an unending Davidic kingdom must look forward to the coming of yet another descendant of David who will reestablish David's throne and rule over an eternal kingdom. For this reason, some Old Testament scholars have described 2 Samuel 7 as the "ideological summit" of the Old Testament as a whole. This promise is the first of many more explicit promises concerning a Davidic Messiah (Isa. 9; 11; 16:5; Jer. 23:5–8; 30:9, 21–22, 31–34; 33:14–26;

---

1. Carl F. Keil, in Carl F. Keil and Franz Delitzsch, *Biblical Commentary on the Old Testament* (Grand Rapids: Eerdmans, 1986), 2:346. Although some commentators see the promised seed that God will raise up as a reference to the resurrected Jesus (Robert Bergen, *1, 2 Samuel*, New American Commentary [Nashville: B&H Academic, 1996], 339–40), the New Testament does not apply this element of the prophecy to Jesus, and the other details of the prophecy seem to preclude this interpretation. For similar exegesis, see A. A. Anderson, *2 Samuel*, Word Biblical Commentary (Dallas: Thomas Nelson, 2000), 121–23; Mary J. Evans, *1 and 2 Samuel*, New International Biblical Commentary (Peabody: Hendrickson, 2000), 168–69; Joyce G. Baldwin, *1 and 2 Samuel*, Tyndale Old Testament Commentary (Downers Grove, IL: IVP Academic, 1988), 227–28.

2. Keil, *Commentary on the Old Testament*, 2:346–47 (emphasis in original).

Ezek. 34:23–24; 36:26–27; 37:21–28; Hos. 3:4–5; Amos 9:11–15; Zech. 3:8; 6:12; 9:9–13; 10:4, 10–12).

The Old Testament descriptions of the Davidic Messiah highlight several important features of this important descendant of David. The Messiah will:

- reign forever and ever;
- reign with righteousness and justice;
- rule over all the peoples of the earth;
- establish peace over all creation;
- be endowed with the Spirit of God;
- be the embodiment of Yahweh;
- destroy the wicked by his mere command;
- act as both King and Priest;
- mediate the new covenant;
- provide forgiveness of sins through his sacrificial death; and
- lead God's people on a new exodus.

Matthew intends his readers to recall this rich Old Testament background when he identifies Jesus as the new David.

The New David Will Reign over the Kingdom of Heaven

One of Matthew's favorite topics is the kingdom of God/heaven. The topic of the kingdom is closely related to the presentation of Jesus as the Son of David, the divinely appointed King. Every king must have a kingdom, a realm over which he exercises his authority. The kingdom of heaven/God is that kingdom over which God rules through the person of the Messiah.

Matthew uses the phrases "the kingdom," "your kingdom," "the kingdom of God," "the kingdom of the Father," and "the kingdom of heaven" forty-nine times in his gospel to refer to the realm of the Messiah.[3] Matthew prefers the phrase "kingdom of

---

3. The word *kingdom* appears fifty-five times in Matthew's gospel. Six of the instances, however, refer either to human kingdoms or to the kingdom of Satan—4:8; 8:12 [?]; 12:25–26; 24:7 (2×).

heaven," used thirty-two times, to the phrase "kingdom of God," used only four or five times.[4] In the past, scholars have often argued that "kingdom of heaven" is a reverent circumlocution for "kingdom of God" that avoids direct reference to deity. This explanation would satisfy if Matthew consistently used the phrase "kingdom of heaven" rather than "kingdom of God." But the use of the phrase "kingdom of God" four to five times in the gospel argues strongly against such an explanation.

Matthew most likely adopts the phrase "kingdom of heaven" in order to squelch contemporary Jewish notions that the Messiah's kingdom would be a mere earthly kingdom ruled by a political Messiah. Matthew's expression "is designed to emphasize that God's kingdom is not like earthly kingdoms, stands over against them, and will eschatologically replace them (on earth)."[5] Matthew's expression thus communicates the same conviction as Jesus' words before Pilate: his kingdom is not of this world (John 18:36).

The Kingdom Is Both Present and Future, Internal and External

Scholars have fiercely debated whether the kingdom is intended to be understood as present and internal or future and external, that is, whether the kingdom refers to the rule of Christ over his disciples here and now or to an eschatological rule that the Messiah will establish. A careful examination of the descriptions of the kingdom in Matthew suggests that the kingdom has both present/future and internal/external facets.[6]

Sometimes Matthew's gospel uses "kingdom" to refer to God's present reign over those who have submitted to the authority of the Messiah. Jesus describes the kingdom as already present in

4. Some manuscripts of Matthew have five instances of "kingdom of God," since they add "of God" to "kingdom" in Matthew 6:33. But the oldest and best manuscripts do not contain "of God."

5. Jonathan T. Pennington, *Heaven and Earth in the Gospel of Matthew* (Grand Rapids: Baker Academic, 2007), 321.

6. For a more extended treatment, see Charles L. Quarles, "Excursus: Nature of the Kingdom in Matthew," in *The Sermon on the Mount: Restoring Christ's Message to the Modern Church* (Nashville: B&H Academic, 2011), 44–53.

some sense in texts such as Matthew 5:3, 10; 12:28; 19:14; and 21:31. Matthew 21:31–32 suggests that tax collectors and prostitutes enter the kingdom when they repent of their former refusal to do the Father's will and believe John the Baptist and his message. These references to the kingdom parallel Paul's teaching that the Father "has delivered us from the domain of darkness and transferred us to the kingdom of his beloved Son" (Col. 1:13).

Despite these descriptions of the kingdom as present, Matthew makes it clear that the kingdom has not yet fully arrived. John the Baptist, the Lord Jesus, and the disciples all insist that the kingdom is near but not yet here (Matt. 3:2; 4:17; 10:7). Most of the references to the kingdom in Matthew present the kingdom as still belonging to the future. In 7:22, disciples enter the kingdom on "that day," the day of final judgment. Similarly, in 25:34, Jesus' followers inherit the kingdom prepared from the foundation of the world on the day of final judgment. In 26:29, Jesus associates the kingdom with the great messianic feast that will occur in the end times. Many of Jesus' parables confirm that the kingdom belongs to the future.

The Background for Jesus' Teaching about the Kingdom Is the Book of Daniel

The primary Old Testament background for Matthew's teaching about the kingdom appears to be the book of Daniel. Several lines of evidence support this conclusion. First, only in Daniel does Jesus' favorite preaching topic, the kingdom of God, appear in connection with Jesus' favorite title for himself, *Son of Man*. Second, the Gospel of Matthew is saturated with allusions to Daniel: e.g., Matt. 13:24–30, 37–43 (Dan. 12:2–3); Matt. 13:31–32 (Dan. 4:21–22); and Matt. 26:64 (Dan. 7:13–14). Altogether, Matthew contains more than thirty possible quotations, verbal parallels, and allusions to Daniel. Thus, a study of Daniel's descriptions of the kingdom is particularly helpful for understanding the references to the kingdom in the Gospel of Matthew.

The first description of God's kingdom in Daniel appears in the dream of Nebuchadnezzar in Daniel 2. King Nebuchadnezzar dreams about a succession of five earthly kingdoms. At the climax of the dream, these earthly kingdoms are destroyed and succeeded by an eternal kingdom (vv. 34–35). Daniel explains the significance of this climax of the dream:

> And in the days of those kings the God of heaven will set up a kingdom that shall never be destroyed, nor shall the kingdom be left to another people. It shall break in pieces all these kingdoms and bring them to an end, and it shall stand forever. (Dan. 2:44)

"Kingdom of God" and "kingdom of heaven" refer to this eternal kingdom established by the God of heaven, a kingdom that brings all human kingdoms to an end. Nebuchadnezzar himself later describes this kingdom: "His kingdom is an everlasting kingdom, and his dominion endures from generation to generation" (Dan. 4:3). Nebuchadnezzar repeats a similar statement in verses 34–35, as does Darius in 6:26–27. When this kingdom replaces the kingdom of men, the will of God will be done on earth as it is done in heaven (Matt. 6:10). None will rebel against him or dare question his authority.

The *kingdom* theme of Daniel climaxes with a picture of the Ancient of Days seated on his throne, with tens of thousands serving him (Dan. 7:9–10). The Ancient of Days grants dominion, glory, and a kingdom to another figure, One "like a son of man" (v. 13). The kingdom given to the Son of Man by God has two essential features. First, the kingdom is universal. Although it does not include every single individual, it does include people of every nation, tribe, and language. Second, the kingdom is eternal. In keeping with a prominent motif of Daniel, the kingdom is an everlasting kingdom that will never be destroyed. The kingdom of heaven in Matthew is this kingdom, the kingdom entrusted by the Ancient of Days to the Son of Man.

The Kingdom of Heaven Is the Focus of Jesus' Parables

Some of the most vivid descriptions of the nature of the coming kingdom in the Gospel of Matthew appear in the collections of

Jesus' parables. His parables typically begin with an introduction such as "the kingdom of heaven is like" (Matt. 13:24, 31, 33, 44, 45, 47; 18:23; 20:1; 22:2; 25:1, 14), and their primary purpose is to unveil some particular characteristic of the kingdom. Unfortunately, space will not permit a detailed examination of the contents of Jesus' parables in the present volume. We can only summarize Jesus' teaching about the kingdom that appears in the parables concentrated in Matthew 13 and 20–23.

- Entering the kingdom requires that one receive the Messiah's very gracious forgiveness and offer forgiveness to others who have sinned against him.
- Entering the kingdom requires that one follow Jesus' teaching, serve his interests, bear the fruit of good deeds, and show kindness to others.
- The Messiah will judge the world to determine who will enjoy his kingdom and who will suffer eternal punishment.
- The kingdom of heaven is so glorious that it is worth any sacrifice.
- The kingdom of heaven is offered even to repentant and believing tax collectors and prostitutes. The blessings and joys of the kingdom vastly exceed anything that Jesus' disciples could ever deserve.
- The kingdom of heaven will extend throughout the earth until it encompasses people of every nation, tribe, and language.

The New David Is Daniel's "Son of Man"

Jesus' favorite teaching topic, the kingdom of heaven, is closely related to his favorite title for himself, *Son of Man*, used eighty-two times in the four Gospels as an apparent self-description of Jesus. The phrase is used thirty times in the Gospel of Matthew. At least five of these occurrences are in material unique to Matthew's gospel. This title is nearly twice as frequent in Matthew as the title translated "Christ" or "Messiah," which appears only sixteen times in the entire gospel. Consequently, *Son of Man* is by far Jesus' favorite title for himself.

Since this title is so significant both to Jesus and to Matthew, it is very important to come to a correct understanding of its meaning. The consistent use of the definite article in this phrase is significant. Either the article identifies the Son of Man as a particular son of man widely recognized by Jesus' audience, or it points to a particular son of man previously described in the Hebrew Scriptures. If the latter, the article would parallel the use of the article in the phrase *the Prophet* in the Gospels, which serves to identify the prophet like Moses previously mentioned in Deuteronomy 18:15.

The previous reference to the Son of Man in the Hebrew Scriptures is easy to locate. The title is clearly drawn from Daniel 7:13–14. Several lines of evidence make this background obvious. Jesus explicitly quotes Daniel 7:13–14 on at least two occasions and makes clear allusions to it in other contexts.

First, in Matthew 24:30, Jesus uses the title *Son of Man*, refers to his coming on the clouds, and describes his great power and glory. Both the title and references are drawn from Daniel's vision of the Son of Man. Furthermore, these allusions to Daniel 7 appear in proximity to a reference to the "abomination of desolation" (v. 15), another allusion to Daniel, this time to 9:27.

Second, in Matthew 26:64, the high priest interrogates Jesus about his messianic claims. Jesus replies, "I tell you, from now on you will see the Son of Man seated at the right hand of Power and coming on the clouds of heaven." Both "Son of Man" and the reference to coming on the clouds of heaven are drawn from Daniel 7:13.

Third, Matthew 25:31, a passage that has no parallel in the other Gospels, describes the Son of Man as One who comes in glory with all the angels, sits on his glorious throne, and judges all the nations. These descriptions are drawn from Daniel 7:13–14, which in turn is interpreted against the background of the preceding vision in verses 9–10.

Jesus' clear dependence on Daniel 7:13–14 raises another important question: Who is the Son of Man in Daniel's vision? Unfortunately, scholars still debate the identification of Daniel's Son of Man. But the oldest interpretation is, in this case, the best. The Son of Man is none other than the Messiah. This interpretation was affirmed by Hellenistic Judaism, rabbinic Judaism, and the early Christian church.[7]

The Son of Man Is the Ruler of a Universal and Eternal Kingdom

This interpretation is strongly supported by the details of Daniel 7:13–14. Daniel outlines several important characteristics of the Son of Man figure. First, the Son of Man is a royal figure who will reign over a universal and eternal kingdom. The universal nature of his reign is affirmed in the statement "all peoples, nations, and languages should serve him." The eternal nature of his reign is expressed in the climactic statement of the vision: "his dominion is an everlasting dominion, which shall not pass away, and his kingdom one that shall not be destroyed." The eternal nature of the reign of the Son of Man is starkly contrasted with the transience of the fourth beast, also identified as a king. This beast was "killed, and its body destroyed and given over to be burned with fire" (v. 11). The point is that the eternal dominion of the Son of Man is remarkably different from the temporary reigns of the world's most powerful human empires.

The Son of Man Comes from Heaven

The Son of Man is a heavenly being, not of this world. The Son of Man comes "with the clouds of heaven" (Dan. 7:13). The use of clouds to depict divine glory in Exodus and the presence of clouds in theophanies such as Ezekiel 1 suggest that the appearance of the Son of Man is the appearance of a divine being. Furthermore, the

7. *1 Enoch* 37–71; *4 Ezra* 13; *Sibylline Oracles* 3; Justin, *Dialogue with Trypho*, 31f.; Hippolytus, *Commentary on Daniel*, 11f.

statement that "all peoples, nations, and languages should serve him" parallels the description of the Ancient of Days: "A thousand thousands served him" (Dan. 7:10). Even more importantly, the Aramaic verb used to describe the service rendered to the Son of Man specifically refers to an act of worship. The verb is used in the Bible to refer exclusively to the veneration or worship of God or gods.[8] A couple of examples should suffice. Daniel 3:17–18 uses this verb in the description of Yahweh as "our God whom we serve." Verse 28 records Nebuchadnezzar's exclamation that Daniel's faithful friends "yielded up their bodies rather than serve and worship any god except their own God." Consequently, the offer of such worship to the Son of Man leads to the suspicion that he is being portrayed as deity appearing in human form, one like a son of man and worthy of worship.

Daniel 7:27 lends support to this interpretation. Although most English translations of the verse render it "all dominions shall serve and obey them," the Hebrew Scriptures, the Septuagint, and Theodotion's Greek text all use the third-person-singular pronoun: "all dominions shall serve and obey *him*." The antecedent of the pronoun is "the Most High." The statement that all dominions shall serve him echoes the description of the Son of Man in Daniel 7:14 and serves to equate the Son of Man with the Most High.

The Septuagint specifically identifies the Son of Man with the Ancient of Days by saying, "He was coming on the clouds of heaven like a son of man, and he was coming like the Ancient of Days, and those who were present were coming to him."[9] From these features, many Jewish interpreters infer that the Son of Man is divine. Additional evidence supporting this understanding will be examined in a later chapter.

8. See Dan. 3:12, 14, 17–18, 28; 6:16, 20; 7:14, 27. Other forms of the root refer to worship or ritual service as well (Ezra 7:19, 24).

9. Translation mine. This reading is supported by the oldest extant manuscript of the Septuagint, MS 967, which dates to the second century. A couple of New Testament texts, 2 Thessalonians 1:7–8 and Revelation 1:13, conflate descriptions of the Son of Man and the Ancient of Days in a manner that suggests that this reading was prevalent in the New Testament era.

The Son of Man Serves as the Eschatological Judge

Daniel's vision of the Son of Man probably also influences Jesus' claim to be the eschatological Judge. This claim is especially prevalent in Matthew's gospel. Matthew 7:21–23 portrays Jesus as the eschatological Judge. He is the One to whom sinners appeal for entrance into the kingdom on the last day. He is the One who delivers the verdict, "I never knew you; depart from me, you workers of lawlessness." Matthew 10:32–33 shows that a sinner's eternal destiny is determined by whether Jesus acknowledges or denies that person before the heavenly Father. In the parable of the weeds, the Son of Man supervises eschatological judgment, and his angels implement that judgment (13:41–42). In 19:28, the Son of Man supervises eschatological judgment, and his disciples implement it. Jesus' cursing of the fig tree depicts his role as Judge in its prefiguring his judgment on the nation of Israel for its spiritual fruitlessness (21:18–19). The climax of Jesus' eschatological teaching in chapter 24 emphasizes the Son of Man's role as eschatological Judge who will cut wicked servants into pieces and sentence them with the hypocrites to a place where there is weeping and gnashing of teeth. In terms that are reminiscent of 7:21–23, Jesus emphasizes his role as eschatological Judge in his description of the Son of Man on a glorious throne judging the nations in 25:31–46.

The description of Jesus as Judge is closely linked to his messiahship. Among the many roles that ancient kings fulfilled was that of judge (1 Kings 3:16–28; Prov. 29:14, 26). This aspect of royal responsibility explains emphasis on the Messiah's ruling with justice and righteousness in Old Testament prophecy.

In Matthew's gospel, allusions to Jesus' role as eschatological Judge are often connected to the *Son of Man* title (Matt. 9:6; 13:41; 16:27; 19:28; 25:31). This suggests that the description of Jesus as eschatological Judge was influenced, at least in part, by Daniel 7, the source of the *Son of Man* title. Although Daniel's vision of the Son of Man does not explicitly refer to his role as Judge, it is implied because kings typically served as judges in Daniel's day.[10] More importantly, both Jesus and Matthew appear to interpret the Son of Man vision in close connection with the vision of the Ancient of Days that immediately precedes it (Dan. 7:9–12). The vision opens with the statement "thrones were placed, and the Ancient of Days took his seat." Daniel describes the throne of the Ancient of Days in a manner similar to the description of God's throne in Ezekiel's vision (Ezek. 1:16; 10:2): "his throne was fiery flames; its wheels were burning fire." The vision of the Ancient of Days climaxes with a judicial setting: "the court sat in judgment, and the books were opened." The statement that the court "sat" refers to sitting upon the thrones mentioned in the opening line of the vision.

The question that naturally arises from careful reflection on the vision is: For whom was the other throne(s) intended? The vision of the Son of Man supplies the answer. The Son of Man, installed as King of the universal and eternal dominion described in Daniel 7:13–14 immediately after the Ancient of Days vision, will occupy the throne alongside the Ancient of Days and judge with him. First Enoch (46:1; 62:5; 69:29) and other early Jewish interpreters argue that the Davidic Messiah (Son of Man) is enthroned with the Ancient of Days. The references to the Son of Man seated "on his glorious throne" (Matt. 19:28; 25:31) show that Jesus and Matthew understand the two visions in Daniel 7 as interrelated in a similar fashion.

Thus, the Son of Man participates with the Ancient of Days in the session of the heavenly court. This Son of Man will open the books (Dan. 7:10) that decree who will suffer punishment and who will be granted life (12:1–2). These books likely record the deeds and words of men (Matt. 7:21–23; 12:33–37; 25:31–46) to which the Son of Man will appeal when he pronounces his just judgment.

One need not worry that judgment based on works undermines in any way the gracious nature of salvation. It is because of Jesus' role as Judge that he bears the authority to forgive sinners and to pronounce them not guilty on the basis of his ransom. As the Son of Man, he has authority on both heaven and earth to

10. See Daniel 3 and 6, in which the king is both legislator and judge, empowered to make law and enforce it.

forgive sins (Matt. 9:2, 6). He forgives sinners on the basis of the ransom that he pays for them (20:28). The parable of the forgiving king (18:21–35) could not be clearer in stating that the heavenly Father has forgiven Jesus' followers of an enormous spiritual debt that they could never repay. The deeds and words of men will not provide the basis on which they are declared righteous in eschatological judgment. These deeds and words will rather provide evidence that they belong to Christ. Just as good trees will inevitably produce good fruit (7:15–20; 12:33–37), so the followers of Jesus, as participants in the new exodus, beneficiaries of the new covenant, and those who have experienced new creation, will inevitably produce the fruit of righteous words and deeds.

Conclusion: Submit to the King

Matthew closely associates Jesus with Old Testament David in order to highlight Jesus' identity as God's Anointed One, the King appointed by heaven. Jesus, as the messianic King, will reign over people of every nation, tribe, and language forever and ever. Jesus' followers belong to the kingdom here and now, since they have surrendered to Jesus' authority to rule over their lives. They will formally inherit the kingdom after Jesus' glorious return, when his kingdom is consummated at last.

Jesus' identity as the messianic King makes it imperative for each individual to kneel before Jesus' throne and submit to his royal authority without delay. In the song of coronation (Ps. 2), the psalmist bluntly describes the choice that a sinner faces: "Kiss the Son, lest he be angry, and you perish in the way, for his wrath is quickly kindled. Blessed are all who take refuge in him" (v. 12). Jesus, God's Son, is the King that God sets on Zion, his holy hill (v. 6). He will either grant sinners refuge (v. 12) or "speak to them in his wrath, and terrify them in his fury" (v. 5). The sinners who declare rebellion against the King by screaming, "Let us burst their bonds apart and cast away their cords from us" (v. 3), will be severely punished and will "perish in the way." But those who "kiss the Son" will be blessed. This kiss is not some romantic gesture. It is a reference to a humble subject's cowering before the king's presence, approaching the throne with head bowed and eyes downcast, falling at the king's feet, and covering his feet with kisses in an expression of obeisance and submission. The King does not plead pitifully for our allegiance; he demands it. And he does not demand some mere halfhearted submission; he orders our complete subjection. Have you "kissed the Son"?

The parable of the wedding feast warns of the wrath of the king against those who do not show proper respect to his son and coregent: "The king was angry, and he sent his troops and destroyed those murderers and burned their city" (Matt. 22:7). Yet the parable of the unforgiving servant shows the refuge that we can find when we bow before the King and plead for his mercy. He will show pity, will have mercy, and will forgive even the most astronomical spiritual debt.

Those who have bowed before the messianic King rise to their feet to live under his rule. Jesus commends highly the Roman centurion's description of submission to authority: "I too am a man under authority, with soldiers under me. And I say to one, 'Go,' and he goes, and to another, 'Come,' and he comes, and to my servant, 'Do this,' and he does it" (8:9). Jesus' disciples, subjects of the King of heaven, likewise go when he says, come when he calls, and do as he orders without question, without hesitation. They recognize that entering the kingdom is so great a privilege that it is worthy of any sacrifice, and Christ is so great a King that he is worthy of our complete submission. Bowing before the throne of the new David, the believer joins a chorus of thousands upon thousands of every nation, tribe, and tongue that exclaims:

> All hail the pow'r of Jesus' name!
> Let angels prostrate fall;
> Bring forth the royal diadem,
> And crown him Lord of all.
> Bring forth the royal diadem,
> And crown him Lord of all.[11]

11. Edward Perronet, "All Hail the Power of Jesus' Name!" (1779).

Part 4

The New Abraham:
Jesus, Our Founder

Matthew's Development of the *New Abraham* Theme

THE FIRST VERSE of the Gospel of Matthew unveils several of the most prominent themes of the gospel. In the previous chapter, we saw that Jesus' identity as the Son of David is key to Matthew's portrait of Jesus. The introduction to the gospel also identifies Jesus as the Son of Abraham. This title further establishes great expectations regarding Jesus' identity and mission in the minds and hearts of Matthew's readers.

Just as *Son of David* implies far more than that Jesus is merely David's descendant, so *Son of Abraham* implies far more than that Jesus is merely born of Abraham's line. The title *Son of David* indicates that Jesus is the fulfillment of God's covenant with David. Similarly, as Son of Abraham, Jesus is the fulfillment of God's covenant with Abraham. He is Abraham's promised seed. *Son of David* implies that Jesus is like David in many remarkable ways. As the Son of Abraham, Jesus is a new Abraham, the Founder of a new chosen people. He will fulfill a role in God's plan similar to the one fulfilled by Abraham himself.

Matthew could have easily traced Jesus' ancestry all the way back to Adam, as Luke does in his genealogy of Jesus (Luke 3:23–38). By beginning the genealogy with Abraham, Matthew places Abraham in a position of special prominence. Furthermore, the fact that Abraham begins the first set of fourteen generations, while David begins the second set of fourteen generations in the

99

genealogical configuration of three sets of fourteen generations, suggests that Abraham and David serve similar purposes in Jesus' genealogy, as the parallel titles *Son of David* and *Son of Abraham* already imply.

Although some suggest that the purpose of beginning the genealogy with Abraham is to present Jesus as a true Jew, later statements in Matthew's gospel make this reason unlikely. A crucial element of the preaching of John the Baptist is the denial that descent from Abraham ensures enjoyment of God's special favor. Matthew 3:9 warns, "Do not presume to say to yourselves, 'We have Abraham as our father,' for I tell you, God is able from these stones to raise up children for Abraham." John warns the Jewish people that they should not presume to be true Jews belonging to God with no need to repent simply because they are descendants of Abraham. In light of this, Jesus' identification as the Son of Abraham must serve a purpose other than marking him as a true Jew. Most likely, *Son of Abraham* identifies Jesus as the fulfillment of God's covenant with Abraham, as the One through whom all nations on earth are to be blessed.

In Genesis 12:1–3, God promises Abraham:

> Go from your country and your kindred and your father's house to the land that I will show you. And I will make of you a great nation, and I will bless you and make your name great, so that you will be a blessing. I will bless those who bless you, and him who dishonors you I will curse, and in you all the families of the earth shall be blessed.

As Son of Abraham, Jesus will be the Founder of a great nation, enjoy God's blessing, be exalted by God, and be the agent through whom God will bless all nations or families on earth. Furthermore, an individual's relationship to and treatment by God will be determined by how that individual responds to Jesus. Blessing the new Abraham invites God's blessing. Dishonoring the new Abraham invites God's curse.

God Has Rejected National Israel as His People

Before examining Jesus' identity as the new Abraham and Founder of a new Israel, it is appropriate to explore Matthew's teaching regarding the fate of national Israel. Many interpreters, particularly those influenced by dispensationalist theology, object to the notion that Jesus' followers constitute a new Israel, insisting that God can in no way abandon national Israel. This view is difficult to reconcile with the express teaching of Jesus in the Gospel of Matthew. Jesus and Matthew, both Jews themselves, insist that God has removed his favor from Israel because of her sin, particularly her failure to embrace Jesus as Messiah.

The Gospel of Matthew contains several graphic statements of Israel's demise. The gospel insists that, because of Israel's sin, God will destroy the nation at large—only a remnant will survive. In doing so, Matthew shows his familiarity with the warnings that God gives to Israel in the Old Testament (Deut. 28:15–68; Isa. 10:20–23).

The cleansing of the temple in Matthew 21:12–13 is an enacted prophecy forewarning the destruction of the temple if Israel does not repent of its failure to fulfill its mission.[1] Jesus immediately reinforces this warning to his disciples by the cursing of a fig tree. In the Old Testament, the prophets often use a tree as a symbol of the nation of Israel.[2] More importantly, in several contexts the withered fig leaves or fruit functions as a symbol of God's judgment on the nations (Isa. 34:4), the kings of Judah and inhabitants of Jerusalem (Jer. 8:13; 24:1–10), or the children of Judah and Israel (Hos. 2:12).[3] The miracle might be intended in particular to prompt readers to recall Micah 7:1–6, in which the prophet bemoans that there is "no first-ripe fig that my soul desires" as a picture of Judah's corruption.[4] In light of this background and the

1. Craig A. Evans, *Matthew–Luke*, Bible Knowledge Commentary (Colorado Springs: Cook, 2003), 389; David L. Turner, *Matthew*, Baker Exegetical Commentary on the New Testament (Grand Rapids: Baker, 2008), 501–2.

2. Jer. 11:16; 24:8; 29:17; Hos. 9:10.

3. W. D. Davies and Dale Allison Jr., *The Gospel according to Matthew*, 3 vols., International Critical Commentary (Edinburgh: T & T Clark, 1988–1997), 3:151.

4. R. T. France, *The Gospel of Matthew*, New International Commentary on the New Testament (Grand Rapids: Eerdmans, 2007), 793.

normal use of fruit in Matthew to speak of the actions and words that God expects, the fruitlessness of the fig tree represents the failure of God's people to produce fruit of righteousness. Through cursing and destroying the fig tree, Jesus distinctly teaches that God's judgment will soon befall the nation of Israel as a whole[5] or, at the very least, Jerusalem and the leaders of Israel.[6]

In the parable of the wicked tenants, the description of the vineyard unmistakably recalls the song of the vineyard in Isaiah 5:1–7, in which the vineyard represents the house of Israel. The allusion to this song guides one in correctly interpreting the parable of the wicked tenants. Isaiah explains his parable by saying, "For the vineyard of the LORD of hosts is the house of Israel, and the men of Judah are his pleasant planting" (Isa. 5:7). The failure of the vineyard to produce good grapes pictures Israel's failure to produce good deeds: "He looked for justice, but behold, bloodshed; for righteousness, but behold, an outcry!" (v. 7b).

The failure of the tenants to deliver the fruit expected by the master also depicts Israel's failure to produce fruit of righteousness. The mistreatment of the master's servants by the tenants depicts Israel's rejection and abuse of the prophets that God sends to call the nation to repentance. Matthew 21:35 basically follows Mark's description of the treatment of the servants but adds "[they] stoned," a statement unparalleled in Mark or Luke, to "[they] beat" and "[they] killed." This addition turns the description into a parallel to Matthew's description of Jerusalem's treatment of the prophets in 23:37: "O Jerusalem, Jerusalem, the city that kills the prophets and stones those who are sent to it!" The parallel signals that Matthew wants his readers to see the tenants' rejection of the servants as a symbol of Israel/Jerusalem's rejection of the prophets.

The tenants' murder of the master's son clearly depicts Israel/ Jerusalem's rejection and crucifixion of Jesus. Once again, subtle

5. Craig Blomberg, *Matthew*, New American Commentary (Nashville: Broadman, 1992), 318; Donald A. Hagner, *Matthew*, Word Biblical Commentary (Dallas: Word, 1993–95), 2:603–4; John Nolland, *Matthew*, New International Greek Testament Commentary (Grand Rapids: Eerdmans, 2005), 852–53; Rudolf Schnackenburg, *The Gospel of Matthew* (Grand Rapids: Eerdmans, 2002), 204–5.
6. Davies and Allison, *Matthew*, 3:148; Turner, *Matthew*, 504.

features of Matthew's gospel suggest this interpretation. Although Mark writes that the tenants first kill the son and then cast him out of the vineyard (Mark 12:8), Matthew inverts the order of the two statements so that the tenants first cast the son out of the vineyard and then kill him. Matthew likely makes this adjustment to conform the parable to events surrounding Jesus' crucifixion, in which Jesus is first taken outside the city of Jerusalem and then killed. By adjusting the order of the clauses, Matthew heightens links between the parable and Jesus' experiences, giving his readers clues to the correct interpretation of the parable. Matthew does not want his readers to miss the fact that the parable depicts Jerusalem's rejection of the Messiah, Jesus.

The response of the master to the tenants' murder of his servants and his son is expressed in Matthew 21:41: "He will put those wretches to a miserable death and let out the vineyard to other tenants who will give him the fruits in their seasons." Later, in 27:25, the Jewish people assume full responsibility before God for the scourging and crucifixion of Jesus by shouting to Pilate, "His blood be on us and on our children!" Jesus' parable lays out the dreaded consequences of their bloodguilt. He warns that the just penalty for rejecting the Messiah is that "the kingdom of God will be taken away from you and given to a people producing its fruits" (21:43). Frederick Bruner correctly notes, "This is one of the most important verses in Matthew, and it says nothing less momentous than that the kingdom of God will be taken away from Israel and given to a new 'nation,' which is usually understood as the church of both Jews and Gentiles."[7]

Christ warns that the kingdom will be taken from "you" (Matt. 21:43). Although Jesus addresses his words particularly to "the chief priests and the elders of the people" (v. 23; see also v. 45), he teaches in the presence of Jews who are assembled in the temple (v. 23). The contrast of "you" with "a people" in verse 43 implies that Jesus addresses these Jews in general at the climax of the parable. The noun *people* (*ethnos*) refers to "a body of persons

7. Frederick Dale Bruner, *The Churchbook: Matthew 13–28*, rev. ed. (Grand Rapids: Eerdmans, 2007), 381.

united by kinship, culture, and common traditions."[8] The giving of the kingdom to a new people recalls several Old Testament texts, but the most important of these is Daniel 7:27, which reads:

> And the kingdom and the dominion
>> and the greatness of the kingdoms under the whole heaven
>> shall be given to the people of the saints of the Most High;
> their kingdom shall be an everlasting kingdom,
>> and all dominions shall serve and obey them.

This apparent allusion to Daniel's prophecy fits well with the allusion to Daniel 2:33–34, 44–45 in Matthew 21:44.[9] Jesus' reference to a stone that crushes all on whom it falls is reminiscent of Daniel's description of the messianic kingdom that struck the image representing human kingdoms. The stone representing the messianic kingdom broke the preceding kingdoms in pieces so that they "became like the chaff of the summer threshing floors; and the wind carried them away, so that not a trace of them could be found" (Dan. 2:35).

Thus, the primary point of the parable of the wicked tenants is that Israel's failure to produce fruit of righteousness, rejection of the prophets, and murder of God's Son will incite God's wrath and lead to the loss of the nation's privileges. As David Hill explains, "The Jewish nation, as a corporate entity, had now forfeited its elect status."[10] God grants the kingdom to a new spiritual Israel who will produce the fruit of righteousness, honor the teaching of the prophets, and welcome the Son—all that national Israel failed to do. God's rejection of Israel opens the way for the creation of a new people.

Matthew refers to the rejection of Israel both explicitly and implicitly in his gospel. Matthew 23:29–36 condemns the scribes

8. "ἔθνος," in *A Greek-English Lexicon of the New Testament and Other Early Christian Literature*, ed. Frederick W. Danker, 3rd ed. (Chicago: University of Chicago Press, 2000), 276.

9. Although Matthew 21:44 is missing from a few ancient manuscripts, internal and external evidence favors its inclusion.

10. David Hill, *The Gospel of Matthew*, New Century Bible (London: Oliphants, 1972), 301.

and Pharisees for murdering the prophets and warns that Christ will send yet more prophets to be persecuted, "so that on you may come all the righteous blood shed on earth, from the blood of innocent Abel to the blood of Zechariah the son of Barachiah, whom you murdered between the sanctuary and the altar" (v. 35). Verse 36, however, shows that the guilt and punishment of the scribes and Pharisees are shared and experienced by the nation in general: "Truly, I say to you, all these things will come upon this generation." The word *generation* indicates that all of Jesus' Jewish contemporaries, not only the scribes and Pharisees, will suffer God's wrath for the rejection of his messengers.

This warning is repeated in Jesus' lament over Jerusalem (Matt. 23:37–38): "See, your house is left to you desolate." John Calvin aptly notes, "By calling it *your house* He indirectly implies it is God's no longer."[11] In 24:1–2, Jesus warns that the temple abandoned by God would also be completely destroyed. The destruction of the temple is a sign of the demise of the holy city, Jerusalem, and the nation in general. When Solomon completes the temple, Yahweh warns that the destruction of the temple would signal God's abandonment of Israel for abandoning him (1 Kings 9:7). The prophets of Israel likewise see the fate of the temple as an indication of the fate of Jerusalem and the nation as a whole (Isa. 64:6–11). The desolation of the temple indicates that Israel has forfeited its privileges as God's covenant people, for "Abraham does not know us, and Israel does not acknowledge us" (63:16). Indeed, the fact that "our adversaries have trampled down your sanctuary" demonstrates that "we have become like those over whom you have never ruled, like those who are not called by your name" (vv. 18–19).

Other texts in Matthew clearly refer to God's rejection of Israel. Matthew 8:12 warns that "the sons of the kingdom will be thrown into the outer darkness. In that place there will be weeping and gnashing of teeth." In this context, the "sons of the kingdom" are Jews that one would expect to participate in the messianic

---

11. John Calvin, *A Harmony of the Gospels Matthew, Mark, and Luke*, ed. D. W. Torrance and T. F. Torrance, trans. A. W. Morrison (Grand Rapids: Eerdmans, 1972), 3:70.

feast, but they are excluded because of their rejection of Jesus. Clearly, this does not mean that all Jews will be excluded from the feast. The preceding verse shows that the patriarchs—Abraham, Isaac, and Jacob—will participate in it. Rather, the verse indicates that belonging to the nation of Israel does not per se qualify one for the blessings of the messianic age.[12]

In Matthew 15:13, Jesus replies to his disciples' concern about offending the Pharisees by saying, "Every plant that my heavenly Father has not planted will be rooted up." Jesus' saying echoes themes from the prophecies of Isaiah. Isaiah describes the righteous within Israel as a plant that the Lord himself had planted to bring himself glory (Isa. 5:7; 60:21; 61:3). Isaiah 60:21 says, "Your people shall all be righteous; they shall possess the land forever, the branch of my planting, the work of my hands, that I might be glorified." Interestingly, this verse is the proof text cited by Jews of this era to prove that "all Israelites have a share in the world to come."[13] Jesus' statement is an intentional critique of the abuse of Isaiah's words by Jesus' contemporaries. By referring to the Pharisees as plants that the Father did not plant, Jesus implies that the Pharisees do not belong to the true Israel. Instead, they are sown by an enemy among the wheat like tares that will be uprooted and destroyed at the time of judgment (Matt. 13:24–30). Jesus' words indicate that many who presume to be Israelites will be proved impostors on judgment day. Jesus' ground for excluding these Pharisees from Israel and the promises made to Israel is likely also based on Isaiah 60:21: "Your people shall all be righteous." Although most in Israel considered the Pharisees to be the epitome of righteousness, Jesus challenges this assumption by the pronouncement of "woes" on the scribes and Pharisees in Matthew 23. Through the woes, Jesus condemns the scribes and Pharisees for their hypocrisy and gives them a scathing rebuke as a "brood of vipers" that will not escape being sentenced to hell.

The parable of the wedding guests in Matthew 22:1–13 also describes God's rejection of national Israel. Several fea-

12. Robert Gundry, *Matthew*, 2nd ed. (Grand Rapids: Eerdmans, 1994), 145–46.
13. *m. Sanhedrin* 10:1.

tures of the parable show that the nation of Israel composed the original guest list for the messianic feast, represented by a wedding feast for the king's son. The servants sent to call the invited guests to the feast clearly represent the Old Testament prophets. The shameful treatment and murder of the slaves mirrors Israel's treatment of the prophets described in 23:29–37. The king's response to the ingratitude and rebellion of the invitees foreshadows God's punishment of Israel. The burning of their city is a clear allusion to the destruction of Jerusalem in A.D. 70. The words "those invited were not worthy" in 22:8 indicate that God has revoked his invitation to national Israel to participate in the messianic feast. As 22:14 warns, many of those who are called are not actually chosen to participate. The parable does not teach that every Israelite will be banned from participation in the messianic feast. But it does teach that Israelites who dishonor God's Son, Jesus, will be uninvited from the messianic feast and sentenced to suffer the wrath of the heavenly King.[14]

The New Abraham Serves as the Founder of a New Israel

Although God rejects national Israel, he acts through the Son of Abraham to found a new chosen people, a new Israel. This theological motif is especially prominent in Matthew's gospel.

The Twelve as Leaders of the New Israel

Matthew 10:1–4 shows that Jesus appoints twelve disciples to call the lost sheep of the house of Israel to repentance. Most scholars are convinced that the number of the disciples is significant. The number of disciples matches the number of the sons of Jacob/Israel and indicates that Jesus regards his disciples as a reconstituted Israel, a new Israel.[15]

14. See Nolland, *Matthew*, 882–92.
15. James D. G. Dunn, *Jesus Remembered*, in *Christianity in the Making*, vol. 1 (Grand Rapids: Eerdmans, 2003), 510.

Three features of the Gospel of Matthew strongly support the view that Matthew associates the twelve disciples with the twelve patriarchs—and thus twelve tribes—of Israel. First, Matthew may have shaped the wording of the account of Jesus' appointment of the Twelve under the influence of the story of Moses' selection of the leaders of the twelve tribes in the introduction to the book of Numbers. God commands Moses, "There shall be with you a man from each tribe, each man being the head of the house of his fathers" (Num. 1:4). Numbers 1:5–16 lists the twelve tribal leaders and introduces the list with the words: "These are the names of the men." Matthew's introduction to the list of the twelve disciples, "The names of the twelve apostles are these," is reminiscent of Numbers 1:5.[16]

Second, the immediate context of the commissioning of the Twelve contains multiple references to Israel. Matthew 9:36 describes the people to whom Jesus proclaims the gospel of the kingdom as "harassed and helpless, like sheep without a shepherd." "Sheep without a shepherd" is stock Old Testament terminology for the people of Israel. In Numbers 27:17, the phrase describes the congregation of the Lord. In 2 Chronicles 18:16 and Ezekiel 34:5, like phrases describe Israel.[17] Similarly, Matthew 10:6 records Jesus' sending of the Twelve to "the lost sheep of the house of Israel." These two references to the lost sheep of Israel form an inclusio that brackets the account of the commissioning of the Twelve, thus associating the twelve disciples with the twelve tribes of Israel. In light of these contextual features, Ulrich Luz concludes: "Matthew knows that the twelve disciples correspond to the twelve tribes of Israel (19:28). Thus the section 9:36–10:6 is entirely about Israel."[18]

Third, the correspondence of the twelve disciples to the twelve patriarchs is explicit in Jesus' words in Matthew 19:28 (cf. Luke 22:30). Jesus promises, "Truly, I say to you, in the new world,

16. France, *Matthew*, 376.
17. In the Septuagint, see also 1 Kings 22:17; Judith 11:19.
18. Ulrich Luz, *Matthew*, Hermeneia (Minneapolis: Augsburg Fortress, 2001–7), 1:66–67.

when the Son of Man will sit on his glorious throne, you who have followed me will also sit on twelve thrones, judging the twelve tribes of Israel." The full significance of Jesus' statement will be explored later. But it is immediately obvious from this verse that, as John Broadus notes, "The number twelve was probably chosen with reference to the number of tribes."[19]

The Church as the New Israel

One of the clearest indications that Jesus is the new Abraham who founds a new Israel is the use of the term *church* in the Gospel of Matthew. Matthew uses the noun only twice (16:18; 18:17). Nevertheless, even his limited use is significant, for Matthew's gospel is the only one of the four Gospels to use the term at all.

A church (*ekklēsia*) is an assembly of people. The Jews of Jesus' audience, as well as the Jewish Christians in Matthew's audience, would have likely interpreted the word in light of its frequent usage in the Old Testament to denote an assembly of the people of God, the congregation of Israel (cf. Deut. 4:10; 9:10; 18:16; 23:1–3, 8; 31:30).

Matthew first uses the term in Jesus' blessing on the apostle Peter: "And I tell you, you are Peter, and on this rock I will build my church, and the gates of hell shall not prevail against it" (Matt. 16:18). Several features of the statement are important for understanding the nature of Jesus' assembly. First, Jesus refers to his disciples as "my church" (or "my assembly"), and the word order of the Greek text places special emphasis on the word *my*. The assembly of the people of God was frequently identified as "the assembly of the Lord" or "the assembly of Israel." The *my* now stands in the place of either *of the Lord* or *of Israel*. If the former, the *my* serves to identify Jesus with the Lord, Yahweh. If the

19. John A. Broadus, *Commentary on the Gospel of Matthew*, American Commentary on the New Testament (Philadelphia: American Baptist Publication Society, 1886), 212–13. France adds to these arguments the observations that the Qumran community had a leading council of twelve members, also apparently based on the number of Israelite tribes, and that the number twelve was so important that the early church replaced Judas Iscariot with Matthias in order to maintain that number. See France, *Matthew*, 744, esp. nn18, 22.

latter, the *my* shows that the people of God have a new identity, one determined not by their relationship to Jacob/Israel, but by their relationship to the Messiah, Jesus. Although both are possible, most commentators adopt the second option.

Second, Jesus contrasts the old Israel with the new Israel by promising that "the gates of hell shall not prevail against it [my church]." "Hell" (lit. *Hades*) refers to the place to which people go after they die. The phrase "gates of hell" is equivalent to the Old Testament phrases "gates of death" (Job 38:17; Pss. 9:13; 107:18) and "gates of Sheol" (Isa. 38:10). Jesus' statement means that, despite the warnings about Israel's demise, death will never be able to imprison the church of the Lord Jesus. The church will never die.

The Promises to Israel Fulfilled in the Church

Jesus also identifies his disciples as the new Israel by transferring to them the promises made to the chosen people of the Old Testament. Perhaps the clearest example of this is the third beatitude, "Blessed are the meek, for they shall inherit the earth" (Matt. 5:5). The closest Old Testament parallel is Psalm 37:11: "The meek shall inherit the land." The psalmist uses the expression "dwell in the land" once (v. 3) and "inherit the land" five times (vv. 9, 11, 22, 29, 34) to describe God's blessings toward those who wait on him with righteousness and meekness. Inheriting the land refers to taking ownership of and residence in Canaan, the land of covenant promise. The phrase is clearly reminiscent of the scores of Old Testament texts that refer to the land as Israel's inheritance. For example, statements such as "When you enter the land of Canaan (this is the land that shall fall to you for an inheritance, the land of Canaan as defined by its borders)" (Num. 34:2) and "You shall cause this people to inherit the land that I swore to their fathers to give them" (Josh. 1:6) prompt the psalmist to write elsewhere, "[The LORD] gave their land as a heritage [lit. *inheritance*], a heritage to his people Israel" (Ps. 135:12). Paul in Acts 13:19 summarizes this Old Testament theme by saying,

"After destroying seven nations in the land of Canaan, he gave them their land as an inheritance."

Although the English translation "they shall inherit the earth" (Matt. 5:5) is legitimate, Matthew's original audience would not have missed the fact that Matthew's Greek is identical to texts such as Psalm 37:11 and Isaiah 61:7.[20] They would likely have been stunned by Jesus' transference of this promise to the disciples he blesses through these beatitudes. Transfer of the promise of inheriting the land to Jesus' disciples unmistakably marks them as the new Israel, the new chosen people.

---

20. For a discussion of the appropriate translation and an explanation of the promise, see Charles L. Quarles, *The Sermon on the Mount: Restoring Christ's Message to the Modern Church* (Nashville: B&H Academic, 2011), 55–58.

8

The Theological Significance
of the *New Abraham* Theme

JESUS' IDENTITY as the new Abraham who will found a new people for God prompts a number of theological questions: How will God form this people? Who will make up this new people? What is the purpose of this new people? The Gospel of Matthew displays the theological significance of the *new Abraham* theme by answering these important questions.

The New Israel Is Graciously Chosen by God

National Israel regarded itself as God's chosen people. The Old Testament frequently refers to God's election of Israel: "I will take you to be my people, and I will be your God" (Ex. 6:7); "The LORD your God has chosen you to be a people for his treasured possession, out of all the peoples who are on the face of the earth" (Deut 7:6; 14:2); "It has pleased the LORD to make you a people for himself" (1 Sam. 12:22). God stresses that his election of Israel is unconditional. Deuteronomy 7:7 reminds Israel that God did not choose her because of her great numbers, since the Israelites were in fact "the fewest of all peoples." He also denies that Israel was granted favor over other nations because of any supposed personal righteousness (Deut. 9:5).

The Psalms of Solomon, written in the first century B.C., celebrate this election, saying, "We are the people whom you have loved," and "you chose the descendants of Abraham above all the nations" (9:8–9). At times, Jewish writers seem to forget the unconditional nature of their election and assume that God chose them because of their greatness. Second Baruch 48:20–24, written in the early second century A.D., exclaims, "These are the people whom you have elected, and this is the nation of which you found no equal."

The prophecies of Amos challenge Israel's presumptions that God elected the entire nation of Israel and that this election guarantees continual blessing. Amos 3:2 describes the divine election of Israel: "You only have I known of all the families of the earth." But rather than agreeing that this election grants some special immunity to the nation, the prophet warns, "Therefore I will punish you for all your iniquities." The prophet's statement "cuts off the root of all false confidence in divine election."[1] Israel's election does not shield her from God's discipline; it actually heightens the nation's accountability to God.[2] Similarly, 9:7 undermines claims of Israel's superiority to other nations by warning that the people of Israel are like the Cushites in God's eyes. The exodus did not prove God's special favor on Israel, since God has rescued pagans as well, such as the Philistines from Caphtor and the Syrians from Kir. By this startling statement, the prophet "tears away from the sinful nation the last support of its carnal security, namely reliance upon its election as the nation of God."[3] Billy Smith correctly observes:

> Amos must have left his audience in shock. Israel's elect status did not excuse their sins or make them superior to other peoples. Rather it gave them a responsibility to reveal God to the nations (Gen. 12:1–3; Isa 42:6), which they had not done; and thus it gave them greater accountability before God, for which they would most assuredly be judged.[4]

1. Carl F. Keil, in Carl F. Keil and Franz Delitzsch, *Biblical Commentary on the Old Testament* (Grand Rapids: Eerdmans, 1986), 1:259.
2. See Billy K. Smith, "Amos," in *Amos, Obadiah, Jonah*, New American Commentary (Nashville: Broadman and Holman, 1995), 70–71.
3. Keil, *Commentary on the Old Testament*, 1:326.
4. Smith, "Amos," 160–61.

Many in first-century Judaism viewed God's election of Israel as a guarantee of salvation. John the Baptist challenges this notion at the beginning of his ministry by urging Judeans to repent in order to prepare for the coming kingdom, preaching, "Do not presume to say to yourselves, 'We have Abraham as our father,' for I tell you, God is able from these stones to raise up children for Abraham" (Matt. 3:9).

Jesus himself challenges Israel's presumption through the parable of the wedding feast, which climaxes with the declaration, "For many are called, but few are chosen" (Matt. 22:14). As explained earlier, this parable contains a strong indictment against Israel for rejecting the prophets and dishonoring God's Son. This disobedience and disbelief disqualifies rebellious sinners in Israel from the privileges of Israel's election as a nation. In harmony with the prophet Amos, Jesus warns that "election . . . will not save sinful Israel from destruction."[5]

The Mishnah taught that "all Israelites have a share in the world to come."[6] This suggests that many first-century Israelites failed to understand the message of the prophet Amos and thus assumed that God's election of Israel guaranteed salvation for all Israelites. The Mishnah did list a few exceptions, such as Israel's most wicked kings, blasphemers, and those that denied the inspiration of the Law (vv. 1–6). This popular theology of many first-century Jews might be summarized by the statement "all are called, and many are chosen." Jesus rejects this theology by insisting that "many are called, but few are chosen" (Matt. 22:14). As will be discussed later, Jesus' teaching implies that God intends to incorporate Gentiles into his redemptive plan. But the more shocking implication to Jesus' original audience is the claim that only a relatively small remnant of Israelites belong to the chosen people of God. R. T. France explains that *chosen* is a term

with strongly ideological overtones deriving from the OT concept of Israel as God's chosen people. But its use here and in 24:31

5. Keil, *Commentary on the Old Testament*, 1:326.
6. *m. Sanhedrin* 10:1.

THE NEW ABRAHAM: JESUS, OUR FOUNDER

introduces a radically new element to that ideological concept: the true "chosen people" is not automatically identified with those who belong to the Israelite community, not even those who are its official leaders: these are the invited, but not necessarily the chosen.[7]

This radical redefinition of the chosen people paves the way for a proper understanding of the term *elect* in Matthew 24. That chapter contains the greatest concentration of the term's use in Jesus' teaching. Verse 22 shows that God will shorten the time of suffering related to the Roman siege of Jerusalem for the sake of the elect. The elect seem to be distinguished from the nation at large. They, by God's mercy, will survive the catastrophe that will claim the lives of so many others. The use of *elect* in this verse implies that they are a subgroup of Israel, not Israel itself. The elect are those who are not merely called but actually chosen. They are the followers of Jesus who, in the terms of the parable of the wedding guests, accept the king's invitation to the marriage feast of his son. These elect are equivalent to the faithful "remnant" described by the prophets (Isa. 10:22; see also Ezek. 6:8). Thus, John Broadus is correct in identifying the elect as "the elect among the Jews (Isa. 65:9), the Jewish Christians."[8]

God not only will protect these elect from the slaughter associated with the Roman war against the Jews in A.D. 68–70, but will also protect them from spiritual deception. In Matthew 24:24, Jesus warns that false messiahs and prophets will perform great signs and wonders that will be so convincing as to deceive, "if possible, even the elect." The parenthetical conditional clause, "if possible," implies that the elect "are in the care of their Father (cf. 10:29–31) and that it is therefore not in the power of these enemies to accomplish their purpose."[9]

7. R. T. France, *The Gospel of Matthew*, New International Commentary on the New Testament (Grand Rapids: Eerdmans, 2007), 827–28.
8. John A. Broadus, *Commentary on the Gospel of Matthew*, American Commentary on the New Testament (Philadelphia: American Baptist Publication Society, 1886), 488.
9. Donald A. Hagner, *Matthew*, Word Biblical Commentary (Dallas: Word, 1993–95), 2:706. Daniel Wallace lists this verse as an example of a second class condition, that is, a condition that the speaker assumes to be untrue. *Greek Grammar: Beyond the Basics*

Matthew's final explicit reference to God's chosen people appears in Matthew 24:31: "And he [the Son of Man] will send out his angels with a loud trumpet call, and they will gather his elect from the four winds, from one end of heaven to the other." Although scholars debate whether this prophecy was fulfilled by the fall of Jerusalem in A.D. 70 or still awaits fulfillment through the second coming of Christ, most commentators agree that the elect are the chosen subjects of the kingdom of the Son of Man, the spiritual Israel, consisting of believing Jews and Gentiles from all over the world.[10]

The description of his disciples as the *elect* is an important part of Jesus' (and Matthew's) presentation of Jesus' followers as the new Israel. The adoption of the term *elect* as part of the *new Israel* theme implies that God's election of new Israel is similar to the election of old Israel. Just as God did not choose Israel because of her great numbers (Deut. 7:7) or superior righteousness (9:5), God did not choose the individuals who would constitute the new Israel because of any perceived good in them. The shocking statement in Matthew 21:31, "the tax collectors and the prostitutes go into the kingdom of God before you," highlights the gracious nature of divine election.

The principle that "many are called, but few are chosen" (Matt. 22:14) implies that divine election is individual rather than

---

(Grand Rapids: Zondervan, 1997), 696. This classification cannot be proved, since the construction omits the verb. Omission of the copulative verb was very common, particularly in impersonal constructions expressing possibility or necessity. See Robert Funk, *A Greek Grammar of the New Testament and Other Early Christian Literature* (Chicago: University of Chicago Press, 1961), § 127. Craig Blomberg, *Matthew*, New American Commentary (Nashville: Broadman, 1992), 361n51, suggests that the construction is a shortened form of the protasis of the fourth class condition, which implies that the fulfillment of the condition is improbable. Perhaps the best analysis recognizes the "encroachment of εἰ on the sphere of ἐάν" that appears to occur both here and in Matthew 5:29–30 and 18:8–9 (cf. Mark 9:43, 45, 47). See Funk, *Greek Grammar*, § 372.3; Charles L. Quarles, *The Sermon on the Mount: Restoring Christ's Message to the Modern Church* (Nashville: B&H Academic, 2011), 123–24. The third class condition may refer to the condition as "a mere *hypothetical* situation or one that probably will not be fulfilled." Wallace, *Greek Grammar*, 696. Matthew's addition of the ascensive conjunction "even" to Mark heightens the implication that the elect will not be deceived.

10. France, *Matthew*, 919–28. See also John Lightfoot, *A Commentary on the New Testament from the Talmud and Hebraica* (1989; repr., Peabody, MA: Hendrickson, 1997), 2:319–20; R. V. G. Tasker, *The Gospel according to St. Matthew*, Tyndale New Testament Commentary (Grand Rapids: Eerdmans, 1961), 225–28.

corporate. Many of Jesus' Jewish contemporaries held a corporate view of election in which God chose the nation and in which all its citizens, except those guilty of the most heinous sins, were chosen as part of that entity. But Jesus' teaching in the parable of the wedding guests (vv. 1–14) insists that many who belong to the nation of Israel are not actually God's chosen people. His chosen ones are a relatively small subgroup within the nation. Their identity as the chosen is manifested by their celebration of the son of the king (Jesus, God's Son) and by the fact that they honor him with proper attire (righteous deeds). Outwardly identifying with the people of God does not guarantee that one truly belongs to the people of God. Similarly, the election of the new Israel is individual rather than corporate. Outwardly identifying with the church does not guarantee that one truly belongs to the chosen people. Jesus implies this in 18:17 by warning that any member of the assembly who does not repent of sin in the process of church discipline should be regarded as "a Gentile and a tax collector." This is also implied by the judgment scenes in Matthew, in which individuals presume to belong to God but are rejected by the eschatological Judge (7:21–23; 25:41–46).

Matthew's gospel also implies that divine election is not only personal but also eternal. In his description of final judgment, the enthroned Son of Man says to his sheep, "Come, you who are blessed by my Father, inherit the kingdom prepared for you from the foundation of the world" (Matt. 25:34). Matthew uses the phrase "the foundation of the world" in his quotation of Psalm 78:2 in Matthew 13:35, and the similar phrase "the beginning of the world" in Matthew 24:21. In all three contexts, the phrases refer to the time when God created the world. God's ancient plan did not merely focus on the preparation of a kingdom. Rather, it focused on the preparation of a kingdom "for you." The statement is reminiscent of 20:23, where Jesus states that it is not his prerogative to reserve spots at his right and left for James and John, since each place "has been prepared by my Father" for a specific individual. Here, too, the kingdom was prepared for specific individuals, "you," the "sheep." Ulrich Luz recognizes the implications of this: "Without explicitly stating it, 'blessed of my Father' implies the idea of predestination that was taken for granted in the Judaism of that day."[11]

Jesus' statement in Matthew 25:34 thus reflects the same theology that prompts Paul to write that "from the beginning God chose you to be saved" (2 Thess. 2:13 NIV) and "chose us in him before the foundation of the world" (Eph. 1:4). First Peter 1:4–5 may well be a reflection on Matthew 25:34. It is no accident that Peter's statement immediately follows his portrayal of the believers throughout Asia Minor as "elect exiles of the dispersion" (v. 1). Peter, too, sees the connection between Jesus' description of his disciples as the chosen people of God and his description of an inheritance prepared for them from eternity past.

The New Israel Consists of Both Jews and Gentiles

A corollary to the truth that Jesus comes to create a new people of God is that Jesus comes to offer salvation to all the peoples of the earth. This theological theme appears quite frequently in Matthew's gospel, beginning even in its opening verses. In his genealogy of Jesus, Matthew normally focuses on the identity of Jesus' male ancestors by using the construction "A was the father of B." In four instances, however, Matthew chooses to also identify the mother by using the construction "A was the father of B by C" (Matt. 1:3, 5 [2×], 6).

Scholars have suggested a variety of motives for Matthew's inclusion of the names of four Old Testament women in his genealogy of Jesus. Some argue that the four women are alike in that they each conceived children under circumstances that were, for one reason or another, irregular and even scandalous. Tamar conceived through an incestuous relationship with her father-in-law (Gen. 38), Rahab through prostitution (Josh. 2:1), Ruth, supposedly,

---

11. Ulrich Luz, *Matthew*, Hermeneia (Minneapolis: Augsburg Fortress, 2001–7), 3:277–78. Luz contrasts this description with the description of "eternal fire" as "prepared for the devil and his angels" and concludes that "the parallel in v. 41 will show clearly that Matthew is somewhat reserved toward the idea of a double predestination."

THE NEW ABRAHAM: JESUS, OUR FOUNDER

through fornication (Ruth 3:7), and Bathsheba through adultery (2 Samuel 11). Raymond Brown explains:

> These women were held up as examples of how God uses the unexpected to triumph over human obstacles and intervenes on behalf of His planned Messiah. It is the combination of the scandalous or irregular union and of divine intervention through the woman that explains best Matthew's choice in the genealogy.[12]

Although this explanation for inclusion of the four Old Testament women is popular with commentators, good reasons exist for flatly rejecting it. First, no evidence suggests that Ruth conceived a child out of wedlock. Even Brown admits that the claim that Ruth 3:7 euphemistically refers to a sexual relationship "is not the overall impression of the book."[13] Early Jewish interpreters do not entertain this view of Ruth's lying at Boaz's feet. On the contrary, Josephus claims that the point of the story is to illustrate "the power of God, who, without difficulty, can raise those that are of ordinary parentage to dignity and splendor, to which he advanced David, though he were born of such mean parents."[14] Although a few modern commentators regard verses 7–15 as a sex scene, the text gives no indication of a sexual union's occurring at this point.[15] On the contrary, the Targum of Ruth notes:

> He [Boaz] restrained his desire and did not approach her, just as Joseph the righteous did, who refused to approach the Egyptian woman, the wife of his master, just as Paltiel bar Laish the Pious did, who placed a sword between himself

12. Raymond Brown, *The Birth of the Messiah* (New York: Doubleday, 1977), 73–74. Also supporting this view are Blomberg, *Matthew*, 55–56; Hagner, *Matthew*, 1:10–11; David Hill, *The Gospel of Matthew*, New Century Bible (London: Oliphants, 1972), 74; Rudolf Schnackenburg, *The Gospel of Matthew* (Grand Rapids: Eerdmans, 2002), 17.

13. Brown, *Birth of the Messiah*, 72n24.

14. Josephus, *Jewish Antiquities*, 5.9.4 § 337.

15. See Robert Hubbard Jr., *The Book of Ruth*, New International Commentary on the Old Testament (Grand Rapids: Eerdmans, 1988), 208–20; Daniel Block, *Judges, Ruth*, New American Commentary (Nashville: Broadman and Holman, 1999), 688–96.

and Michal daughter of Saul, wife of David, whom he refused to reproach.[16]

Ruth 4:13 seems to present the sexual act that consummates Boaz and Ruth's marriage as their first.

Second, the miraculous conceptions by Old Testament women such as Sarah had much more in common with the miraculous conception of Jesus by Mary than those of the women named in the genealogy. Appealing to the scandalous births of women in the genealogy to silence objections to the mysterious circumstances of Jesus' birth would have sounded like a tacit admission of Mary's impurity, undermining Matthew's repeated claim of Jesus' virginal conception. As Robert Gundry argues, "such a counterattack would have deepened suspicions concerning the legitimacy of Jesus' birth."[17]

Far more likely is that the women are included because all four are Gentiles. Ancient Jewish texts describe Tamar as a "foreigner."[18] Rahab is a Canaanite from Jericho (Josh. 2:8–24). Ruth is a Moabite (Ruth 1:4).[19]

Some argue that Bathsheba breaks this pattern because it is assumed that she is an Israelite. Second Samuel 11:3 identifies her as the daughter of Eliam. If this Eliam is identical to the one named in 2 Samuel 23:34, Bathsheba is a Gilonite (from the city of Gilo). Nevertheless, Bathsheba bears the status of a Hittite because of her marriage to Uriah the Hittite (11:3). Although the genealogy that Matthew follows from 1 Chronicles 3:5 refers to the mother of Solomon as "Bathsheba daughter of Ammiel" (NIV), Matthew emphasizes her association with her Hittite husband by

16. D. R. G. Beattie, *Targum of Ruth*, Aramaic Targum 19 (Collegeville, MN: Liturgical, 1994), 26–27.

17. Robert Gundry, *Matthew*, 2nd ed. (Grand Rapids: Eerdmans, 1994), 15.

18. Philo, *Virt.*, 220–22.

19. The Talmud claims that Ruth is actually the great-granddaughter of King Balak. See *b. Sanhedrin* 105b. Also, *b. Yebamot* 63a describes Ruth of Moab and Naaman of Ammon as two good shoots grafted into the line of Abraham. *b. Yebamot* 76b states that Doeg the Edomite challenged David's identity as an Israelite because of his descent from Ruth. *b. Baba Qamma* 38b describes Ruth of Moab and Naaman of Ammon as two beautiful doves from among the Gentiles.

referring to her not by her name or her father's name, but as "the wife of Uriah" (Matt. 1:6).

The mention of these four Gentile women in the genealogy of the Messiah signals God's intention to include Gentiles in his redemptive plan.[20] The genealogy thus serves to support Matthew's identification of Jesus as the "son of Abraham" (v. 1), the seed of Abraham through whom all nations on earth will be blessed.

This theme resurfaces in Matthew's account of the summons of the magi to worship Jesus in Bethlehem in Matthew 2. The journey of the magi to celebrate the birth of the Jewish Messiah is stunning. First-century Eastern magi epitomized the false religion that characterized the Gentile world. They mixed together the false religion of Zoroastrianism with astrology, the interpretation of dreams and visions, and black magic.[21] Eastern magi are described in some detail in Daniel 2:2, 4–5, and 10, in which the magi are associated with magicians, enchanters, and sorcerers in the court of Nebuchadnezzar, king of Babylon. Jews avoided associations with magi, as the Talmud taught: "He who learns from a *magus* is worthy of death."[22]

Strikingly, these Gentiles are the first worshipers of Jesus in the Gospel of Matthew. The humble and reverent worship of Jesus by pagan leaders of the Gentile world stands in stark contrast to the apparent apathy of the chief priests and scribes and their refusal to investigate the possibility that the Messiah has been born. This foreshadows Jesus' rejection by the Jewish leaders and his acceptance by Gentiles later in the gospel.

In Matthew 3:9, John the Baptist warns that the Pharisees and Sadducees should no longer boast in their physical descent

20. Richard Bauckham, "Tamar's Ancestry and Rahab's Marriage: Two Problems in the Matthean Genealogy," *Novum Testamentum* 37 (1995): 313–29, esp. 313; W. D. Davies and Dale Allison Jr., *The Gospel according to Matthew*, 3 vols., International Critical Commentary (Edinburgh: T & T Clark, 1988–1997), 1:170–72; Gundry, *Matthew*, 15; Craig Keener, *A Commentary on the Gospel of Matthew* (Grand Rapids: Eerdmans, 1999), 78–80; Luz, *Matthew*, 1:84–85.

21. See G. Delling, "μάγος," in *Theological Dictionary of the New Testament*, ed. Gerhard Kittel and Gerhard Friedrich, trans. Geoffrey W. Bromiley, 10 vols. (Grand Rapids: Eerdmans, 1964–76), 4:356–59; Brown, *Birth of the Messiah*, 167–74. Also see the use of the term in Acts 13:8 and Paul's description in verses 10–11.

22. *b. Shabbat* 75a.

from Abraham, since God bears the power to raise up children for Abraham even from among the stones scattered across the landscape. John's words, which contain an important allusion to Isaiah 51:1–2, hint that God might form a new Israel that is not composed merely of Abraham's physical descendants. This implication is confirmed by the added warning that the children of Abraham are like a tree that has failed to produce fruit of righteousness. According to John, the sharp axe of the Lord is at this moment poised to fall and cut down the tree at its root and cast it into the fire. If Israel does not repent, judgment is imminent. God's judgment will be so fierce as to require the miraculous creation of a new people of God, just as John implies.

Matthew 4 marks the beginning of numerous extensions of the ministry of Jesus beyond the Jewish people to those of Gentile backgrounds. Verses 12–16 describe Jesus' decision to establish his ministry headquarters in Capernaum as a fulfillment of God's promise in Isaiah 9:1–2 to bring light to "Galilee of the Gentiles." In Matthew 4:4, people from Syria, most likely including Gentiles, begin to bring sick and diseased friends and family members to Jesus for healing. The crowds from the Decapolis that follow Jesus (v. 25) are probably largely composed of Gentiles.

In Matthew 8:5–13, Jesus offers to enter the house of a Roman centurion. This defies the Jewish taboo against entering the house of a Gentile (cf. Acts 10:28). Jesus exclaims that the faith of this Gentile has exceeded any faith that he has encountered in Israel. He clearly implies the inclusion of the Gentiles in the kingdom of God by claiming that many from the East and the West will enter the kingdom and feast with Abraham, Isaac, and Jacob. He also warns that many "sons of the kingdom," Jews who reject Jesus, will be excluded from the kingdom.

In Matthew 12:15–21, Matthew identifies Jesus as the fulfillment of Isaiah 42:1–4, a prophecy that climaxes with the promise that "in his name the Gentiles will hope." In Matthew 12:41–42, Jesus reminds the scribes and Pharisees about the Ninevites and the queen of the South, who repented and sought true wisdom from the ends of the earth. He warns that these Gentiles will stand up on the day of judgment and condemn the Jewish leaders who rejected Jesus.

In Matthew 15:21–28, Matthew describes Jesus' kindness to a Gentile woman. He specifically describes the woman as a "Canaanite" (cf. Mark 7:26), probably to associate this woman with the most notorious pagan enemy of Israel. Jesus' kindness to the woman shows that the Gentiles whom first-century Jews would have regarded as most despicable may follow Christ and be blessed by him. In verses 29–31, Jesus heals the sick on the northern shores of the Sea of Galilee in what is apparently Gentile territory. The people's praise to "the God of Israel" implies that Gentiles were glorifying the God associated with the Israelites.

The theme of God's inclusion of the Gentiles is prominent at Jesus' crucifixion. A Roman centurion and his guards exclaim, "Truly this man was the Son of God!" (Matt. 27:54). Their bold confession is in stark contrast to the refusal of the Jewish leaders to believe, even after the soldiers report Jesus' resurrection. Finally, the theme is clearly stated in the Great Commission, in which Jesus urges his followers to make disciples of "all nations" (28:19–20).

Although Luke's gospel is commonly recognized as the gospel that emphasizes that God has incorporated Gentile believers into the new Israel, this great theological theme is just as prominent in the gospel penned by one of Jesus' own Jewish followers. If this theme had been fully appreciated by other Jewish Christians in the early church, the tensions between Jewish and Gentile Christians that Paul addresses so frequently in his letters might have never arisen. Although Paul is recognized as the great apostle to the Gentiles, Matthew's gospel demonstrates that at least one of the Twelve was equally committed to Gentile outreach. The convictions that Paul expresses in Ephesians 2:11–22 were cherished by Matthew also. Though Gentiles had once been "separated from Christ, alienated from the commonwealth of Israel and strangers to the covenants of promise, having no hope and without God in the world," now those who were far away had been "brought near by the blood of Christ." Gentile disciples of Jesus were "no longer strangers and aliens, but . . . fellow citizens with the saints and members of the household of God."

The New Israel Will Fulfill Its Mission of Producing Righteousness and Being a Light to the Nations

God appointed the nation of Israel to fulfill two important purposes. Israel was to display the character of Yahweh by being holy as he is holy (Ex. 19:6; Lev. 11:45; Deut. 26:19). Israel was also to be the instrument by which God would bless other nations (Gen. 18:18; 22:18; 26:4; 1 Chron. 16:31, 35; Ps. 96:1–3).

The nation of Israel fails to fulfill either of these aspects of its mission. Consequently, the nation incurs the judgment that both John the Baptist and Jesus repeatedly threaten. God then turns to another people with whom he establishes his new covenant to fulfill the mission that Israel neglected. The new Israel will complete the mission first assigned to national Israel.

The New Israel Will Be Holy

The people founded by the new Abraham display God's holy character. The holy character of God's new chosen people is prominent in the Gospel of Matthew. In Matthew 3:7–10, John warns the descendants of Abraham regarding the fate that will befall them if they fail to bear good fruit. In this context, "God is able from these stones to raise up children for Abraham" suggests that if God should raise up a new chosen people, they will bear the good fruit of good works.

In his famous Sermon on the Mount, Jesus describes his disciples as "the pure in heart" (Matt. 5:8), those who "hunger and thirst for righteousness," whose longings for righteousness "shall be satisfied" (5:6). He describes his disciples as those who are both characterized by righteousness and prepared to suffer persecution "for righteousness' sake" (vv. 10–12). Jesus' disciples are those who display "good works" that "give glory to your Father who is in heaven" (v. 16).

The section of the Sermon on the Mount that contrasts Jesus' expectations of his disciples with the teachings of the rabbis (Matt. 5:21–48) is bracketed with references to the extraordinary righteousness of Jesus' disciples. Jesus commands them to honor even the least of the commandments and to be characterized by righteousness that "exceeds that of the scribes and Pharisees" (vv. 17–20). At the close of the section, Jesus commands, "You therefore must be perfect, as your heavenly Father is perfect" (v. 48). Jesus' disciples would recognize this climactic command as a clear echo of Leviticus 11:45, in which God commands Israel, "You shall therefore be holy, for I am holy."

Matthew 6:1–18 is focused on the proper practice of righteousness (see esp. v. 1). Matthew 7:15–20 recalls the teaching of John the Baptist and insists that true disciples of Jesus are like good trees that produce good fruit. Verse 21 promises that Jesus' disciples will do the will of the Father who is in heaven. The concluding parable of the Sermon on the Mount shows that Jesus' true disciples are wise because they both hear Jesus' words and do them (vv. 24–27).

The promise of reward for those who give a cup of cold water to one of Jesus' disciples (Matt. 10:42) alludes to the promise that "one who receives a righteous person because he is a righteous person will receive a righteous person's reward" (v. 41). Jesus' words thus portray his disciples as those who are righteous. A survey of the use of the terms *righteous* and *righteousness* in the Gospel of Matthew shows that the word group refers to the expression of holy character through good works.

Matthew 12:46–50 portrays Jesus' disciples as members of his family ("my brother and sister and mother") who do "the will of my Father in heaven." The parable of the soils (13:1–8, 18–23) portrays the true disciples as fertile soil that produces a harvest of righteousness nothing short of miraculous ("some a hundredfold, some sixty, some thirty"). Similarly, the parable of the weeds (vv. 24–30, 36–43) describes Jesus' disciples as the "sons of the kingdom"[23] who bear good fruit. These disciples are

23. This phrase is particularly significant. It is the same expression used in Matthew 8:12 to describe Israelites as "the sons of the kingdom." Jesus warns, however, that those

"the righteous" who will "shine like the sun in the kingdom of their Father." Jesus' teaching about final judgment in 25:31–46 concludes with a description of his disciples as "the righteous" who will receive eternal life.

Perhaps the most important text in Matthew demonstrating that the new Israel will manifest the righteousness that Old Testament Israel failed to produce is the parable of the wicked tenants (Matt. 21:33–44). In response to the parable, the chief priests and elders indict themselves by admitting that the vineyard owner's just reaction to the tenants would be to "put those wretches to a miserable death and let out the vineyard to other tenants who will give him the fruits in their seasons." The statement demonstrates that Israel deserved God's judgment for failing to produce the fruit of good works, while the new Israel will produce fruit of righteousness.

The New Israel Will Bless the Nations

God promised Abraham that all the nations on earth would be blessed through him. In keeping with that promise, God entrusted Israel with the task of being a "light for the nations" (Isa. 49:6). In Matthew, Jesus transfers this mission of Israel to his own disciples.

Jesus describes his disciples as the "light of the world" (Matt. 5:13–14). Since 4:15–16 applies Isaiah 9:1–2 to Jesus, the gospel clearly identifies Jesus as the "light." The description of Jesus' disciples as the "light" demonstrates that they "are to be extensions of the Messiah's ministry by taking up His mission of bringing salvation to the world."[24] Isaiah 60:1–3 probably serves as the background for Matthew 5:14–16. Matthew's text describes the disciples as a shining light that displays the glory of the Father through good works. Similarly, Isaiah encourages Israel, "Arise,

---

"sons of the kingdom will be thrown into the outer darkness," where there is "weeping and gnashing of teeth." In 13:38, the "sons of the kingdom" are the new spiritual Israel who are promised the "kingdom of their Father." Thus, there are two very different destinies for two very different groups known as "sons of the kingdom."

24. Quarles, *Sermon on the Mount*, 84.

shine, for your light has come, and the glory of the LORD has risen upon you." Then Isaiah 60:21 promises, "Your people shall all be righteous; they shall possess the land forever, the branch of my planting, the work of my hands, that I might be glorified." Matthew 5:16 seems to echo Isaiah's statement: "Let your light shine before others, so that they may see your good works and give glory to your Father who is in heaven."

Isaiah 60 is a prophecy concerning Israel that describes the restored Zion. But Jesus uses an emphatic construction to insist that "you" (i.e., "my disciples") are "the" light of the world, thereby implying that Jesus' disciples alone are the true light of the world. Craig Keener observes that through the description of the disciples as the light of the world, "Jesus depicts his disciples' mission in stark biblical terms traditionally used for the mission of Israel."[25] By applying this label to his disciples, Jesus implies that they have "supplanted national Israel as God's covenant people"[26] and have taken up Israel's mission to the nations.

Isaiah 60 stresses Israel's role in summoning the nations to God. For as God's glory was manifested through Israel, "nations shall come to your light" (v. 3). The prophecy emphasizes that all the peoples of the earth, from Midian and Ephah to Sheba and Tarshish, will be drawn to Zion to worship Yahweh and offer him their treasures. God will use these nations to restore Israel, for "foreigners shall build up your walls" (v. 10). Jesus' allusion to Isaiah 60 demonstrates that his disciples, the new Israel, will assume Israel's role in manifesting the glory of God to the nations and drawing the peoples of the world to worship him.

The new Israel will be a blessing to the nations primarily by propagating the gospel of the kingdom to all the peoples of the world. Consequently, Matthew's gospel stresses the church's role as a witness to the world. Matthew's gospel makes it clear that Jesus' disciples were to focus their initial ministry efforts on the "lost sheep of the house of Israel," so much so that Jesus could even instruct them to "go nowhere among the Gentiles and enter

25. Keener, *Matthew*, 174–75.
26. Quarles, *Sermon on the Mount*, 85.

no town of the Samaritans" (Matt. 10:5). Numerous statements in Matthew, however, assume or command the disciples' mission to Gentiles in other nations. Verse 18 warns: "You will be dragged before governors and kings for my sake, to bear witness before them and the Gentiles." Jesus' eschatological discourse says, "This gospel of the kingdom will be proclaimed throughout the whole world as a testimony to all nations" (24:14). Finally, the Gospel of Matthew climaxes with Jesus' commission to "go therefore and make disciples of all nations" (28:19–20).

The inclusion of the Gentiles from far and wide in the new Israel is a prominent theme in Matthew's gospel. This proclamation of the gospel to the nations is, of course, the means by which God includes Gentiles in his plan of redemption.

Conclusion: Share the Good News

Because of its sinful rebellion against God and its rejection of the prophets and the Messiah, the nation of Israel forfeited its privileges as the chosen people of God. As the Son of Abraham, Jesus is the Founder of a new chosen people. With regard to the new Israel, Jesus fills the role that Abraham filled with regard to national Israel. The new Israel consists of the followers of Jesus Christ and includes both Jews and Gentiles. The new Israel founded by the Son of Abraham fulfills the mission originally assigned to Israel, a mission that the nation miserably failed to fulfill. The new Israel manifests the holy character of God and offers blessing to all the families of the earth by proclaiming the good news about Jesus Christ to the ends of the earth.

Jesus' role as the new Abraham founding a new people has important practical implications for believers today. The gracious, unconditional election of the new chosen people promotes humility and gratitude. The assurance that God will protect his people from spiritual deception grants the believer a profound sense of security. The holiness that is to characterize the chosen people stirs hunger and thirst for righteousness. The diverse makeup of the chosen people prompts disciples to abandon old prejudices and to see others with new eyes.

Perhaps most importantly, the ancient promise that the new Abraham will be One through whom all the nations of the earth will be blessed, combined with the new Israel's call to be a light to the nations, prompts Jesus' disciples to be zealous in sharing the good news of salvation both near and far. The Master's words—that the gospel of the kingdom will be proclaimed throughout the whole world as a testimony to all nations—inspire them to give sacrificially to support the propagation of the gospel, pray for the advancement of the kingdom to the ends of the earth, and proclaim the gospel boldly and compassionately. Led by the new Abraham, the new Israel hears the old appeal:

> Rescue the perishing, Care for the dying,
> Snatch them in pity from sin and the grave;
> Weep o'er the erring one, Lift up the fallen,
> Tell them of Jesus the mighty to save.
> Rescue the perishing, Care for the dying;
> Jesus is merciful, Jesus will save.[27]

---

27. Fanny Crosby, "Rescue the Perishing" (1869).

Part 5

The New Creator:
Jesus, Our God

Matthew's Development of the *New Creator* Theme: The Titles of Jesus

ALTHOUGH MATTHEW presents Jesus as Savior, Ruler, and Founder of a new people, Jesus is far greater than even these roles imply. Matthew's gospel is characterized by a high Christology that worships Jesus as God himself, the Creator who made all that exists.

Although this part of this book is titled "The New Creator," the title does not function exactly as one might expect based on the titles of previous parts. As the new Moses, Abraham, and David, Jesus is similar to but distinguished from the Old Testament Moses, Abraham, and David. The application of the title *New Creator* to Jesus, however, is not intended to distinguish him from the Creator described in the Old Testament. On the contrary, Jesus is the agent of original creation, as Matthew's portrayal of Jesus as Wisdom will show. The title *New Creator* simply denotes that Jesus, as God with us, is not only the One who made the universe, but also the Author of the miracle of new creation. He is the One who will restore God's creation and make his people new.

This chapter will explore some of the titles of Jesus that Matthew uses to communicate the deity of Christ. The next chapter will explore other descriptions of Jesus that express his deity. A final chapter will examine the practical ramifications of Jesus' deity for the life of his disciples.

Son of Man

Matthew's gospel assigns several titles to Jesus that strongly imply his deity. Jesus' favorite self-designation is the title *Son of Man*. Jesus uses this title of himself thirty-one times in Matthew's gospel. Although scholars hotly debate the meaning of the title, the interpretation of the phrase best supported by the Gospels views *Son of Man* as a messianic title drawn from Daniel 7:13–14.[1] The discussion of Jesus as the new David has shown that *Son of Man* identifies Jesus as a King of heavenly origin who will reign over a kingdom composed of people of every nation, tribe, and tongue forever. A closer examination of the *Son of Man* title, however, shows that the Christological implications of Jesus' use of the title are even greater. The title clearly implies Jesus' deity.

The vision of Daniel 7:9–14 belongs to the Aramaic portion of this Old Testament book. The text portrays the "one like a son of man" as a heavenly figure.[2] Several features of the vision combine to mark this intention of the author's portrayal. First, the one like a son of man comes "with the clouds of heaven." The use of the cloud to depict the divine glory in the Pentateuch and the presence of clouds in theophanies such as the vision of Ezekiel 1 (which has a close relationship to Daniel 7) mark the Daniel 7 vision as a theophany as well.[3] The image of riding on the clouds or being surrounded by clouds implies that Daniel is describing an appearance of God himself.

Daniel 7:14 highlights the exalted status and divine nature of the figure with the words "all peoples, nations, and languages should serve him." The statement parallels the description of the Ancient of Days: "A thousand thousands served him, and ten thousand times ten thousand stood before him" (v. 10). Although both texts speak of throngs that serve heavenly figures, the

1. Delbert Burkett, *The Son of Man Debate: A History and Evaluation* (Cambridge: Cambridge University Press, 2000), 122–23.
2. Chrys C. Caragounis, *The Son of Man: Vision and Interpretation* (Tübingen: J. C. B. Mohr, 1986), 80–81.
3. Like Ezekiel 1, the Daniel 7 vision speaks of a divine throne with wheels engulfed in flames. Cf. Dan. 7:9–10 with Ezek. 1:15–28.

thousands who serve the Ancient of Days are evidently angelic figures, while those who serve the one like a son of man are clearly human.

The text uses distinct vocabulary to describe the service rendered to the Ancient of Days and the Son of Man. The verb *shmsh*, used to describe angelic service to the Ancient of Days, is a common verb denoting service in many different forms. Strikingly, the verb *plkh*, used to describe the service to the Son of Man, is a different verb that may be properly translated "worship." In biblical literature, this particular verb is exclusively used to refer to the veneration or worship of God or gods.[4] This usage is prominent in Daniel leading up to the Son of Man vision. For example, Daniel 3:12 uses this verb in the Chaldeans' complaint that Shadrach, Meshach, and Abednego "do not serve your gods or worship the golden image that you have set up." The verb also appears in the bold affirmation of the three Jewish men, "Our God whom we serve is able to deliver us from the burning fiery furnace," and "we will not serve your gods" (vv. 17–18). The verb is also used in the climactic expression of monotheism and polemic against idolatry: "His servants . . . yielded up their bodies rather than serve and worship any god except their own God" (v. 28). Against this background, the use of the verb *to serve* has clear connotations. It refers to service, veneration, or worship reserved particularly for Yahweh.[5] That the author uses a generic term to describe service to the Ancient of Days, yet a term reserved for divine worship to describe service to the Son of Man, is unexpected and telling. The offer of such worship to the Son of Man rather naturally leads to the

---

4. See Dan. 3:12, 14, 17–18, 28; 6:16, 20; 7:14, 27. Ezra 7:24 uses the participial form to refer to "servants of this house of God" who officiate in ritual worship in the Jerusalem temple. Furthermore, the derivative noun form *palkhan* (פָּלְחָן) refers to worship or ritual service in the temple as well (v. 19). See "פלח" and "פָּלְחָן" in Ludwig Köehler and Walter Baumgartner, *Hebrew and Aramaic Lexicon of the Old Testament* (Leiden: Brill, 2002), 1957.

5. The verb was also used to speak of divine worship in extrabiblical Aramaic. See Marcus Jastrow, *Dictionary of the Targumim, Talmud Babli, Yerushalmi, and Midrashic Literature* (New York: Judaica, 1996), 1178. M. Shepherd correctly observes that the meaning of the verb is closer in sense to סגד than to עבד. See his "Daniel 7:13 and the New Testament Son of Man," *Westminster Theological Journal* 68 (2006): 99–111, esp. 101n6.

suspicion that he is being portrayed as deity, the embodiment of the glory of Yahweh.

One final feature of the Daniel 7 vision is significant. Verse 9 indicates that "thrones were placed, and the Ancient of Days took his seat." This raises the question of who will occupy the other throne or thrones. The context suggests that the throne is intended for the Son of Man. He is to be seated on that throne and granted "dominion and glory and a kingdom" (v. 14). The idea that this figure is seated beside the Ancient of Days on a heavenly throne has far-reaching implications for his nature and stature. This enthronement strongly implies that this Son of Man is a divine figure. Furthermore, since the vision of the Ancient of Days is a scene of divine judgment in which a court is convened and books of evidence are opened, if the Son of Man occupies a throne beside the Ancient of Days, he likely participates in divine judgment as well.

Although many modern scholars dispute the claim that the author intended these features to portray the Son of Man as both a divine and a royal figure, the features of Daniel's vision discussed above clearly prompted later Jewish interpreters who carefully reflected on the details of the vision to portray the Son of Man as a divine King, eternal Ruler, and cosmic Judge. That later Jewish interpreters understood the text in the manner suggested above is evident from a survey of interpretations in later Jewish literature.

The Septuagint text of Daniel 7:9–14 contains a reading different from that which appears in the Hebrew Bible and later Greek translations. Both the Hebrew Bible and Theodotion's Greek version distinguish the Son of Man from the Ancient of Days. In the Old Greek text, however, the Ancient of Days and the "one like a son of man" are one being rather than two:

> I was watching in the nightly visions and behold, he was coming on the clouds of heaven like a son of man, and he was coming like the Ancient of Days, and those who were present were coming to him.[6]

6. Translation mine.

This reading is supported by the earliest known manuscript of the Septuagint (MS 967), dating to the second century A.D. Although some scholars argue that this reading is a product of unintentional scribal error, most critics now conclude that the original Greek translation equated the Son of Man and Ancient of Days in order to express a carefully thought-out interpretation of the Aramaic text.[7] Some have even argued that the original Greek translation preserves the original Hebrew reading that stands behind the current Aramaic text.[8] Second Thessalonians 1:7–8 and Revelation 1:13–14 conflate descriptions of the Son of Man and the Ancient of Days in a manner suggesting that the reading of MS 967 was known in the first century A.D. If this reading is original and intentional, the interpretation assumed in the Septuagint reflects the earliest known interpretation of the Son of Man vision after the composition of Daniel.

The Similitudes of Enoch offer important evidence for pre-Christian Jewish interpretation of Daniel 7:13–14. The Similitudes (1 Enoch 37–71) assign the revered divine name to the Son of Man and describe all creation as worshiping the Son of Man. The Babylonian Talmud shows that Aqiba, the famous rabbi of the early second century, taught that Daniel 7 implies that the Son of Man is enthroned alongside the Ancient of Days, a conclusion that Aqiba's critics considered blasphemous.[9]

Jesus' reply to the high priest during his trial shows that Jesus interpreted Daniel 7 much as Aqiba later would. Jesus identifies himself as the Son of Man whom Caiaphas would eventually see "seated at the right hand of Power" (Matt. 26:64). Like Aqiba's critics, Caiaphas is outraged by Jesus' statement, for in his view the messianic Son of Man has no place beside the Ancient of

---

7. See F. F. Bruce, "The Oldest Greek Version of Daniel," *Old Testament Studies* 20 (1975): 22–40; S. Kim, "The 'Son of Man' as the Son of God," *Wissenschaftliche Untersuchungen zum Neuen Testament* 30 (1983): 22–25.

8. J. Lust has argued that the Septuagint preserves the most ancient form of the text. See his "Daniel 7,13 and Septuagint," *Ephemerides Theologicae Lovanienses* 54 (1978): 62–69.

9. See Charles L. Quarles, "Lord or Legend? Jesus as the Messianic Son of Man," in *Can We Trust the New Testament on the Historical Jesus? Bart Ehrman and Craig Evans in Dialogue* (Minneapolis: Fortress, forthcoming).

Days. In his view, Jesus' claim to be the Son of Man, enthroned as Yahweh's coregent at his side, is both shocking and blasphemous.

Many of Jesus' contemporaries recognize the title *Son of Man* as referring to One who bears the very name *Yahweh*, worthy of worship in the highest sense and enthroned beside the Ancient of Days. Jesus uses the title to describe himself in this lofty sense. His use of the title in this manner prompts the high priest to charge him with blasphemy and sentence him to death.

Wisdom

An important Christological title that is often overlooked appears in Matthew 11:19: "The Son of Man came eating and drinking, and they say, 'Look at him! A glutton and a drunkard, a friend of tax collectors and sinners!' Yet wisdom is justified by her deeds." The first part of the verse is clear. In contrast with the ascetic and austere nature of the wilderness ministry of John the Baptist, Jesus' ministry involves feasting with notorious sinners (9:10–13). This stirs objections to Jesus' ministry, particularly from the Pharisees, who spread rumors that unfairly caricature Jesus as a glutton and drunkard. The final part of the verse is much more difficult. But strong evidence suggests that Jesus is not offering a pithy description of wisdom in general. Instead, he is identifying himself as Wisdom personified. The vocabulary, context, and structure of the passage—as well as other references to wisdom in Jesus' teaching—support this understanding.

First, Jesus describes wisdom as justified or vindicated. This implies that false accusations have been made against wisdom, but that the righteous character of wisdom will ultimately be demonstrated. Furthermore, wisdom is described as performing deeds. Luke's parallel (Luke 7:35) refers to wisdom's "children." These descriptions appear to personify Wisdom as an innocent defendant who performs deeds and has a family.

Second, the portrayal of wisdom as one falsely accused closely associates wisdom with Jesus. The context shows that because Jesus does not dance to the tune piped by his critics, the Son of Man is falsely accused of gluttony and drunkenness. This context prompts the reader to expect a reference to Jesus' future vindication. Instead, Jesus refers to wisdom's vindication. The flow of the dialogue thus suggests that Jesus identifies himself as Wisdom.

Third, the structure of the text suggests that Matthew sees Jesus as Wisdom personified. Matthew 11:2–19 is a single narrative unit. The references to "deeds" in the first and final verses of the unit serve as structural brackets that mark the section as a literary unit. Verse 2 refers to the deeds of the Messiah that vindicate Jesus' claim to be the Messiah. Verse 19 refers to the deeds that justify wisdom. The inclusio implies that Matthew equates the deeds of the Messiah and the deeds of wisdom in a manner that personifies Wisdom and identifies Jesus with it.[10]

Finally, other references to wisdom in the Gospels show that Jesus personifies Wisdom and identifies himself as such. Matthew 11:25–30 is the most important and convincing example. The references to wisdom hidden from the wise, as well as the statement that only the Father knows the Son, are reminiscent of descriptions of personified Wisdom in Jewish texts.[11] More importantly, verses 28–30 contain multiple allusions to the Wisdom of Ben Sira. "Come to me" (v. 28) echoes Wisdom's call to "draw near to me" (Sir. 51:23).[12] "Take my yoke upon you, and learn from me" (Matt. 11:29) is reminiscent of the command, "Put your neck under her [Wisdom's] yoke, and let your souls receive instruction" (Sir. 51:26).[13] The reference to those who "labor and are heavy laden," who are those to whom Jesus gives

10. Ulrich Luz, *Matthew*, Hermeneia (Minneapolis: Augsburg Fortress, 2001–7), 2:149, notes that Matthew's reference to "deeds" in 11:19 "is probably taking up the thread of 11:2."

11. See Job 28; Wisd. Sol. 9. For other possible parallels, see Celia Deutsch, *Hidden Wisdom and the Easy Yoke: Wisdom, Torah and Discipleship in Matthew 11.25–30* (Sheffield, UK: JSOT Press, 1987), 103–30.

12. See also Wisdom's command, "Come to me," in Sirach 24:19.

13. See a similar statement in Sirach 6:24–31 in which a person accepts the fetters and collar of wisdom only to discover that the fetters become a purple cord and the collar a golden necklace, and that she gives rest to her slaves by transforming them into kings.

"rest" (Matt. 11:28), and the promise that Jesus' yoke is easy and burden light recall the confession that "I have labored just a little and found for myself much rest" (Sir. 51:27).[14] Jesus' words in Matthew are a clear allusion to Sirach, but they adapt Sirach's words in a significant way. Although the sage of Sirach speaks *for* Wisdom, Jesus speaks *as* Wisdom. As R. T. France observes, "Jesus is not merely Wisdom's messenger, but himself fills the role of Wisdom."[15]

In Luke 11:49–51, Jesus says:

> Therefore also the Wisdom of God said, "I will send them prophets and apostles, some of whom they will kill and persecute, so that the blood of all the prophets, shed from the foundation of the world, may be charged against this generation, from the blood of Abel to the blood of Zechariah, who perished between the altar and the sanctuary. Yes, I tell you, it will be required of this generation."

The capitalization of the title *Wisdom of God* in the ESV is fully appropriate. The fact that Wisdom speaks confirms that Jesus intends to refer to Wisdom personified. Matthew's parallel in 23:34–36 adapts the earlier reading preserved in Luke by having Jesus say, "Therefore I send you prophets and wise men and scribes, some of whom you will kill." Matthew's adaptation clearly identifies Jesus as the Wisdom of God personified.[16]

The identification of Jesus with personified Wisdom is very significant. In the personification of Wisdom in Proverbs 8, Wisdom is described as a preexistent being who lived "before the beginning of the earth" (Prov. 8:23). Wisdom was an agent through whom God made the world and who stood beside God in the act of creation "like a master workman" (v. 30). Similarly, Job 28

14. Translations of Sirach are mine. See also Sir. 6:28.
15. R. T. France, *Matthew: Evangelist and Teacher*, New Testament Profiles (Downers Grove, IL: InterVarsity Press, 1989), 304.
16. Donald A. Hagner, *Matthew*, Word Biblical Commentary (Dallas: Word, 1993–95), 1:311; Luz, *Matthew*, 2:149–50. By the time that Luz wrote his comments on Matthew 23:34, he had become more skeptical of Wisdom Christology in Matthew. See Luz, *Matthew*, 3:152–53.

states that God saw and established Wisdom "when he gave to the wind its weight and apportioned the waters by measure, when he made a decree for the rain and a way for the lightning of the thunder" (Job 28:25–26).

In intertestamental literature, descriptions of Wisdom become more detailed, vivid, and exalted. Wisdom of Solomon describes Wisdom as "a breath of the power of God and a pure emanation of the glory of the Almighty," "a reflection of eternal light, a spotless mirror of the working of God, and an image of his goodness" who "can do all things," "renews all things," and "is fashioner of what exists" (Wisd. Sol. 7:25–8:5). Wisdom of Solomon 10 and 11 recount the history of God's people from Adam to Moses and assign to Wisdom the works of God. Wisdom delivered Adam from his transgression, rescued God's people from the flood, saved Lot from the destruction of Sodom, protected Joseph and gave him the scepter of Egypt, brought about the exodus, became a cloud by day and a flame by night to guide the people, parted the waters of the Red Sea, and provided water from a rock. The book even refers to a kind of incarnation of this figure: "Send her forth from the holy heavens, and from the throne of your glory send her, that she may labor at my side, and that I may learn what is pleasing to you" (9:10). Baruch 3:36–37 speaks of a similar descent and incarnation of Wisdom, for after God gave Wisdom to Israel, "afterward she appeared on earth and lived with humankind."

Consequently, Jesus' portrayal of himself as Wisdom in the Gospel of Matthew implies that Jesus is the agent through whom Yahweh performed his greatest works, One who existed before the first act of creation and descended to earth to live among humankind.[17] This Wisdom Christology is an important component of the exalted descriptions of Jesus in texts such as Colossians 1:15–20 and Hebrews 1:1–4. Thus, the title serves to reinforce the implications of titles such as *Immanuel*, *Son of Man*, and *Son of God*. Although the title does not play as prominent a role in the

17. France, *Matthew: Evangelist and Teacher*, 305–6.

Gospel of Matthew as these other titles do, its implications for understanding Matthew's Christology are highly significant.

Lord

Various individuals call Jesus "Lord" numerous times in the Gospel of Matthew (Matt. 7:21–22; 8:2, 6, 8, 21, 25; 9:28; 14:28, 30; 15:22, 25, 27; 16:22; 17:4, 15; 18:21; 20:30 (possibly), 31, 33; 21:3; 25:37, 44; 26:22). "Lord" (*kyrios*) may serve as a title of authority and thus denote the master of a slave (24:50) or the ruler of a subject (27:63). On the other hand, the title also serves as the Greek translation of the divine name *Yahweh* in the Septuagint and thus often refers to deity. On many occasions in Matthew, "Lord" clearly refers to Yahweh. The "angel of the Lord" in Matthew 1:24; 2:13, 19; and 28:2 is the messenger of Yahweh of the Old Testament. In the Old Testament texts that Matthew quotes, "Lord" consistently refers to Yahweh (3:3; 4:7, 10; 21:9, 42; 22:37, 44; 23:39), with the possible exception of the second of two occurrences of "Lord" in the quotation of Psalm 110:1 in Matthew 22:44, in which "Lord" translates the Hebrew title *Adonai*.

The context or structure of several of Matthew's descriptions of Jesus as Lord strongly suggests that "Lord" functions as a title of deity. One important example is the use of the double vocative "Lord, Lord" in Matthew 7:21 and 22. This double vocative appears eighteen times in the Septuagint.[18] Every single occurrence is an indisputable reference to Yahweh, and most occurrences translate the combined title and name *Adonai Yahweh*. Matthew assumes his readers' familiarity with the Old Testament, and it is likely that they would have recognized the construction "Lord, Lord" as an echo of the Old Testament, seeing "Lord" as having divine connotations.[19] Both of the occurrences of the double vocative

18. Deut. 3:24; 9:26; Judg. 6:22; 16:28; 1 Kings 8:53; 1 Chron. 17:24; Est. 13:9; Pss. 68:7; 108:21; 129:3; 139:8; 140:8; Jer. 28:62; Ezek. 21:15; Amos 7:2, 5; 2 Macc. 1:24; 3 Macc. 2:2. See also Judg. 2:1; 2 Sam. 7:18–20, 22, 25, 28–29.

19. For a more extensive argument in support of this view, see Charles L. Quarles, *The Sermon on the Mount: Restoring Christ's Message to the Modern Church* (Nashville: B&H Academic, 2011), 330–32.

"Lord, Lord" in Matthew are addressed specifically to Jesus. Matthew 7:21 says, "Not everyone who says *to me*, 'Lord, Lord,' will enter the kingdom of heaven." Similarly, verse 22 says, "On that day, many will say *to me*, 'Lord, Lord.'" The dual application of the double vocative to Jesus in appeals for admission into the kingdom indicates that confession of Jesus' identity as Yahweh is a condition for becoming Jesus' disciple.

On several occasions in Matthew, petitioners appeal to Jesus for miracles of healing or exorcism with the cry, "Lord, have mercy," or close variations of this cry:

- 15:22: "Have mercy on me, O Lord" (entire expression unique to Matthew);
- 17:15: "Lord, have mercy on my son" (entire expression unique to Matthew);
- 20:31: "Lord, have mercy on us" (title "Lord" unique to Matthew).

Matthew's readers, steeped as they apparently were in the Old Testament Scriptures, would likely have recognized these appeals as echoes of descriptions of Yahweh and impassioned appeals to him offered by saints of old. In the theophany of Exodus 33:19, in which Yahweh reveals his glory and his name, he says, "I will make all my goodness pass before you and will proclaim before you my name 'The LORD.' And I will be gracious to whom I will be gracious, and will show mercy on whom I will show mercy." Reflection on this revelation of God's name and merciful character prompts petitions such as "Have mercy on me, LORD" (Pss. 6:2; 9:13; 30:9; 86:3), and "LORD, have mercy on me" (41:4, 10).[20] Psalm 123:3 expresses the same petition in the plural: "Have mercy on us, LORD, have mercy on us." Isaiah 33:2 similarly phrases the petition, "LORD, have mercy on us."

20. These are my personal translations from the Septuagint. The translations in the ESV may be slightly different, since they are based on the Hebrew text rather than the Greek translation.

Intertestamental literature also picks up this refrain. Odes of Solomon 14:40 says, "Lord, have mercy on me." Baruch 3:2 likewise pleads, "Listen, Lord, and have mercy."

In the Septuagint, all appeals for mercy that utilize the verb "to have mercy" (*eleeō*) in the second-person-singular imperative, in combination with the vocative singular form of "Lord" (*kyrios*), are addressed to Yahweh. Thus, when Matthew's readers hear petitioners approach Jesus with pleas such as "Have mercy, Lord," they immediately recognize that these petitioners are addressing Jesus in the same way that psalms and prophets address Yahweh himself.

All three of the accounts in Matthew in which petitioners plead to Jesus for mercy and address him as "Lord" are paralleled in Mark. But the plea itself is unique to Matthew in 15:22 (cf. Mark 7:25) and 17:15 (cf. Mark 9:17). The plea in Matthew 20:31 is paralleled by Mark 10:47, but in Mark Jesus is addressed simply as "Son of David," not as "Lord." This suggests that this construction is related to a theological theme that Matthew deems particularly important to his readers.

Other appeals to Jesus for help in Matthew seem designed to stir similar reminiscences of Old Testament pleas to Yahweh. The appeals "Save us, Lord" in Matthew 8:25 and "Lord, save me" in 14:30 recall texts such as 2 Kings 19:19; Psalms 3:8; 6:4; 12:1; 20:9; 106:47; 109:26; 118:25; Isaiah 37:20; and Jeremiah 17:14. In fact, of the eleven combinations of the vocative "Lord" and the second-person imperative "save!" in the Septuagint, every instance except 2 Kings 6:26 is an appeal to Yahweh. Once again, these forms of the plea are unique to Matthew (cf. Matt. 8:25 with Mark 4:38/Luke 8:24) and are likely part of the Matthean emphasis on the deity of Jesus.

Finally, Matthew 15:25 records the plea of the Canaanite woman, "Lord, help me." This plea is reminiscent of Old Testament appeals such as Psalms 44:26 (Septuagint: "Rise up, LORD, help us!") and 109:26 ("Help me, O LORD my God!"). These two verses are the only combinations of the vocative "LORD" with the second-person-singular imperative "help!" in the Septuagint.

Although Matthew's account is paralleled in Mark 7:24–30, this plea is unique to Matthew.

Matthew's unique and consistent use of "Lord" to address Jesus in pleas that are reminiscent of Old Testament appeals to Yahweh can hardly be an accident. Desperate people needing Jesus' miraculous intervention address him as Old Testament saints addressed Yahweh in confirmation of the portrayal of Jesus as Immanuel, God with us.

Perhaps the most important use of "Lord" in describing Jesus in the Gospels appears in Matthew 12:8 (cf. Mark 2:28). Jesus refers to himself as "lord of the Sabbath." What does such a title mean? Many scholars simply interpret "Lord" as a title of authority, so that "lord of the Sabbath" simply means that Jesus or humanity in general has authority over the Sabbath. Jesus' original Jewish audience would likely have suspected that the title implied far more than Jesus' authority over the Sabbath. Anthony Saldarini has suggested that the title is an allusion to Leviticus 23:3, "a Sabbath to the LORD," in which "LORD" is a reference to Yahweh, who instituted and commanded the Sabbath.[21] This title would likely have evoked memories of the fourth commandment:

> Remember the Sabbath day, to keep it holy. Six days you shall labor, and do all your work, but the seventh day is a Sabbath to the LORD your God. On it you shall not do any work, you, or your son, or your daughter, your male servant, or your female servant, or your livestock, or the sojourner who is within your gates. For in six days the LORD made heaven and earth, the sea, and all that is in them, and rested on the seventh day. Therefore the LORD blessed the Sabbath day and made it holy. (Ex. 20:8–11)

The implications of Jesus' claim are staggering. France observes:

> Not only is the Son of Man greater than David and the temple, but he is "Lord" of the institution which is traced in the OT to God's direct command (Gen. 2:3), enshrined in the Decalogue

21. Anthony J. Saldarini, *Matthew's Christian-Jewish Community* (Chicago: University of Chicago Press, 1994), 129.

which is the central codification of God's requirements for his people, and described by God as "my Sabbath" (Ex. 31:13; Lev. 19:3, 30; Isa. 56:4, etc.; cf. the recurrent phrase "a Sabbath to/for Yahweh," Ex. 16:23; 20:10; 35:2, etc.). Against that background to speak of humanity in general as "lord of the Sabbath" would be unthinkable; to speak of an individual human being as such is to make the most extraordinary claim to an authority on a par with that of God himself.[22]

Son of God

At first glance, the title *Son of God* does not appear to have a prominent role in the Gospel of Matthew. The title appears only eight times (Matt. 4:3, 6; 8:29; 14:33; 26:63; 27:40, 43, 54). Only two of these occurrences show Jesus proper respect (14:33; 27:54). The other occurrences involve attempted manipulations by Satan (4:3, 6), exclamations by demons (8:29), interrogation by the high priest (26:63), or the sneers of Jesus' persecutors (27:40, 43). Furthermore, the use of the title by the high priest places *Son of God* in an appositional position to *Christ*, which seems to indicate that the title functions as a simple synonym for *Messiah* with no further significance, at least for Jesus' Jewish opponents. Psalm 2 was widely regarded as a messianic psalm, and many Jews recognized the Messiah as One who would be adopted by God into a special relationship because of the statement, "You are my Son; today I have begotten you" (Ps. 2:7).

A closer look suggests that the title is of great significance to Matthew, expressing far more than merely Jesus' identity as the Messiah. Matthew also sometimes uses shorter expressions to convey Jesus' identity as the Son of God. In Matthew 3:17, God proclaims at Jesus' baptism, "This is my beloved Son," and 17:5 repeats this proclamation at the transfiguration. The climactic confession of the centurion and bystanders in 27:54, "Truly this was the Son of God," answers the earlier dismiss-

22. R. T. France, *The Gospel of Matthew*, New International Commentary on the New Testament (Grand Rapids: Eerdmans, 2007), 462–63.

als of the bystanders, "If you are the Son of God, come down from the cross" (v. 40), and "He trusts in God; let God deliver him now, if he desires him. For he said, 'I am the Son of God'" (v. 43). These factors suggest that Jesus' identity as the Son of God is a very important theme of Matthew's gospel and worthy of careful consideration.

Since, as we have seen, abundant evidence suggests that Matthew utilized the Gospel of Mark in writing his own gospel, Matthew 1:1 first seems to be a puzzling downgrade of the identity of Jesus. Mark's introduction to his gospel identifies Jesus as "the Son of God," while Matthew's gospel identifies Jesus as "the son of David" and "the son of Abraham." Despite first impressions to the contrary, Matthew is not diluting Mark's high Christology. Jack Kingsbury rightly observes, "The theme of the divine sonship of Jesus runs like an unbroken thread through 1:14–16, becoming ever more visible and thus alerting the reader to the manner in which Matthew would have him comprehend the person of Jesus."[23]

Although the title *Son of God* is absent from the introduction to Matthew's gospel, the earliest portions of the gospel still stress Jesus' divine sonship. The conclusion of the genealogy clearly identifies Jesus as the Son of God. The discussion of Jesus' direct descent in Matthew 1:16, unlike the preceding generations of the genealogy, identifies a human mother—but no human father—of Jesus. Furthermore, it utilizes the divine passive to indicate that God is responsible for Jesus' miraculous conception.

What is implied in the genealogy is made explicit in the account of Jesus' birth. Matthew writes that Mary "was found to be with child from the Holy Spirit" (Matt. 1:18). Furthermore, the angel tells Joseph, "That which is conceived in her is from the Holy Spirit" (v. 20). The narrative that follows repeatedly implies the miraculous conception of Jesus by the Spirit by referring to Jesus as "the child" in contexts in which one would ordinarily expect "your [Joseph's] child."

23. Jack D. Kingsbury, *Matthew: Structure, Christology, Kingdom* (Philadelphia: Fortress, 1975), 17.

The theme of Jesus' divine sonship in these early chapters of Matthew reaches its pinnacle in the exclamation of the Father at Jesus' baptism: "This is my beloved Son, with whom I am well pleased" (Matt. 3:17). Matthew's readers would not have missed the allusion to Psalm 2:7, which implies Jesus' identity as the Davidic King and hence Son of David. In the context of Matthew's narrative, however, the title *my beloved Son* assumes even greater significance. Kingsbury notes:

> And the theme of the divine sonship pervades all four chapters [Matthew 1–4]. With reference to the latter, Jesus Messiah is, to be sure, Son of Abraham, Son of David, and King, but foremost he is the Son of God, for his origin can be traced to God. The conjecture is surely correct that the title "Son of God" is absent from 1:1 because Matthew intends that God himself should be the first to make this pronouncement.[24]

The prominence of this exclamation is clear from the repeated use of "Son of God" by the Tempter in the narrative that immediately follows the baptism (Matt. 4:1–11). Satan begins the first two temptations with the challenge, "If you are the Son of God . . ." (vv. 3, 6). The narrative seam in 4:17 (cf. 16:21) shows that 1:1–4:16 constitutes the first major section of Matthew's gospel. A close examination shows that Jesus' identity as the Son of God is the most prominent feature of this first section.

The title is also prominent in the second major section of Matthew, 4:17–16:20. Explicit use of the title is rare in the early chapters of this section. Yet Jesus' identity as the Son of God is clearly implied by his use of the expression "my Father" in 7:21; 10:32–33; 11:27; 12:50; and 16:17.[25] Except for Jesus' reference to God as "my Father" in 11:27, which is paralleled in Luke 10:22, the descriptions of God as "my Father" are unique to Matthew and thus of special importance to this gospel. Although Luke occasionally uses the phrase, Matthew uses it much more frequently.

24. Ibid.
25. See also Matt. 18:10, 19; 20:23; 25:34; 26:39, 42, 53.

Matthew 11:27 uses the bare title *Son* in a manner that emphasizes Jesus' exclusive relationship with the Father: "No one knows the Son except the Father, and no one knows the Father except the Son and anyone to whom the Son chooses to reveal him." This exclusive relationship between the Father and Son implies that "Son" functions as far more than a mere royal title. This same exclusive relationship is implied by the use of the definite article in the reference to Jesus as "*the* Son" in 24:36 and Jesus' frequent use of the expression "my Father" mentioned above.

One feature of the title *Son of God* that indicates its special importance for Matthew is its confessional usage. In response to Jesus' miracle of walking on the water, Jesus' disciples "worshiped him" and exclaimed, "Truly you are the Son of God" (Matt. 14:33). As will be discussed in the next chapter, the miracle involves a reenactment of the deeds of Yahweh described in the Old Testament. The disciples apparently recognize the profound significance of the event and express their worship of Jesus by affirming his divine sonship. The title seems important to Matthew, since the use of the title by Jesus' disciples in 14:33 has no parallel in Mark.[26] The use of the adverb *truly* places special emphasis on the conviction of the disciples that their confession is undoubtedly true.

The final and climactic pericope of this central section of the gospel relates Peter's great confession that Jesus is "the Christ, the Son of the living God" (Matt. 16:16). Jesus affirms Peter's confession and states that the confession is evidence that Peter is a recipient of the divinely given revelation described in 11:27. "Flesh and blood has not revealed this to you, but my Father who is in heaven" (16:17) evokes memory of the statement, "No one knows the Son except the Father, and no one knows the Father except the Son and anyone to whom the Son chooses to reveal him" (11:27). Just as the Son must reveal the Father to others, so also the Father, who has unique knowledge of the Son, must reveal him to others. Once again, the powerful reference to divine

---

26. Compare Mark 6:51, which describes the response of the disciples: "And they were utterly astounded."

sonship is part of a Matthean emphasis. The parallel account of Peter's confession in Mark 8:29 merely has "You are the Christ." Matthew's addition of the title "Son of the living God" suggests its importance to him.

The third major section of Matthew (16:21–28:20) is permeated with important references to Jesus' identity as the Son of God. Just as the first section of the gospel climaxes with the Father's confession "This is my beloved Son" at Jesus' baptism (3:17), the final section begins with the Father's confession "This is my beloved Son" at the transfiguration (17:5). Important features of the account allude to Old Testament descriptions of Yahweh's appearances and show clearly that *Son* functions here as more than a mere messianic title, recalling the divine origin of Jesus described in the opening chapters of the gospel.

This section also contains two major parables in which the fate of individuals is determined by their treatment of the son of the leading character. The parable of the wicked tenants (Matt. 21:33–46) focuses on the fate of those who fail to offer God the fruits of righteousness, reject and abuse his servants, the prophets, and murder his Son. Several features of the parable clearly demonstrate that the vineyard owner represents God and that the son of the vineyard owner represents Jesus. Matthew even reverses Mark's order by describing the son as first thrown out of the vineyard and then killed to match Jesus' expulsion from Jerusalem that precedes his crucifixion. This adaptation is designed to aid his readers in recognizing that the murdered son represents the crucified Jesus. Although the parable stresses the failure of Israel to produce fruit of righteousness, it clearly teaches that the coming destruction of Jerusalem and subjugation of her people is, more than anything else, God's punishment of those who kill his Son.

The parable of the wedding feast (Matt. 22:1–14) describes the destructive fury of a king against subjects who ignore an invitation to the wedding feast of his son. Because the treatment of the king's servants recalls Israel's treatment of the prophets, and the destruction of their city anticipates the destruction of Jerusalem, the parable clearly warns of the punishment that will befall those who reject Jesus, God's Son. Admittedly, this parable does not focus on the son or emphasize his role to the extent that the parable of the wicked tenants does. But Matthew likely places the parable of the wicked tenants immediately before the parable of the wedding feast because he wants the latter parable to be interpreted in light of the former.

The Christological purpose of the two parables is highlighted by the dialogue between Jesus and the Jewish leaders that follows the two parables in Matthew's gospel. This dialogue climaxes with the question posed by Jesus to the Pharisees, "What do you think about the Christ? Whose son is he?" (Matt. 22:42). The Pharisees reply that the Christ is "the Son of David." Jesus argues in response that the Scriptures teach that the Messiah is far more than merely a son of David. In Psalm 110:1, David refers to the Messiah as his "Lord." Jesus' statement clearly teaches that the Messiah is more than a reigning king; he is also Lord. Yet his discussion implies even more. His original question—"Whose son is he?"—prompts readers to conclude that Jesus is more than the Son of David—he is also the Son of God. This answer is already on the tip of the tongue of readers already familiar with Matthew's genealogy, birth narrative, pronouncements by the Father, and confessions by Jesus' disciples. The interaction of Jesus and the Jewish leaders that climaxes with the discussion of the Messiah's sonship immediately follows the parables of the wicked tenants and the wedding feast in order to confirm that the son in those parables is none other than the Son of God.

The theme of Jesus' divine sonship continues in this final section with references to Jesus as "the Son" (Matt. 24:36) and the messianic King's reference to God as "my Father" (25:34). Then Jesus identifies himself as the messianic King and divine Son in Gethsemane by addressing God as "my Father" (26:39, 42).

Jesus' trial and crucifixion are dominated by interrogation regarding his identity as the Son of God (Matt. 26:63) and mockery of his divine sonship (27:40, 43). But Jesus' identity as Son of God is confirmed by the climactic confession of the gospel. Matthew 27:54 states, "When the centurion and those who were with him, keeping watch over Jesus, saw the earthquake and what took place, they were filled with awe and said, 'Truly this was the Son of God!'" This confession is verified by Jesus' resurrection and by the climactic statement of the entire gospel. In 28:18, Jesus says, "All authority in heaven and on earth has been given to me." The statement deliberately recalls 11:27, "All things have been handed over to me by my Father." This handing over of all things to Jesus exhibits his exclusive relationship to God as Son to Father.

If any doubt about the full significance of the title *Son of God* in Matthew remains, it is dissolved by the use of *Son* in the Trinitarian formula of 28:19–20.[27] In the confession that accompanies baptism, the Father, Son, and Holy Spirit share the same name, for the baptismal formula refers not to the names (plural) of the Father and of the Son and of the Holy Spirit, but to the name (singular) of the three persons. This shared name is apparently the divine name, *Yahweh*. Earlier descriptions of the Son's exclusive relationship to the Father now give way to an affirmation of the ontological unity of the Son with the Father and the Spirit. Clearly, *Son of God* is more than a mere messianic title inspired by Psalm 2. In Matthew's gospel, the title is an expression of Jesus' divine origin, divine authority, and divine status.

Immanuel

Matthew 1:23 quotes Isaiah 7:14 and applies it to Jesus. Although readers might be tempted to assume that Isaiah 7:14 is quoted merely to confirm that Jesus is conceived by a virgin, the translation Matthew offers of the name *Immanuel* suggests that he also intends his readers to apply it to Jesus and recognize its Christological significance.

The Hebrew name *Immanuel* means "God is with us" and is likely an allusion to God's promise to be with the line of David (2 Sam. 7:9; 1 Kings 1:37; 11:38; Ps. 89:21, 24). This suggests that

27. France, *Matthew*, 1118.

the child named *Immanuel* will be a king in the line of David.[28] Since later prophecy in Isaiah describes this same child as "Mighty God" (Isa. 9:6), however, the name seems to communicate more than that God is with David's descendants. It seems to suggest that God is present with his people in the person of this child.

What the Old Testament prophecies imply, the Gospel of Matthew confirms.[29]

The importance and significance of the name *Immanuel* are reinforced by the final words of Jesus in the Gospel of Matthew: "And behold, I am with you always, to the end of the age" (Matt. 28:20). Matthew 1:23 and 28:20 serve to bracket the entire gospel. The promise that "God [is] with us" at the beginning of the gospel is ultimately fulfilled in Jesus' assurance "I am with you" at the end of the gospel. The connection between the two texts suggests that Matthew intends to identify Jesus who is "with you" with God who is "with us."

This interpretation is strongly supported by the Old Testament background of the promised presence in Matthew 28:20. Jesus' promise is a verbatim repetition of the promise of Yahweh in Haggai 1:13: "I am with you, declares the LORD."[30] The promise "I am with you" is reminiscent of many other Old Testament texts that assure God's people of his presence (Gen. 26:24; 28:15; Ex. 3:12; Josh. 1:5, 9; Isa. 41:10; 43:5; Jer. 1:19; 15:20; 42:11; Hag. 2:4).[31]

The literary context of Jesus' promise heightens the connection to these Old Testament promises. Jesus' promise is part of his commission to his disciples. The promise of God's presence frequently accompanies his commissioning of Old Testament leaders, in which "the assurance of God's presence was to empower his often inadequate servants to fulfill the task he had called them

---

28. Hans Wildberger, *Isaiah 1–12: A Commentary*, Continental Commentaries (Minneapolis: Fortress, 1991), 311–12; Gary V. Smith, *Isaiah*, New American Commentary (Nashville: B&H Academic, 2007–9), 1:213.

29. Kingsbury, *Matthew: Structure, Christology, Kingdom*, 96.

30. There is, however, a difference in word order.

31. Hagner, *Matthew*, 2:888. For an extensive treatment of the Old Testament promises of the divine presence using "I am with you," see David D. Kupp, *Matthew's Emmanuel: Divine Presence and God's People in the First Gospel* (Cambridge: Cambridge University Press, 1996), 138–56.

to (Ex. 3:12; 4:12; Josh. 1:5, 9; Judg. 6:16; Jer. 1:8; cf. also the angel sent with the Israelites in Ex. 23:20–23)."[32] The promise of his presence in the commissioning of the disciples parallels the promise of the divine presence in the commissioning of God's servants in the Old Testament. Thus, Jesus is speaking as Yahweh speaks and is claiming divine status, authority, and power.

These two promises of God's presence among his people in the person of Jesus in Matthew's gospel are matched by yet a third. In Matthew 18:20, Jesus promises, "For where two or three are gathered in my name, there am I among them." The relationship of these three texts is "generally acknowledged by students of Matthew."[33] Some scholars have objected that the difference in wording between 18:20 and 1:23/28:20 makes a relationship between the three texts doubtful. But Hubert Frankemölle has demonstrated that the phrases *with them* and *among them* are used interchangeably in both the Old Testament and Qumran literature.[34] Thus, 18:20 is an element of a triad affirming God's presence with his people in the person of Jesus.

Readers may tend to minimize the importance of the title *Immanuel* in the Gospel of Matthew, since it appears only once in the entire gospel. This is unfortunate. Based on the data surveyed above, Kingsbury reasonably concludes that "the entire first Gospel may be regarded as an attempt on the part of Matthew to draw out the implications of what it means to say in 1:23 that in him God dwells with his people."[35] Because of the presence of the *Immanuel* theme at the beginning, middle, and end of the gospel, it appears that Jesus' identity as the Immanuel is a highly important Christological theme of the first gospel.

32. France, *Matthew*, 1119.
33. Kingsbury, *Matthew: Structure, Christology, Kingdom*, 69.
34. Hubert Frankemölle, *Jahwebund und Kirche Christi* (Münster: Aschendorff, 1974), 32–34.
35. Kingsbury, *Matthew: Structure, Christology, Kingdom*, 96.

Matthew's Development of the *New Creator* Theme: Other Descriptions of Jesus

MATTHEW EXPRESSES Jesus' deity in ways other than the mere use of divine titles. He also appeals to Jesus' supremacy, the extraordinary circumstances of his birth, his fulfillment of the Old Testament, his miracles, and his use of characteristic expressions of Yahweh to emphasize his own identity as God.

Jesus' Supremacy Demonstrates His Deity

The supremacy of Jesus is implied in subtle ways in the account of his birth and infancy. But Jesus' supremacy becomes abundantly clear in Matthew 12. Jesus describes himself as greater than the temple (Matt. 12:6) and, using slightly different vocabulary, greater than the prophet Jonah (v. 41) and Solomon (v. 42). Because the Greek adjectives translated "something greater than" are neuter in gender, some commentators argue that Jesus must be referring to some object (such as the kingdom) or trait (such as mercy) rather than to himself. Yet in verses 41 and 42, in which the point of comparison is a person (Jonah and Solomon), the most natural sense is that the One greater than these is also a person. Thus, Jesus is greater than the famous prophet who preached with such great effect that thousands repented, and he is greater than the wisest of Israel's kings, the one first regarded as the son of David. Since neuter forms of the comparative adjective are used in a comparison with persons in verses 41 and 42, it is plausible that the neuter adjective in verse 6 applies to a person as well. Greek grammarians have long argued that the neuter gender may sometimes be used to refer to persons in cases in which a general quality of the person rather than his individual identity is emphasized.[1] Many commentators find such a usage here.[2] A number of the early Christian scribes who copied manuscripts of Matthew read the text in this manner and changed the adjective to the masculine gender as a result.[3]

The most important clue for identifying who or what is "greater than" the temple is the context of the discussion. Jesus' words are spoken in defense of the behavior of his disciples, accused by the Pharisees of breaking the Sabbath. In Jesus' first argument (Matt. 12:3–4), his disciples correspond to David's men, suggesting that Jesus is to be associated with David. In the second argument (v. 5), Jesus' disciples correspond to the priests in the temple who break the Sabbath, yet remain innocent. This raises the question that if Jesus' disciples are like the priests in the temple, to whom is Jesus himself to be compared? Jesus ultimately answers that question by identifying himself as the "Lord of the Sabbath" (v. 8), a title that I have argued clearly identifies Jesus as Yahweh. In such a context, wise readers of Matthew's gospel recognize that which is greater than the temple as none other than Jesus, Lord of the Sabbath.

This interpretation also finds support in references to the temple in Matthew 26:61 and 27:40. Witnesses accuse Jesus of teaching something about tearing down the temple and rebuild-

1. Robert Funk, *A Greek Grammar of the New Testament and Other Early Christian Literature* (Chicago: University of Chicago Press, 1961), § 138.
2. See W. D. Davies and Dale Allison Jr., *The Gospel according to Matthew*, 3 vols., International Critical Commentary (Edinburgh: T & T Clark, 1988–1997), 2:314; Robert Gundry, *Matthew*, 2nd ed. (Grand Rapids: Eerdmans, 1994), 223; David L. Turner, *Matthew*, Baker Exegetical Commentary on the New Testament (Grand Rapids: Baker, 2008), 310.
3. See, for example, C, L, Δ.

ing it in three days. Matthew's readers would likely interpret the "three days" as a reference to the period between Jesus' death and resurrection (12:40; 16:21; 17:23; 20:19; 27:63) and thus identify Jesus' body as the new temple torn down and rebuilt. This would prompt them to recognize Jesus as the One greater than Herod's temple.

Yahweh is greater than the temple, and it is his presence that gives the temple its significance. Jesus teaches in Matthew 5:35 that Jerusalem is to be regarded with reverence, since "it is the city of the great King." His words allude to Psalm 48:2, in which a description of Jerusalem as "the city of the great King" parallels "the city of our God" in the previous verse. Just as Jerusalem derives its significance from the presence of God, the great King, so also the temple derives its significance from the presence of God.

The glaring deficiency of the temple was its incapacity to house the presence of God. Even when the temple was first completed and dedicated, Solomon questioned, "Will God indeed dwell on the earth? Behold, heaven and the highest heaven cannot contain you; how much less this house that I have built!" (1 Kings 8:27). Yet as One "greater than the temple," Jesus houses the glory and presence of God in a way that the temple never could. Thus, this statement of Jesus in Matthew approximates descriptions of Jesus' body as the tabernacle and temple of God in the Gospel of John (John 1:14; 2:21). The theme of Jesus' supremacy to even the temple strongly attests to his deity.

Jesus' Virginal Conception Demonstrates His Deity

Matthew does not wait until the account of Jesus' birth to inform his readers of Jesus' miraculous conception. He implies the virginal conception at the conclusion of his genealogy of Jesus. As we saw in chapter 8, the genealogy proceeds with a familiar pattern: A was the father of B. And again, in the four instances in which a mother is identified, Matthew names the mother by adding the construction "by C." For example, Matthew 1:3 states, "Judah [was] the father of Perez and Zerah by Tamar." The description of Jesus' birth in verse 16 deviates significantly from the typical formula: "Jacob the father of Joseph the husband of Mary, of whom Jesus was born, who is called Christ." In the Greek text, the pronoun *whom* is in the feminine gender and thus refers unambiguously to Mary as the one "of whom" (literally "by" whom, the same Greek preposition that identified the mothers in verses 3, 5, and 6) Jesus was born. Unlike the other generations of the genealogy, which emphasize the identity of the father, the description of the circumstances of Jesus' birth identifies Mary as his biological mother but does not identify a human father. The Greek verb translated "was born" in verse 16 is the same verb translated "was the father of" in verse 2. Throughout the genealogy, the verb refers to the act of conception. In verse 16, however, the verb appears in the passive voice. Most scholars recognize that the passive form functions as a "divine passive," which describes a divine action without explicit reference to God as the actor.[4] The grammar demonstrates that God miraculously conceived Jesus by Mary. Thus, the climax of the genealogy of Jesus briefly introduces the reader to the virginal conception and prepares him to understand the amazing narrative of Jesus' birth that follows in verses 18–25.

The introduction to the account of Jesus' birth in Matthew 1:18 emphasizes the uniqueness of his birth. In the Greek text, the phrase translated "of Jesus Christ" is shifted ahead of its normal position following the noun it modifies ("birth") to the front of the sentence. This unusual word order places emphasis on "of Jesus Christ" and highlights that Jesus' birth was different from every other birth described in the preceding genealogy. Furthermore, the conjunction translated "Now" in the ESV is probably adversative and should be translated "But," as it is in verse 20. After describing dozens of normal births in the genealogy, Mat-

4. See the discussion of the "divine or theological passive" in Daniel Wallace, *Greek Grammar: Beyond the Basics* (Grand Rapids: Zondervan, 1997), 437–38; and Funk, *Greek Grammar*, §§ 130(1), 313, 342(1). See also Davies and Allison, *Matthew*, 1:184.

thew contrasts Jesus' birth with the words "But *Jesus'* birth took place in this way." ·

Matthew makes it clear that Joseph and Mary are already betrothed but have not "[come] together" when Mary is "found to be with child" (Matt. 1:18). Some scholars have argued that the phrase "before they came together" means only that Joseph and Mary were not yet cohabitating, thus leaving open the possibility that Joseph fathered Jesus during the betrothal period. But although sexual relations are not necessarily implied by the verb, the verb commonly refers to sexual relations, as the usage by Josephus and Philo demonstrates.[5] Furthermore, when Matthew describes the marriage and the beginning of their cohabitation, he twice uses a form of the verb *took* (*paralambanō*; Matt. 1:20, 24). The verb means "to take into close association" and was used of a husband's bringing his wife into his home to live with him.[6] If Matthew had merely wanted to state that Joseph and Mary were not yet cohabitating, his later usage suggests that he would have written "before Joseph took her" rather than "before they came together." Matthew's choice of vocabulary makes it clear that Joseph and Mary abstained from sexual relations during their betrothal period.[7]

The angel of the Lord who appears to Joseph clearly states that "that which is conceived in her is from the Holy Spirit" (Matt. 1:20). The application of Isaiah 7:14 to Mary and Jesus explicitly identifies Mary as a "virgin" (*parthenos*). In the Septuagint, the word often serves as the translation of the Hebrew term *bethulah*, which often refers to a "grown-up girl without any sexual experience with men."[8]

---

5. Raymond Brown, *The Birth of the Messiah* (New York: Doubleday, 1977), 124.

6. "παραλαμβάνω," in *A Greek-English Lexicon of the New Testament and Other Early Christian Literature*, ed. Frederick W. Danker, 3rd ed. (Chicago: University of Chicago Press, 2000), 786. This meaning is attested in Herodotus, Lucian, Josephus, Song of Solomon, and Gospel of James.

7. For a defense of the historicity of the virgin birth, see Charles L. Quarles, "Why Not 'Beginning from Bethlehem'? A Critique of James D. G. Dunn's Treatment of the Synoptic Birth Narratives," in *Memories of Jesus: A Critical Appraisal of James D. G. Dunn's Jesus Remembered*, ed. Robert B. Stewart and Gary R. Habermas (Nashville: B&H Academic, 2010), 173–96.

8. "בְּתוּלָה," in Ludwig Köehler and Walter Baumgartner, *Hebrew and Aramaic Lexicon of the Old Testament* (Leiden: Brill, 2002), 167.

Thus, it is not surprising that the Greek term frequently emphasizes virginity.[9] In non-Matthean New Testament usage, virginity
is consistently implied by the term.[10] Mary's question in Luke
1:34—"How can this [conception of a child] be, since I do not
know a man?" (NKJV)—clearly uses the verb *to know* in a sexual
sense (paralleling the usage in Gen. 4:1, 17; 19:8; Judg. 11:39;
21:12; and 1 Sam. 1:19) and thus demonstrates that *parthenos* in
Luke's account of Jesus' birth means one who has not previously
engaged in sexual intercourse.[11]

Several explicit statements in the Matthean birth narrative
weigh decidedly in favor of true virginity. Matthew's statements
that Mary's pregnancy is due to the activity of the Holy Spirit
(Matt. 1:18, 20) imply that Jesus was not conceived by the ordinary
means, showing that Matthew has the stricter sense of *virgin* in
mind.[12] Furthermore, the statement that Joseph "knew her not
until she had given birth to a son" (v. 25) clearly indicates that
Joseph did not have sexual relations with Mary before Jesus'
birth. Verse 25 is a clear example of the use of the verb *to know*
to refer to sexual relations.

The unique circumstances of Jesus' birth, particularly the
activity of the Holy Spirit in conceiving Jesus by Mary, identifies him as *Immanuel*, which as we have seen is a term meaning
"God with us." The Hebrew name means more precisely "God
is with us" and is likely an allusion to God's promise to be with

9. See Lev. 21:13–15; Deut. 22:23, 28; Judg. 19:24; 21:11–12; 2 Sam. 13:2, 18; Ezek.
44:22. See also G. Delling, "παρθένος," in *Theological Dictionary of the New Testament*,
ed. Gerhard Kittel and Gerhard Friedrich, trans. Geoffrey W. Bromiley, 10 vols. (Grand
Rapids: Eerdmans, 1964–76), 5:832–33.

10. Danker confidently defines the term as "one who has never engaged in sexual
intercourse, virgin, chaste person" and later as "female of marriageable age w. focus
on virginity." See "παρθένος," in *Greek-English Lexicon*, 777.

11. I. Howard Marshall, *Commentary on Luke*, New International Greek Testament Commentary (Grand Rapids: Eerdmans, 1978), 69; Darrell Bock, *Luke 1:1–9:50*,
Baker Exegetical Commentary on the New Testament (Grand Rapids: Baker, 1994),
108, 118–21.

12. Davies and Allison, *Matthew*, 1:199–208; Rudolf Schnackenburg, *The Gospel
of Matthew* (Grand Rapids: Eerdmans, 2002), 18–20. For a helpful introduction to historical issues surrounding Jesus' birth, readers should consult Ben Witherington, "The
Birth of Jesus," in *Dictionary of Jesus and the Gospels* (Downers Grove, IL: InterVarsity
Press, 1992).

the line of David (2 Sam. 7:9; 1 Kings 1:37; 11:38; Ps. 89:21, 24). This suggests that the child named *Immanuel* will be a king in the line of David.[13]

The prophecy about the birth of the child named *Immanuel* is closely connected to the prophecy about the birth of a Davidic Ruler in Isaiah 9:6–7. The second prophecy says that the Ruler will be called *Mighty God*. This is clearly a title of deity.[14]

Matthew's citation of Isaiah 7:14 in reference to Jesus implies that he is the fulfillment of the entire complex of messianic prophecies in the early chapters of Isaiah (7:14; 9:1–7; 11:1–5). Thus, Jesus is the promised Messiah, the descendant of David who will rule over God's people with righteousness and justice. Yet his titles *God with us* and *Mighty God* convey that the child born of David's line will be fully God, deity incarnate, God in human flesh.

Jesus' Fulfillment of the Old Testament Demonstrates His Deity

One of the greatest indications of the high Christology of the Synoptic Gospels is the usage of Old Testament texts that describe Yahweh to describe Jesus. This feature of the Synoptic Gospels is especially prominent in Matthew. Matthew's gospel is written to demonstrate that Jesus is the fulfillment of the greatest promises of the Old Testament. His gospel is packed with quotations of and allusions to the Old Testament. Many of the texts to which he appeals are distinctly messianic. In a number of important texts, however, he presents Jesus as the fulfillment of Old Testament prophecies about or describing Yahweh.

Matthew 3:3 (cf. Mark 1:2) introduces the ministry of John the Baptist by saying, "For this is he who was spoken of by the prophet Isaiah when he said, 'The voice of one crying in the wil-

13. Hans Wildberger, *Isaiah 1–12: A Commentary*, Continental Commentary (Minneapolis: Fortress, 1991), 311–12; Gary V. Smith, *Isaiah*, New American Commentary (Nashville: B&H Academic, 2007–9), 1:213.
14. John Oswalt, *Isaiah*, New International Commentary on the Old Testament (Grand Rapids: Eerdmans, 1986), 1:246–47.

derness: "Prepare the way of the Lord; make his paths straight." ' " The text quoted by Matthew, Isaiah 40:3, is about preparation for the coming of Yahweh. The preparation of the road is a symbolic portrayal of the spiritual preparations that people must make for God's arrival. The purpose of God's coming is to reveal his glory to all flesh (Isa. 40:5). In Matthew's application of this text, John the Baptist assumes the role of the voice calling sinners to prepare. But Matthew 3:11 identifies Jesus with the words "he who is coming," the One for whose judgment the people must prepare. Thus, just as John the Baptist assumes the role of the voice in Isaiah 40:3, Jesus takes the place of the Lord whose way must be prepared and the God whose paths must be made straight.

Matthew employs a similar literary strategy by applying Isaiah 9:1–2 to Jesus in Matthew 4:16. Matthew argues that Jesus' residence in Capernaum fulfills important details of the Isaiah 9 prophecy, which climaxes with the promise of a child who will rule over David's kingdom and bear four exalted titles, including *Mighty God*, a title specifically reserved in the Old Testament for Yahweh.[15]

I argued earlier that Matthew's citation of Isaiah 7:14 in reference to Jesus implies that he is the fulfillment of the entire complex of messianic prophecies in the early chapters of Isaiah (7:14; 9:1–7; 11:1–5). Matthew's application of Isaiah 9 to Jesus in Matthew 4:12–16 confirms this view and demonstrates that Matthew regards Jesus as the embodiment of Mighty God. Matthew's application of this text to Jesus is particularly important. Although Matthew often utilizes Old Testament allusions to Yahweh in descriptions of Jesus, in this case he explicitly states that the prophecy of Isaiah describing a child who is "Mighty God" is fulfilled by Jesus.

In Matthew 11:10, another important Old Testament text is applied to John the Baptist. This time, however, Jesus himself interprets and applies the text. Jesus explains the significance of John the Baptist by quoting Malachi 3:1: "Behold, I send my

15. William Holladay, *Isaiah: Scroll of a Prophetic Heritage* (Grand Rapids: Eerdmans, 1978), 107.

messenger before your face, who will prepare your way before you." Although some of Matthew's wording is very similar to Exodus 23:20, it is clear that the Malachi text is predominant in his mind, since Matthew 11:14 identifies John as "Elijah who is to come," a clear allusion to Malachi 4:5: "Behold, I will send you Elijah the prophet before the great and awesome day of the LORD comes." Both the messenger of Malachi 3:1 and the Elijah of Malachi 4:5 prepare for the coming of Yahweh. The context of Jesus' discussion is very important. The discussion immediately follows John's questioning of Jesus to determine whether Jesus is the "one who is to come," which matches Malachi's description of the messenger of the covenant: "Behold, he is coming" (3:1). John's question—"Shall we look for another?" (Matt. 11:3)—may allude to the description of Yahweh as "the Lord whom you seek" (Mal. 3:1). Jesus confirms his identity as the Coming One by pointing to his miracles, which fulfill the conditions that the prophets said would accompany the dawn of the new era.

The pronouns "you" and "your" in Jesus' quotation interpret the prophecy as a prophecy about Jesus. Thus, Jesus is the Lord who is coming, just as John is the Elijah (the messenger) who is to come. As W. D. Davies and Dale Allison Jr. state bluntly, "So Jesus has replaced Yahweh: 'the way of God is the way of Christ.'"[16]

In Matthew 25:31, Jesus refers to the time when "the Son of Man comes in his glory" to "sit on his glorious throne." This statement conflates several important Old Testament texts. The reference to the Son of Man's coming in his glory is an allusion to the Son of Man vision in Daniel 7:13–14. The "glorious throne" appears to be a reference to the vision of the reign of the Ancient of Days in Daniel 7:9–10. In that vision, the Ancient of Days takes his seat on a throne of "fiery flames." This implies that the Son of Man is enthroned with the Ancient of Days and thus reigns as his equal. The clause "and all the angels with him" is potentially a reference to the "ten thousand times ten thousand" who stand before the throne in the Ancient of Days vision. But the wording

16. Davies and Allison, *Matthew*, 2:250.

is apparently derived from Zechariah 14:5, which describes the eschatological Day of the Lord: "Then the LORD my God will come, and all the holy ones with him."[17] This Day of the Lord results in the enthronement of Yahweh as King over all humanity, for "the LORD will be king over all the earth. On that day the LORD will be one and his name one" (v. 9). Matthew, following Jesus, has conflated descriptions of the reigns of the Son of Man and Yahweh in a manner that substitutes the Son of Man for Yahweh, thereby equating the Son of Man with Yahweh. Furthermore, the gathering of the nations in Matthew 25:32 seems to allude to Joel 3:2, where Yahweh's judgment of the nations accompanies his restoration of Judah: "I [Yahweh] will gather all the nations. . . . And I will enter into judgment with them." In the span of just two verses, three different Old Testament texts describing Yahweh have been applied to the Son of Man.

Matthew's frequent application of descriptions of Yahweh to Jesus implies a very high Christology. It is unlikely that someone like Matthew from a reverent Jewish background would apply these texts to Jesus unless he were convinced that Jesus, the Immanuel, truly embodies deity and thus manifests the presence of God.

Jesus' Deeds Demonstrate His Deity

The Cleansing of the Leper

Jesus heals a leper in Matthew 8:1–4. The leper's approach to Jesus prepares the reader for a revelation of Jesus' deity. The leper worships Jesus and addresses him by the divine title *Lord*. The leper also expresses his unflinching faith that Jesus bears

17. The Septuagint of Zechariah 14:5 reads "and all the holy ones with him." Matthew's text is identical except for substituting "angels" for "holy ones": "and all the angels with him." R. T. France observes, "In a passage so loaded with OT echoes it is also likely that the phrase 'all the angels with him' echoes not only the imagery of Daniel 7:10 but also the last clause of Zechariah 14:5, where very similar words depict the eschatological coming of God." R. T. France, *The Gospel of Matthew*, New International Commentary on the New Testament (Grand Rapids: Eerdmans, 2007), 960–61.

the power to cleanse him of his leprosy. Jesus cleanses the leper with a mere touch and a single command, "Be clean." The healing is immediate and so complete that the former leper can pass the inspection of the priests based on the guidelines in Leviticus 13–14 and be fully restored to the congregation of Israel.

Jesus not only possesses the personal power to cleanse people of leprosy, he is able to grant that power to others. Although all three Synoptic Gospels record Jesus' commissioning of the Twelve, Matthew is the only one to preserve the charge: "And proclaim as you go, saying, 'The kingdom of heaven is at hand.' Heal the sick, raise the dead, cleanse lepers, cast out demons" (Matt. 10:7).

Matthew 11:5 appeals to the fact that Jesus cleanses lepers to confirm his identity as the Coming One. Most of the features of Jesus' ministry described in 11:5 are mentioned explicitly in Old Testament prophecies. Isaiah 26:19; 29:18; 35:5; 42:18; and 61:1 foretell the blind receiving sight, the lame walking again, the deaf hearing, and the dead being raised. Isaiah 61:1 foretells the preaching of good news to the poor. The only element of Jesus' ministry not specifically mentioned in Old Testament prophecies is the cleansing of lepers.

Jesus' inclusion of the reference to cleansing lepers in his reply to John, even though the messianic prophecies make no reference to such a miracle, indicates that he sees this miracle as having special significance. R. T. France comments, "Jesus' ministry is seen to exceed its scriptural models by catering also to the reputedly incurable conditions of leprosy and death."[18] The promise of resurrection in Isaiah 26:19 likely explains its inclusion in Jesus' list. The Messianic Apocalypse of the Dead Sea Scrolls (4Q521) shows that the Qumran sectarians expected the Messiah to raise the dead. Nevertheless, no extant texts suggest that first-century Jews associated healing leprosy with the ministry of the Messiah. Thus, by cleansing the leper, Jesus does more than merely perform a messianic act.

18. France, *Matthew*, 424.

Readers familiar with Old Testament descriptions of leprosy would likely have been more astounded by the cleansing of lepers than any other healing miracle that Jesus performs. The cleansing of lepers is a conscious reenactment of the deeds of Yahweh in the Hebrew Scriptures. In the entire Old Testament, only three people are healed of leprosy: Moses in Exodus 4; Miriam in Numbers 12; and Naaman in 2 Kings 5. Moses' healing is clearly an act of Yahweh. God inflicts Moses' hand with leprosy and then heals him of that leprosy, offering to repeat the act as a sign to confirm to the Hebrews that he has indeed appeared to Moses. Miriam's leprosy is inflicted as punishment for rebelling against Moses' authority. Evidently her condition was severe. Moses compares the condition of her skin to that of a stillborn infant "whose flesh is half eaten away when he comes out of his mother's womb" (Num. 12:12). Miriam's healing is an act of God in response to Moses' prayer, "God, please heal her" (v. 13). Similarly, although the leper Naaman sought out Elisha to seek healing, he acknowledges that only Yahweh could perform the healing. In 2 Kings 5:11, Naaman expresses that he expects the prophet to "call upon the name of the LORD his God, and wave his hand over the place and cure the leper." Furthermore, when Naaman is healed after washing seven times in the Jordan, he exclaims, "Behold, I know that there is no God in all the earth but in Israel" (v. 15). In addition to the claim that God heals Naaman, details in the narrative clearly indicate that he alone is capable of healing Naaman. When the king of Syria sends Naaman to Israel to be healed of his leprosy, the king of Israel responds, "Am I God, to kill and to make alive, that this man sends word to me to cure a man of his leprosy?" (v. 7). This statement shows that one could just as easily raise the dead as heal a leper. God alone has the power to do either. Consequently, when Naaman is healed, he becomes a worshiper of Yahweh, exclaiming, "Your servant will not offer burnt offering or sacrifice to any god but the LORD" (vv. 15–17).

Matthew emphasizes the miracle of the leper's cleansing by adjusting the order of miracles in Mark 1:29–45 so as to place the story of the leper first in the sequence. In light of 2 Kings 5:7,

Jesus likely includes the reference to cleansing lepers in his list of proofs that he is the "one who is to come" (Matt. 11:3) in order to demonstrate that he will exceed the expectations his contemporaries had for the Messiah by performing miracles associated exclusively with the deeds of Yahweh. Matthew likely places the miracle first because, of all the healing miracles, it is the most powerful display of Jesus' authority as the Immanuel, God with us.

Interestingly, the primary source for the descriptions of Jesus' miracles in Matthew 11 appears to be Isaiah 35:4–6. Isaiah does not merely say that these miraculous acts of healing will accompany the Messiah's coming; he insists that they will accompany Yahweh's coming. These miracles signal the fulfillment of Isaiah's momentous announcement, "Behold, your God will come . . . . He will come and save you" (v. 4). Thus, Jesus' healing miracles and the claim that they fulfill Isaiah 35 imply Jesus' identity as Yahweh.

Psalm 103:3 describes Yahweh as the One "who forgives all your iniquity, who heals all your diseases." One may detect an echo of this text in Matthew's statement that Jesus went through all the villages "healing every disease" (Matt. 9:35). Leprosy was one disease generally recognized to be incurable by any medical means. Thus, Jesus' cleansing of the leper in 8:1–4 powerfully demonstrates the claim that 9:35 ultimately makes: Jesus really did heal every disease, even incurable ones. These acts demonstrate that Jesus is Yahweh who forgives and heals.

The Nature Miracles

Matthew explicitly describes Jesus' authority over the weather in Matthew 8:23–27, as Jesus stills the storm on the Sea of Galilee with a mere rebuke, producing an immediate calm. The disciples immediately recognize that the stilling of the storm has enormous implications for Jesus' identity, asking, "What sort of man is this, that even winds and sea obey him?" (v. 27). Sadly, modern interpreters so quickly spiritualize the miracle with talk of how Jesus calms the storms of life that many miss the true significance of the event. Jesus controls the weather! This amazing feat should prompt readers to react with the same marvel that characterized the observers of the miracle and to ask the same question that they asked: "What sort of man is this?"

Matthew's readers, familiar as they were with the Old Testament, would likely have recalled a number of texts. Psalm 89:8–9 says, "O LORD God of hosts, who is mighty as you are, O LORD, with your faithfulness all around you? You rule the raging of the sea; when its waves rise, you still them." "Who is mighty as you are?" implies that the stilling of the waves requires power that God alone possesses. Psalm 107:25–32 climaxes with the words, "He [Yahweh] made the storm be still, and the waves of the sea were hushed. Then they were glad that the waters were quiet, and he brought them to their desired haven." Similarly, Psalm 65:7 describes Yahweh as the One "who stills the roaring of the seas, the roaring of their waves."

As discussed earlier, the implications of the miracle for Jesus' identity are heightened by the plea expressed in Matthew 8:25, "Save us, Lord." This appeal recalls texts such as 2 Kings 19:19; Psalms 3:8; 6:4; 12:1; 20:9; 106:47; 109:26; 118:25; Isaiah 37:20; and Jeremiah 17:14. In fact, as we saw in the previous chapter, of the eleven combinations of the vocative "Lord" and the second-person imperative "save!" in the Septuagint, every instance except 2 Kings 6:26 is an appeal to Yahweh. This distinct appeal is unique to Matthew (cf. Matt. 8:25 with Mark 4:38/Luke 8:24) and likely part of the Matthean emphasis on the deity of Jesus.

Immediately following the feeding of the five thousand, Matthew 14:23–33 (Mark 6:45–52; John 6:16–21) records a similar nature miracle: Jesus' miraculous crossing of the sea. This is reminiscent of one of the great deeds of Yahweh associated with the exodus: the Hebrews' miraculous crossing of the Red Sea. These events signal that Jesus is none other than the One responsible for the miracle of the manna and none other than the One responsible for the crossing of the Red Sea. He is Yahweh.

Although the association of the miraculous crossing of the sea with Moses implies that the new Moses has arrived to lead a new exodus, the miracle exceeds expectations of the prophet like Moses. The Old Testament makes it clear that it was Yahweh, not Moses, who was responsible for the miraculous crossing of the sea (Ex. 14:29–31; 15:8–11; Ps. 78:12–13).[19] In light of this Old Testament background, Jesus' miraculous feeding and a miraculous crossing of the sea display the power of the God of the exodus and demonstrate Jesus' identity as God.

The fact that Jesus crosses the sea by walking upon it, rather than parting it and walking through it (Ex. 14:21–22; Josh. 3:14–17; 2 Kings 2:8, 14), suggests that despite the allusions to the miracles of the exodus, Jesus and Matthew have another group of texts in mind as the primary Old Testament background. Job 9:8 describes God as the One "who alone stretched out the heavens and trampled the waves of the sea." Similarly, Psalm 77:19 may imply that Old Testament saints believed that God walked ahead of Israel in crossing the Red Sea. Although the preceding context refers to Yahweh's control of the weather, the psalm says, "Your way was through the sea, your path through the great waters; yet your footprints were unseen," and then adds, "You led your people like a flock by the hand of Moses and Aaron" (v. 20). Isaiah 43:16 likewise describes Yahweh as the One "who makes a way in the sea, a path in the mighty waters."

In addition to walking on water, the narrative implies that Jesus exercises control over the wind (Matt. 14:32). This also closely associates Jesus with Yahweh, as the texts discussed related to the stilling of the storm show. Jesus' words "Take heart; it is I" (v. 27) may be translated "Take heart; I AM." Although the disciples might have originally regarded the words as a simple expression of identification, later and more careful reflection would likely have led them to conclude that the words were intended to recall the divine name. Matthew probably intends his readers to hear the statement "I AM" as an echo of Yahweh's revelation of the significance of the divine name in Exodus 3:14 (cf. Isa. 41:4; 43:10; 47:8, 10).[20] D. A. Carson notes:

19. See also Pss. 105:40; 106:7–12; 136:4, 13–15.
20. Davies and Allison, *Matthew*, 2:506. They point to the rabbinic tradition that clubs engraved with the divine name *I am that I am* would still waves high enough to capsize

169

Although the Greek *ego eimi* can have no more force than that [a calming exhortation], any Christian after the Resurrection and Ascension would also detect echoes of "I am," the decisive self-disclosure of God (Ex. 3:14; Isa. 43:10; 51:12). Once again we find Jesus revealing himself in a veiled way that will prove especially rich to Christians after his resurrection.[21]

The command "Do not be afraid" (Matt. 14:27) reinforces the nuance of divine self-disclosure, since the singular form of Jesus' command is the familiar way in which Yahweh addresses the patriarchs and the nation of Israel (Gen. 15:1; 26:24; 28:13 [Septuagint]; 46:3; Isa. 41:13). This is all the more likely in the context of Peter's cry, "Lord, save me" (Matt. 14:30), which, like the cry in 8:25, is reminiscent of cries to Yahweh in the Old Testament. The disciples' "worship" of Jesus, expressed by the confession "Truly you are the Son of God" (14:33) (both of which are unique to Matthew's account), also contributes to the deeper significance of the words "I am" and suggests that Matthew intends his readers to interpret the pericope as a revelation of Jesus' deity.

Eschatological Judgment and the Forgiveness of Sins

In numerous texts in the Gospels, Matthew insists that Jesus bears authority to judge and forgive sinners. In Matthew 3:11–12, John the Baptist affirms Jesus' authority to judge:

> I baptize you with water for repentance, but he who is coming after me is mightier than I, whose sandals I am not worthy to carry. He will baptize you with the Holy Spirit and fire. His winnowing fork is in his hand, and he will clear his threshing floor and gather his wheat into the barn, but the chaff he will burn with unquenchable fire.

---

a ship. They conclude, "By walking on and subduing the sea Jesus has manifested the numinous power of Yahweh." See also Donald A. Hagner, *Matthew*, Word Biblical Commentary (Dallas: Word, 1993–95), 2:423; Ulrich Luz, *Matthew*, Hermeneia (Minneapolis: Augsburg Fortress, 2001–7), 2:320; Turner, *Matthew*, 373.

21. D. A. Carson, "Matthew," in *Matthew, Mark, Luke*, Expositor's Bible Commentary (Grand Rapids: Zondervan, 1984), 344.

Later, in Matthew 11:1–6, Jesus clearly identifies himself as "the one who [was] to come" expected by John. Thus, Matthew's gospel demonstrates that Jesus is the One coming to separate his disciples (the wheat) from the wicked (the chaff) in eschatological judgment.

The two accounts examined above appear in both Matthew and Luke. Jesus' identity as eschatological Judge, however, literally saturates unique portions of Matthew. In the Sermon on the Mount (Matt. 7:21–23), people appeal to Jesus for their entrance into the kingdom. Jesus has the authority to turn sinners away. At the conclusion of the sermon, Jesus tells the parable of the wise man and the foolish man (vv. 24–27), in which he teaches that a sinner's verdict in eschatological judgment will be based on his response to Jesus' teaching.

The parable of the wheat and the weeds (Matt. 13:24–30, 37–43) states that "the Son of Man will send his angels, and they will gather out of his kingdom all causes of sin and all law-breakers, and throw them into the fiery furnace. In that place there will be weeping and gnashing of teeth" (vv. 41–42). In 16:27 Jesus says, "The Son of Man is going to come with his angels in the glory of his Father, and then he will repay each person according to what he has done." Later, in the description of the scene of final judgment (25:31–46), also unique to Matthew, Jesus describes himself as the Son of Man who sits on the throne of his glory and judges the nations. He will say to the righteous, "Come, you who are blessed by my Father, inherit the kingdom prepared for you from the foundation of the world" (v. 34). He will say to the wicked, "Depart from me, you cursed, into the eternal fire prepared for the devil and his angels" (v. 41).

Matthew's Jewish Christian readers were familiar enough with the Old Testament to discern the significance of Jesus' role as eschatological Judge. They were keenly aware that the Old Testament insists that God is the ultimate Judge of all human beings. The patriarch Abraham describes Yahweh as "the Judge of all the earth" (Gen. 18:25). The Psalms repeatedly affirm that Yahweh is the eschatological Judge (Pss. 7:8–11; 9:7–8; 50:3–6).

171

Jesus' identity as eschatological Judge in Matthew is closely related to his authority to forgive sins. In Matthew 9:2, Jesus says to the paralytic, "Take heart, my son; your sins are forgiven." Some of the scribes immediately respond, "This man is blaspheming" (v. 3). The scribes rightly recognize that in claiming to forgive sins, Jesus is claiming a divine prerogative. The scribes recognize that only a divine Judge could acquit sinners. Thus, Jesus' claim to bear the authority to forgive sins implies a claim to be the eschatological Judge, a claim to deity itself.

Matthew's claim that Jesus will preside over humanity's final judgment is paralleled by statements made in Paul's letters. The day of judgment is described in the Old Testament as the day of the Lord (*Yahweh*; Isa. 13:6, 9; Ezek. 13:5; 30:3; Joel 1:15; 2:1, 11, 31; 3:14; Amos 5:18, 20; Obad. 15; Zeph. 1:7, 14). Paul refers to that great day as the day of the Lord Jesus Christ (1 Cor. 1:8; 5:5; 2 Cor. 1:14; Phil. 1:6, 10; 2:16; 1 Thess. 5:2; 2 Thess. 2:1–2; 2 Tim. 1:18). Thus, Paul, like Matthew, not only affirms Jesus' role as eschatological Judge but also implies Jesus' identity as Yahweh.

Jesus' Words Demonstrate His Deity

On several occasions in Matthew's gospel, Jesus speaks in a manner in which one would expect only Yahweh to speak. Jesus' words imply that he is assuming the role of Yahweh. One example of this phenomenon appears in Jesus' lamentation over Jerusalem in Matthew 23:37–39.

Two elements of Jesus' statement contain echoes of descriptions of Yahweh in the Old Testament. First, Jesus expresses his longing to gather the Israelites in Jerusalem: "O Jerusalem, Jerusalem, the city that kills the prophets and stones those who are sent to it! How often would I have gathered your children together as a hen gathers her brood under her wings, and you would not!" (Matt. 23:37). The reference to the "gathering" of the people of Jerusalem recalls texts such as Psalm 106:47: "Save us, O LORD our God, and gather us from among the nations." This psalm remembers how Israel was handed over to her enemies because of her failure to keep the covenant. God, however, remembers his covenant with Israel, delivers her from her exile, and restores her. The psalmist prays for Yahweh to bring an end to Israel's exile once more and regather the scattered people in the Land of Promise. Psalm 147:2 expresses a similar plea: "The LORD builds up Jerusalem; he gathers the outcasts of Israel." This text is particularly important because Yahweh "gathers" the outcasts of Israel, and these outcasts parallel "Jerusalem." Jesus' words portray him as the One who gathers Jerusalem, while the Old Testament portrays Yahweh as the One who gathers Jerusalem.

Furthermore, the Old Testament portrays Yahweh as the One who shelters his people as a mother bird protects her young under her wings (Pss. 17:8–9; 91:4). More importantly, similar imagery is used to describe Yahweh's protection of Jerusalem specifically (Isa. 31:5). Gary Smith observes that this promise alludes to Deuteronomy 32:11, in which God is portrayed as an eagle flying over its nested young.[22] In light of this background, Jesus' portrayal of his desire to protect Jerusalem as a bird seeking to protect its young evokes reminiscence of the Old Testament descriptions of Yahweh's protection of Jerusalem.[23] Such descriptions are used only of Yahweh's loving care for his people. Thus, when Jesus speaks of protecting Jerusalem beneath his wings, "Jesus' statement . . . recalls the imagery of God's care and protection."[24]

The rabbis also reserved such imagery for Yahweh. The Babylonian Talmud frequently speaks of one's coming under the wings of the presence of God.[25] These factors prompted Apollinaris of Laodicea (d. A.D. 390) to write, "By speaking of wings and shelter

22. Smith, *Isaiah*, 1:533.
23. See also Ruth 2:12; Pss. 36:7; 57:1; 61:4; 63:7.
24. Craig A. Evans, *Matthew*, New Cambridge Bible Commentary (New York: Cambridge University Press, 2012), 398.
25. *b. Shabbat* 31a; *b. Sanhedrin* 96b (2×); *b. Avodah Zarah* 13b (2×); *b. Nedarim* 32a; *b. Ta'anit* 9a; *b. Yevamot* 46b, 48b; *b. Sotah* 13b; *b. Bava Metzi'a* 84a. See the references to other Jewish literature in Craig Keener, *A Commentary on the Gospel of Matthew* (Grand Rapids: Eerdmans, 1999), 558.

Jesus teaches in a way appropriate for God."[26] Consequently, in Matthew 23:37, Jesus speaks as only Yahweh speaks.

In Jesus' statement about the demise of the temple, his association with Yahweh becomes even more pronounced. "See, your house is left to you desolate" (Matt. 23:38) refers to the coming destruction of the temple. Although "house" could refer to the nation of Israel, which Matthew elsewhere designates the "house of Israel" (10:6; 15:24), 12:4 also uses the phrase "house of God" to describe the temple.[27] The close proximity of the warning about the desolation of the "house" to Jesus' clear prophecy of the destruction of the temple in 24:1–2 strongly suggests that the "house" is the Jerusalem temple.

The verb translated "left" (*aphiēmi*) in this context means "to move away," with "implication of causing a separation"—to leave or depart from.[28] When referring to impersonal objects, the verb commonly means "give up, abandon." Furthermore, the adjective *desolate* means "abandoned, deserted, uninhabited."[29] The abandonment does not refer to desertion by Israel through the people's neglect of temple rituals. Their continuing commitment to the temple is clearly expressed in the description of the temple as "your" house that is left "to you." Thus, the abandonment of the temple must refer to God's abandonment of his house. Jesus' words are reminiscent of Ezekiel 10 and 11, where the glory of the Lord leaves the temple, thereby presaging the coming destruction of the temple. By describing the temple as "your house" rather than as the "house of God" (Matt. 12:4), Jesus implies that the temple has been completely abandoned by God and that his glory no longer resides there. The temple is now just like any other hovel in Jerusalem, the house of men but not the house of God.

Matthew 23:39 introduces a shocking explanation for the divine abandonment of the temple. The verse begins with the

26. Manlio Simonetti, ed., *Matthew 14–28*, Ancient Christian Commentary on Scripture (Downers Grove, IL: InterVarsity Press, 2002), 184.

27. See also the description of the temple as "my house" in Matthew 21:13, which quotes Isaiah 56:7.

28. "ἀφίημι," in *Greek-English Lexicon*, 156.

29. "ἔρημος," in ibid., 391.

explanatory "For" to demonstrate that the words of verse 39 explain the cause or ground of the claim that God has departed from the temple. Readers would expect an explanation along the lines of: "For I tell you, you will not see God's glory again . . ." Instead, one reads, "For I tell you, you will not see *me* again, until you say, 'Blessed is he who comes in the name of the Lord.'" This clarifies that it is Jesus himself whose departure will signal the temple's desolation. Unless the people of Jerusalem repent of their rejection of Jesus and join the Galilean pilgrims mentioned in 21:9 in welcoming Jesus as the Messiah, Jesus warns, "You will not see me again."[30] France notes, "It is significant that he speaks of seeing 'me' (not God, whose house it was) again. As we have noted before, . . . for Matthew the presence of Jesus *is* the presence of God."[31] Davies and Allison likewise explain Matthew's use of the Old Testament description of the departure of the *shekinah* from the temple to portray Jesus' abandonment of the temple: "Perhaps the distinction is without a difference, for Matthew identified Jesus with the *shekinah*."[32] God's presence abandons the temple when Jesus turns his back on the temple and walks away from it.[33] Immanuel's abandonment of the temple constitutes Yahweh's abandonment of the temple.

Interestingly, Matthew 24:1 says that "Jesus left the temple," and verse 3 names the Mount of Olives, the mountainside just east of the Temple Mount, as his first destination after abandoning the temple. The most natural route from the temple to the Mount of Olives would have taken Jesus through the eastern gate of the temple, across the valley, and to the Mount of Olives. From the vantage point of the Mount of Olives, Jesus could point to the temple and warn of its coming destruction.

Jesus' movement may well be a conscious reenactment of the movement of the glory of God that abandoned the temple in

---

30. See France, *Matthew*, 884. France references his notes on Matthew 3:3, 11; 11:10, 14; 21:16, 44; see also ibid., 784–85.

31. Ibid., 884.

32. Davies and Allison, *Matthew*, 3:322–23.

33. "That God has abandoned his house means also that 'Immanuel' will no longer be seen." Luz, *Matthew*, 3:162.

Ezekiel 10–11. Ezekiel 10:19 shows that the glory of God exited the temple through the eastern gate. Ezekiel 11:23 adds, "And the glory of the LORD went up from the midst of the city and stood on the mountain that is on the east side of the city." That mountain is, of course, the Mount of Olives. Thus, in his lament over Jerusalem and accompanying actions, Jesus is speaking and acting as Yahweh speaks and acts.[34]

Conclusion

Matthew's gospel emphasizes the deity of Jesus in many remarkable ways. Jesus' supremacy, origin, and numerous exalted titles point to his identity as God. Matthew applies Old Testament texts about Yahweh to Jesus in a way that would seem blasphemous if Jesus were not divine. The gospel insists that Jesus performs the deeds associated with Yahweh in the Old Testament, in some cases performing deeds that the Old Testament claims only Yahweh could perform. Jesus also speaks the words of Yahweh. He talks as God talks. He makes statements that one would expect only God to make. These features of Matthew's gospel confirm Jesus' identity as Immanuel, God with us.

34. France, *Matthew*, 887.

The Theological Significance of the *New Creator* Theme

MATTHEW'S INSISTENCE on Jesus' identity as Yahweh, the Creator, is motivated in part by a very practical concern. Matthew recognizes that salvation involves a new genesis, a new creation, in which the catastrophic consequences of sin on God's creation are reversed and the world is restored according to God's desire. Because Jesus is Yahweh, the Creator, he is vested with the power of new creation. Because Jesus is divine, he is more than capable of making his people new here and now, ultimately restoring all creation to its original design.

The Gospel of Matthew Is a New Book of Genesis

The genealogy of Jesus implies his deity and, more specifically, his identity as the Author of the new creation in two powerful and profound ways. First, Matthew opens his gospel with the words "the book of the genealogy of Jesus Christ." The Greek word translated "genealogy" (*genesis*) literally means "origin." The only other occurrence of the word *genesis* in Matthew—and, for that matter, the entire New Testament—is Matthew 1:18, a text in which the term clearly means "origin." The phrase "the book of origin" was a common way of referring in Greek to Genesis, the first book of the Bible. Determining precisely when all the

Old Testament books received titles is difficult. Nevertheless, the first book of the Greek Scriptures clearly bore the name *Genesis* in Matthew's day. Philo of Alexandria (c. 20 B.C.–A.D. 50) refers to the book as *Genesis* three different times in his writings and even claims that Moses himself assigned this title to the book.[1] Early Jewish and Christian writers such as Justin, Origen, Eusebius, Melito of Sardis, and the second-century author of an anonymous Greek transcription of names of Old Testament books utilized this title as well.[2]

Christian Jews reading Matthew's Greek gospel would have immediately recognized an allusion to Genesis in the first phrase of the book. Thus, the opening words of Matthew's gospel are part of the same literary strategy that prompts John to begin his gospel with the phrase "In the beginning." This phrase clearly alludes to the initial phrase of Genesis 1:1, a phrase that serves as the title for Genesis in the Hebrew Bible.[3] Just as John begins his gospel with an allusion to the title of the Hebrew Scriptures' first book ("In the beginning"), so Matthew begins his gospel with a reference to that same book's title in the Greek Scriptures (*Genesis*).

Even a casual reading of Matthew's gospel shows that his presentation of Jesus' life and ministry constantly beckons readers to glance back at the Old Testament to understand his significance. This is obvious in Matthew's frequent claim that Jesus fulfills explicit quotations of the Old Testament. The Old Testament also appears to provide the key for a proper understanding of the phrase "the book of genesis" at the beginning of the gospel. This phrase appears only twice in the entire Old Testament, in Genesis 2:4 and 5:1. The first text states: "These are the generations [Septuagint: This is the book of the origin] of the heavens and the earth when they were created, in the day that the LORD God made the earth and the heavens." It is important to note that this

---

1. Philo, *Posterity*, 127; *Abraham* 1; *Eternity* 19.
2. See W. D. Davies and Dale Allison Jr., *The Gospel according to Matthew*, 3 vols., International Critical Commentary (Edinburgh: T & T Clark, 1988–1997), 1:151.
3. So also R. T. France, *The Gospel of Matthew*, New International Commentary on the New Testament (Grand Rapids: Eerdmans, 2007), 28.

use of the phrase clearly does not merely introduce a genealogical list, as it is often assumed that the phrase does in Matthew 1:1. Instead, the phrase serves as the title of what might be called a "creation account" of the origin of the heavens and earth. The second text (Gen. 5:1–2) states:

> This is the book of the generations [Septuagint: This is the book of the origin] of Adam. When God created man, he made him in the likeness of God. Male and female he created them, and he blessed them and named them Man when they were created.

The next verse begins a genealogy that lasts an entire chapter. But the phrase "book of origin" does not appear to serve primarily as the title of the genealogy but as the title of the account of the creation of humanity that precedes that genealogy. The normal introduction to genealogies in Genesis is the phrase "these are the generations" (6:9; 10:1; 11:10, 27; 25:12, 19; 36:1, 9; 37:2). If Matthew had intended to introduce merely the genealogy, one would have expected him to use the common introduction to genealogies. By using the introduction to "creation accounts," Matthew implies that he, too, is introducing a creation account.[4]

The use of the title of a creation account in Matthew 1:1 leaves the befuddled interpreter with a host of questions. Does the title refer to the content of the genealogy, the entire birth narrative, the beginning of Jesus' ministry, or the entire gospel? What kind of creation is Matthew describing? How does the phrase "of Jesus Christ" relate to the creation account? Is Matthew describing the origin of Jesus, his incarnation and entrance into the world? Or is Matthew describing a creation wrought by Jesus?

---

4. The most extensive argument for this interpretation is Davies and Allison, *Matthew*, 1:149–55. For other scholars who see Matthew 1:1 as an allusion to the creation accounts of Genesis, see F. W. Beare, *The Gospel according to Matthew* (Oxford: Blackwell, 1981); Donald A. Hagner, *Matthew*, Word Biblical Commentary (Dallas: Word, 1993–95), 1:9 (although Hagner argues that interpreters should not go so far as to see the reference to a new creation accomplished by Jesus); David Hill, *The Gospel of Matthew*, New Century Bible (London: Oliphants, 1972), 74–75; Leon Morris, *Matthew*, Pillar New Testament Commentary (Grand Rapids: Eerdmans, 1992), 18–19; Michael J. Wilkins, *Matthew*, NIV Application Commentary (Grand Rapids: Zondervan, 2004), 55.

These are difficult questions that cannot be fully explored here. The weight of evidence, however, favors viewing the title "the book of the genesis of Jesus Christ" as a title for the entire gospel. In New Testament vocabulary, the word *book* (*biblos*) consistently refers to a full-length book or scroll rather than to a small portion of a literary work, such as a genealogy or birth narrative.[5] When Matthew refers to a brief document, such as a certificate of divorce (Matt. 19:7), he prefers the diminutive form (*biblion*), which may be translated "little book" and indicates a "brief written message."[6] Several scholars have pointed out that "origin" in the first phrase of the gospel matches the reference to the "end of the age" in the final phrase of the gospel (28:20).[7] This, too, supports the view that the opening phrase serves as a title for the entire gospel. It suggests that Matthew wants readers to view his entire gospel as a new account of creation—a new creation wrought by the new Creator, Jesus Christ.

Jesus Bears the Power of New Creation

If the title of the gospel refers to a new creation wrought by Jesus, one would expect the theme of new creation not only to appear elsewhere in the gospel, but to be prominent enough to justify the description of the gospel as a book about a new genesis. The gospel does not disappoint this expectation.

John the Baptist prophesies about One who will come who is "mightier than I" (Matt. 3:11), the Messiah. This Coming One will demonstrate that he is more powerful than John by offering a more powerful baptism. Although John baptizes with water, the Messiah will baptize "with the Holy Spirit and fire."

5. Davies and Allison, *Matthew*, 1:151.

6. "βιβλίον," in *A Greek-English Lexicon of the New Testament and Other Early Christian Literature*, ed. Frederick W. Danker, 3rd ed. (Chicago: University of Chicago Press, 2000), 176.

7. W. L. Kynes, *A Christology of Solidarity: Jesus as the Representative of His People in Matthew* (Lanham, MD: University Press of America, 1991), 171; John Nolland, *Matthew*, New International Greek Testament Commentary (Grand Rapids: Eerdmans, 2005), 71.

The baptism with the Holy Spirit refers to the baptism received by those represented by the good trees that bear good fruit and the useful wheat winnowed by the Messiah and stored in his barn. The good fruit is obviously the "fruit in keeping with repentance" (Matt. 3:8), the good works that display the genuine repentance of the disciple. The context suggests that the baptism with the Holy Spirit refers to a transformation effected by the Holy Spirit to cause the Messiah's followers to produce fruit of righteousness.

The events accompanying Jesus' own baptism by John positively identify Jesus as the Messiah who baptizes with the Holy Spirit, confirming that this baptism will result in a new genesis, a new creation, of his disciples. Matthew explains: "And when Jesus was baptized, immediately he went up from the water, and behold, the heavens were opened to him, and he saw the Spirit of God descending like a dove and coming to rest on him" (Matt. 3:16). Interpreters have long puzzled over the description of the Spirit's descending "like a dove," and myriad explanations have been offered. The most plausible explanation for the association of the Spirit with a dove points to Genesis 1. Genesis 1:2 describes the activity of the Spirit in creation: "the Spirit of God was hovering over the face of the waters." The Hebrew verb translated "hovering" was the same verb used to describe a bird's flapping its wings in order to remain in a stationary position in the air.[8] Since this verb was commonly associated with birds, Jewish writers sometimes portrayed the Holy Spirit as a bird. Later rabbinic writings sometimes associated the Spirit with the eagle. But a number of early texts associated the activity of the Spirit in creation with the hovering of a dove over the young in its nest. Ben Zoma, a rabbi of the late first century, said that the activity of the Spirit in Genesis 1:2 was "like a dove that hovers over her young without actually touching them."[9] The rabbis do not explain why they associate the Spirit in Genesis 1 with the

8. See "רחף," in Ludwig Köehler and Walter Baumgartner, *Hebrew and Aramaic Lexicon of the Old Testament* (Leiden: Brill, 2002), 1219.
9. *b. Hagigah* 15a. See also *Targum of the Writings* 2.12.

dove rather than some other species of bird. The association was probably influenced by Genesis 8:6–11. After the destruction that accompanies Noah's flood, a dove brings Noah a sign that the earth is being renewed. Perhaps this association of the dove with the new creation that followed the flood led to an association of the dove with the original creation. What is clear is that the Jews of Matthew's time expected the Spirit to reenact the miracle of creation in the hearts of his people. A fragment of the Dead Sea Scrolls describes the Spirit as "hovering" over the repentant in an apparent allusion to Genesis 1:2.

These background data suggest that the association of the Spirit with the dove at Jesus' baptism is designed to remind observers (and readers) of the creation account. The original readers would not likely miss the similarities between the Spirit's hovering like a bird over the primordial waters of Genesis 1 and the Spirit's hovering like a dove over the waters of baptism. This allusion to the activity of the Spirit in creation serves to mark Jesus' ministry as the beginning of a new creation.

Many of the early church fathers recognized a connection between Genesis 1 and the baptisms of Jesus and his followers. Such fathers include Tertullian, Theodotus, Cyril of Jerusalem, and Didymus the Blind.[10] Many modern scholars also recognize the theological significance of the Old Testament allusion. W. D. Davies and Dale Allison Jr. write, "The events of Gen[esis] 1 were being recapitulated or repeated in Messiah's life; the eschatological creation had begun."[11]

Matthew appears to associate the Messiah's performance of the baptism of the Spirit with the descent of the Spirit like a dove. The Spirit's descent imparts to the Messiah the power to baptize with the Spirit. The baptism with the Spirit is equivalent to the act of new creation. The baptism of the Spirit is the fulfillment of the promise of the new covenant in Ezekiel 36:25–27.

10. Davies and Allison, *Matthew*, 1:334.
11. See ibid., 1:334–35; Hagner, *Matthew*, 1:58; William Lane, *Gospel of Mark*, New International Commentary on the New Testament (Grand Rapids: Eerdmans, 1974), 56–57; C. K. Barrett, *The Holy Spirit and the Gospel Tradition* (London: SPCK, 1947), 38–39.

Jesus Promises to Bring a New Creation

The theme of new creation becomes explicit in Jesus' teaching in Matthew 19:28: "Truly, I say to you, in the new world, when the Son of Man will sit on his glorious throne, you who have followed me will also sit on twelve thrones, judging the twelve tribes of Israel." The marginal notation in the ESV remarks that the Greek term translated "new world" means "regeneration." The Greek term prefixes the adverb meaning "again" (*palin*) to the noun meaning "beginning" (*genesia*, a cognate of *genesis*).[12] The Son of Man will be enthroned over a "new world," a new creation that results from a second genesis.

Matthew did not coin the term that refers to this "beginning again."[13] Jesus' contemporary Philo of Alexandria used the term to describe the resurrection of Abel and other individuals.[14] He also used the term to refer to the restoration of the world after Noah's flood.[15] Josephus used the term to describe the restoration of Israel after the exile[16] and used a related construction to describe resurrection.[17]

The concept behind the term translated "new world" was derived from the Old Testament. The Old Testament prophets describe the eschatological hope as a "new heavens and a new earth." Isaiah 65:17–25 describes the new heavens and new earth as a return to the state of creation before the fall. The prophet announces that the new creation will not be plagued by the curse of death (vv. 20–22), fruitless toil (vv. 22–23), agonizing childbirth (v. 23), broken fellowship with God (v. 24), or enmity with God's other creatures (v. 25). The theme of the reversal of the curse and the renewal of creation climaxes with the statement: "And dust shall be the serpent's food" (v. 25). God's judgment on the serpent will

12. The noun γενέσια is used in Matthew 14:6 to refer to a "birthday celebration" that commemorates a person's birth or "origin."

13. For the usage by the Stoics and in Jewish literature, see F. Büschel, "παλιγγενεσία," in *Theological Dictionary of the New Testament*, ed. Gerhard Kittel and Gerhard Köehler, trans. Geoffrey W. Bromiley, 10 vols. (Grand Rapids: Eerdmans, 1964–76), 1:686–89.

14. Philo, *Posterity*, 124; *Cherubim*, 114.

15. Philo, *Moses*, 2.65.

16. Josephus, *Jewish Antiquities*, 11.66.

17. Josephus, *Against Apion*, 2.218.

continue and be intensified. Rather than merely crawling in the dust, he will be forced to eat it, like other enemies of God debased by him (49:23; cf. Ps. 72:9). This final note ensures that the new heavens and earth will not be corrupted like God's first creation. The serpent will be powerless to deceive, corrupt, and destroy.

Based on these prophecies, first-century Judaism regarded the fulfillment of God's purpose as a period of renewal and new beginning.[18] The Dead Sea Scrolls teach that the two spirits of good and evil strive in the heart of man "until the determined end, and until the Renewal."[19] This "renewal" is equivalent to Matthew's "new world." The author of 4 Ezra describes the messianic kingdom and the end of the world as a new genesis:

> And the world shall be turned back to primeval silence for seven days, as it was at the first beginnings; so that no one shall be left. And after seven days the world, which is not yet awake, shall be roused, and that which is corruptible shall perish. And the earth shall give up those who are asleep in it.[20]

Early Christians understood this notion well. The author of the Epistle of Barnabas wrote, "Again, I will show you how the Lord speaks to us. He made a second creation in the last days. And the Lord says: 'Behold, I make the last things as the first.'"[21] In Acts 3:21, Peter refers to "the time for restoring all the things about which God spoke by the mouth of his holy prophets long ago." This reference confirms that the concept of the "restoration" or "renewal" of all things was derived from Old Testament prophecies.

Teaching prominent in Matthew regarding the new genesis wrought by Jesus is also articulated clearly by Paul (2 Cor. 5:17;

18. See the discussion in D. C. Sim, "The Meaning of παλιγγενεσία in Matthew 19.28," *Journal for the Study of the New Testament* 50 (1993): 3–12, esp. 5–7.

19. 1QS 4:25, trans. from Geza Vermes, *The Dead Sea Scrolls in English*, 3rd ed. (Sheffield, UK: JSOT Press, 1987), 67. France, *Matthew*, 743n14, translates the phrases "the appointed end and the new creation."

20. 4 Ezra 7:30–32, trans. from Bruce Metzger, "Fourth Book of Ezra," in *Old Testament Pseudepigrapha*, ed. James Charlesworth, 2 vols. (New Haven, CT: Yale University Press, 1983), 1:537–38.

21. *Barnabas* 6:11–13.

Gal. 6:15; Eph. 2:10). Paul frequently refers to the restoration of the divine image in believers, an extension and application of the *new creation* theme (Rom. 8:29; 1 Cor. 15:49; 2 Cor. 3:18; Col. 3:10).

Old Testament figures such as David long for the miracle of new creation. David's adultery with Bathsheba makes him very conscious of the wickedness of his own heart. He begs God to change him with the plea, "Create in me a clean heart, O God, and renew a right spirit within me" (Ps. 51:10). David's plea for renewal and transformation uses the very same verb employed in Genesis 1:1 to describe God's creation of the universe. David prays for a new genesis, an act of creation to make his heart what God desires. Through Jesus' baptism with the Spirit, his disciples are experiencing the answer to David's prayer.

Matthew makes it clear that sinners desperately need the miracle of new creation. His gospel insists that every sinner is depraved (Matt. 5:28; 12:34; 15:8; 19:8). The clearest and most extensive description of the sinner's spiritual condition in his book is in 15:18–20: "But what comes out of the mouth proceeds from the heart, and this defiles a person. For out of the heart come evil thoughts, murder, adultery, sexual immorality, theft, false witness, slander. These are what defile a person." Jesus reinforces this teaching by speaking later of the sinner's inner corruption (23:25–28).

Shockingly, Jesus' blessings on his disciples at the beginning of the Sermon on the Mount pronounce them to be "the pure in heart" (Matt. 5:8). The pure heart is the heart on which God has inscribed his law (Jer. 31:33), a heart of flesh that prompts God's people to follow his statutes and carefully observe his ordinances (Ezek. 11:19–20; 36:26–27). The pure heart is one newly created, a heart over which the Spirit hovers with creative power, a heart that has experienced a new genesis.

Conclusion: Worship Jesus

Good theology necessarily intersects with praxis. Biblical convictions prompt particular actions. The truths that the believer sincerely confesses must be expressed through daily living. Thus, the study of Matthew's description of Jesus as Immanuel, the incarnation of deity, the One who performs the miracle of new creation, inspires the reader of the gospel to ask, "How am I to respond to the doctrine of the deity of Jesus?"

Matthew reveals the proper response through a related theological theme: the worship of Jesus. Matthew, more than any other gospel, shows that Jesus is worthy of all worship and is the proper object of our most sincere adoration and praise.

Matthew introduces the theme of the worship of Jesus in the narrative of Jesus' birth and infancy. In fact, the greatest concentration of references to the worship of Jesus appears in the narrative about the infant Jesus in Matthew 2. When the magi from the east address Herod, inquiring about where they might find the infant Messiah, they query, "Where is he who has been born king of the Jews? For we saw his star when it rose and have come to worship him" (v. 2). When Herod later sends the magi to Bethlehem based on his inquiry of the chief priests and scribes, he attempts to deceive the magi by claiming that he also desires to "come and worship him" (v. 8). He obviously recognizes that the magi believe worship to be the only proper response to the infant Messiah, even from a king like himself. Verse 11 tells us that when the magi entered the house where the infant Jesus was, "they fell down and worshiped him." Although some commentators view this worship as merely the act of prostrating oneself in the presence of a king, Matthew's verb seems to imply more. The participle translated "they fell down" already indicates that the magi prostrated themselves before Jesus, and it is unlikely that the verb "worship" is a meaningless redundancy.[22]

Matthew likely intends his readers to interpret this reference to worship against the backdrop of Jesus' temptation experience in Matthew 4:9–10. There the devil attempts to entice Jesus to worship him by offering him all the kingdoms of the world and

22. Hagner, *Matthew*, 1:28. Hagner's view is taken up by Grant R. Osborne in *Matthew*, Zondervan Exegetical Commentary on the New Testament (Grand Rapids: Zondervan, 2010), 87.

their glory. Jesus refuses to worship Satan, quoting Deuteronomy 6:13, "You shall worship the Lord your God and him only shall you serve." Since Jesus teaches that worship must be reserved for God alone, the worship of Jesus by the magi reminds the thoughtful reader of Jesus' identity as Immanuel and demonstrates that others should follow the example of the magi by worshiping Jesus. David Garland writes, "The story will reveal that Jesus is not only worthy of reverence as a king but is due the same adoration that previously was reserved only for God."[23] In light of Jesus' words during the temptation, Matthew and his readers would likely have regarded the magi's act of veneration of Jesus as blasphemous if not for their conviction that Jesus is Immanuel, the incarnation of deity.

As this theme of the gospel unfolds, a leper (Matt. 8:2), a synagogue ruler (9:18), Jesus' disciples (14:33), a Canaanite woman (15:25), and the mother of James and John (20:20) worship Jesus. Although some commentators dispute the claim that these episodes are examples of religious worship, in each case clues from the context suggest that Matthew intends his readers to see the act as a prelude to their own worship of Jesus. His Jewish Christian readers would certainly be familiar with texts such as Deuteronomy 6:13. They would also be familiar with the interpretation of that text that guided conduct later in Jewish life, such as the refusal of the three Jewish youths to worship the king's golden image (Dan. 3:28) and Mordecai's refusal to pay homage to Haman (Est. 3:1–6). Their contemporaries conscientiously avoided using the verb *to worship* to describe homage paid to kings by Jews of that time and considered such homage a "barbaric custom" not in keeping with the Jewish conviction that there is one true God.[24] Thus, Matthew likely intends his readers to interpret this worship as proper religious worship rather than merely homage paid to a dignitary.[25]

23. David E. Garland, *Reading Matthew: A Literary and Theological Commentary* (Macon, GA: Smyth and Helwys, 2001), 27.
24. Josephus, *Jewish War*, 2.336, 350; Philo, *Embassy*, §§ 115–16.
25. Robert Gundry, *Matthew*, 2nd ed. (Grand Rapids: Eerdmans, 1994), 172.

After the resurrection of Jesus, one finds a concentration of references to the worship of Jesus that is rivaled only by the concentration of references in Matthew 2. After the women leave the empty tomb to tell the disciples of Jesus' resurrection, Jesus meets and greets them. Matthew 28:9 describes the reaction of the women: "And they came up and took hold of his feet and worshiped him." Clearly, the verb cannot refer merely to prostrating oneself before Jesus. The verbs of verse 9 are in chronological order. The women approach Jesus, then take hold of his feet, and then worship him. Kneeling or prostrating precedes taking hold of Jesus' feet and thus cannot be the sense of "worship." The resurrection is powerful confirmation of Jesus' identity as the Son of God (27:40, 43). The women recognize that as the resurrected Son of God, Jesus is worthy of worship in the highest sense of the term.[26]

The climax of the theme of worship of Jesus appears in Matthew 28:17. The eleven disciples go to Galilee to meet Jesus according to the instructions given in verses 7 and 10. Verse 17 states: "And when they saw him they worshiped him, but some doubted." Several features of the context confirm that "worshiped" refers to the worship of Jesus as deity. First, the juxtaposition of the term with "doubted" implies that "worshiped" is used in its religious sense. Second, Jesus claims to bear all authority both on earth and in heaven. Third, Jesus claims that he as Son shares the name (singular) of the Father and the Spirit. Finally, Jesus expresses his abiding presence with his disciples in a manner reminiscent of God's presence with his people in Old Testament promises.

The worship of Jesus as divine is not only a prominent theme of the Gospel of Matthew, but also a pervasive theme in New Testament theology as a whole. In Hebrews 1:6, God commands his angels to worship Jesus (cf. Deut. 32:43). Philippians 2:10–11 quotes the description of the worship of Yahweh in Isaiah 45:23 in order to describe eschatological worship of Jesus. Texts such as Revelation 5:12–13 draw phrases from the doxology of Yahweh in 1 Chronicles 29:11–12 to describe the worship of Jesus. The

---

26. D. A. Carson, "Matthew," in *Matthew, Mark, Luke*, Expositor's Bible Commentary (Grand Rapids: Zondervan, 1984), 589.

Christian hymns preserved in Philippians 2:6–11 and Colossians 1:15–20 show that the early church sang praises to Jesus as God. Even early pagan descriptions of Christian worship claimed that Christians gathered early in the morning on a particular day of the week in order to sing "hymns to Christ as to God."[27]

The deity of Jesus is a crucial element of Christian doctrine. Indeed, Matthew 28:19–20 implies that disciples confess Jesus' deity through the act of baptism. But the theme of the worship of Jesus in Matthew prevents the reader from viewing the deity of Jesus only as an article of belief to which the disciple merely gives mental assent. It precludes the reader from viewing the deity of Jesus merely as the element of a creed that one confesses in ritual. Instead, the deity of Jesus drives the disciple to his knees, bowing both head and heart before him to worship him in spirit and in truth. The disciple recognizes that to do anything other than to worship Jesus as God is at best sacrilege and at worst blasphemy. The disciple eagerly kneels beside magi, lepers, Canaanites, slaves, and other disciples and adores Jesus as the God before whom men and angels bow. The disciple joins in the angels' song:

> Christ, by highest heav'n adored,
> Christ, the everlasting Lord!
> Late in time behold him come,
> Offspring of the Virgin's womb.
> Veiled in flesh the Godhead see;
> Hail th'incarnate Deity,
> Pleased as man with men to dwell,
> Jesus, our Emmanuel.[28]

His identity as *God with us* demands nothing less.

---

27. Pliny, *Epistles*, 10.96.7. Pliny's letters date to approximately A.D. 111–15.

28. These words, originally written by Charles Wesley in 1739, were later adapted by George Whitefield, Martin Madan, and William Hayman Cummings. See Gordon Giles, *O Come Emmanuel: A Musical Tour of Daily Readings for Advent and Christmas* (Brewster, MA: Paraclete Press, 2006).

Conclusion

IN THE INTRODUCTION to this book, I expressed concern about the doctrinal anemia that plagues the contemporary church. You probably sensed that I am alarmed by the modern church's ignorance of basic Christian doctrines. When I read the statistics cited in the introduction, I do not just see numbers on a page. I see the faces of real people with real souls headed to a very real eternity. And I am haunted by those faces.

I see the faces of people like Doug. Doug was a state university student who happened to be sitting at a table in the library where I was conducting some research. I struck up a conversation with Doug, and soon he was pouring out his life's story. I discovered that he had been a Navy SEAL and had traveled across the world. During his travels he had experimented with several of the world's major religions. He had concluded that all religions were "basically the same."

I explained that despite some superficial similarities to other world religions, Christianity was profoundly different from other religions. He asked, "How?" I replied, "Moses claimed to be a prophet of God. Muhammad claimed to be a prophet of God. But Jesus did not just claim to be a prophet of God; he claimed to be the God of the prophets."

Doug, who claimed to be quite the religious expert, rolled his eyes and asked, "How did you come up with a ridiculous idea like that?" I explained that Jesus' identity as God was affirmed by the most important ecumenical creeds in the history of the Christian church. I insisted that Jesus' deity was clearly taught in the Bible, and I offered to show Doug a few of the relevant texts, if he was interested. Doug smugly replied, "Give it a try."

191

For the next half hour, Doug and I examined one text after another. Doug tried to explain away the first few texts that we examined. After looking at four or five texts, he fell silent. After looking at a dozen or so, he finally held up his hands in a gesture of surrender. "Okay, okay, it's there. The Bible really does teach that Jesus is God!" Then he scratched his head with a puzzled expression and added, "How could I, of all people, have missed that?"

"What do you mean, 'I, of all people'?" I asked.

Doug replied, "Believe it or not, I am the son of a Christian pastor. I listened to my dad preach every Sunday morning, Sunday night, and Wednesday night for the first eighteen years of my life. I considered myself an expert on Christianity. But I have never heard what you just showed me—that Jesus is God."

I wish I could say that Doug's experience is a rare one. Unfortunately, I constantly encounter people who have attended churches for their entire lives and yet are unaware of the most elementary teachings of the Christian faith. Do not misunderstand. I am not at all surprised that church folks cannot define the hypostatic union or explain the difference between supralapsarian and infralapsarian views. But I am stunned and saddened to encounter people who profess to be Christians and yet do not know essential truths such as Jesus' deity and bodily resurrection.

The modern church needs a good dose of the Gospel of Matthew. Matthew's gospel is a great cure for doctrinal anemia. This gospel presents the essential truths of the Christian faith in powerfully compelling and beautiful ways.

Matthew shows that Jesus is the new Moses, our Savior, Redeemer, and Deliverer. He has led a new spiritual exodus and initiated the new covenant. He is the Servant of the Lord who suffered the wrath of God against sin so that believers can be forgiven. We should respond to the new Moses by repenting of our sins and trusting him to deliver us from the punishment that our sins deserve and redeem us from the spiritual slavery that these sins imposed.

Jesus is the new David, our King. He is the fulfillment of God's covenant with David. He will rule over a kingdom composed of people from every nation, tribe, and tongue forever and ever. We must kneel before his throne as humble subjects, recognizing that he bears all authority and that he deserves and demands our fullest submission.

Jesus is the new Abraham, our Founder. He fulfills God's covenant with Abraham by creating a new chosen people composed of both Jews and Gentiles who will be holy as God is holy and who will serve as a light to the nations. The new Israel must proclaim the gospel boldly and compassionately to others.

Jesus is the new Creator, Immanuel, Yahweh in human flesh. He performs the miracle of new creation, transforming his people from the inside out, so that they become the people he desires. Those who experience the new creation never cease to be awed by his glory and greatness and offer him their sincerest adoration, worship, and praise.

Matthew, the scribe of the kingdom (Matt. 13:51–52), still has more treasures to unpack. No book or series of books could exhaust the riches of Matthew's treasures old and new. Yet we have been privileged to take a close look at some of the most stunning of these treasures.

As amazing as it is to see Matthew's awe-inspiring treasures on display, Matthew intends far more than this. Neither he nor I can be content with readers' merely gazing upon these treasures, mumbling an "ooh" or "ahh," and then walking away impressed but unchanged. Matthew intends to share his treasure, not merely to show it. He longs for his treasure to become ours. He knows that some treasures are so valuable, they are worth any sacrifice, like treasure hidden in a field or a pearl of great price (Matt. 13:44–46). And he is gripped by the truth that "where your treasure is, there your heart will be also" (6:21).

By God's grace, may each of us truly treasure Jesus, the new Moses, the new David, the new Abraham, the new Creator. May we offer him any sacrifice that he demands. May our hearts always be captivated by him. May we labor to ensure that the church never forgets who he really is. And may we proclaim his gospel to the ends of the earth. How could we do anything less?

Questions for Study and Reflection

Chapter 1: Introduction to the Gospel of Matthew

1. Why is it important for modern Christians to study biblical theology, and particularly the theology of Matthew?

2. Who wrote the Gospel of Matthew? What evidence supports this identification of the author? Why is this authorship significant?

3. When was the Gospel of Matthew written? Does this date fit with the claim that the gospel was written by an eyewitness of Jesus' ministry?

4. Where was the gospel probably written?

5. For what kind of reader did Matthew intend his gospel? How were these original readers different from modern readers? Does this explain why modern readers often miss much of Matthew's message?

6. What are the two major structures that have been proposed for Matthew's gospel? Can these two structures be combined?

7. What is the primary purpose of the Gospel of Matthew?

Chapter 2: Introduction to the Theological Study of Matthew

1. What are some helpful steps for discovering the theology of Matthew? Explain each step and give examples of what may be found through each step.

2. What is the key text in the Gospel of Matthew for understanding how Matthew envisioned his work as a gospel writer? How is Matthew like the Jewish scribes? How is Matthew different? What is Matthew's "old" treasure? What is his "new" treasure?

3. How did Matthew view the Old Testament? How did he view the relationship of the Old Testament to Jesus?

Chapter 3: Matthew's Development of the New Moses Theme

1. What Old Testament prophecy prompted God's people to expect the coming of a new Moses?

2. One ancient rabbi taught, "As the first redeemer was, so shall the latter Redeemer be." Who is the first redeemer? Who is the latter Redeemer? According to the rabbi, how would the two resemble each other?

3. What other New Testament figures saw Jesus as the new Moses?

4. How is the Old Testament description of Moses' birth and infancy similar to Matthew's description of Jesus' birth and infancy? Did later Jewish traditions about Moses' birth have more or less in common with Matthew's account of Jesus' birth? How?

5. What are some examples of Old Testament quotations related to Moses that Matthew applies directly to Jesus?

6. How is Matthew's description of Jesus' teaching similar to Old Testament descriptions of Moses' teaching?

7. How is Matthew's description of Jesus' fasting similar to Old Testament descriptions of Moses' fasting?

8. What are some of the miracles of Jesus that resemble miracles performed by Moses? What are the similarities?

9. What are some of the similarities between Jesus' transfiguration and the experience of Moses?

10. Is the recognition of similarities between Moses and Jesus of recent origin, or did ancient Christians notice these similarities also?

11. Is Matthew's gospel historical or fictional? In particular, did he invent the similarities between Jesus and Moses in order to make a theological point?

Chapter 4: The Theological Significance of the New Moses Theme

1. How did ancient Jews view Moses? Was he seen primarily as a lawgiver or as something else?

2. What is the new exodus? How is it similar to the exodus led by Moses? How is it different? Is Matthew the first biblical writer to speak of a new exodus?

3. What are the most important Old Testament references to the new covenant? What are the primary features of this covenant? How is it different from the old covenant?

4. What are some important references in Matthew to the new covenant? What other New Testament writers refer to this covenant?

5. How is Matthew's portrayal of Jesus as Isaiah's Servant of the Lord related to his portrayal of Jesus as the new Moses?

6. What are the hallmarks of the ministry of the Servant of the Lord?

7. How should readers of Matthew's gospel respond to the presentation of Jesus as the new Moses?

Chapter 5: Matthew's Development of the New David Theme

1. In what three ways does the genealogy of Jesus emphasize his relationship to King David?

2. Which of the four Gospels applies the title *Son of David* to Jesus most frequently? What is the significance of this?

3. What circumstances of Jesus' birth serve to associate him with David?

4. How does Jesus' identity as a Nazarene fit with a prominent theme of Old Testament messianic prophecy?

Chapter 6: The Theological Significance of the New David Theme

1. What is the most important Old Testament promise concerning the coming of a new David?

2. How does the Old Testament describe the Davidic Messiah?

3. Is the kingdom of heaven present and internal, future and external, or both?

4. What is the primary Old Testament background for Jesus' understanding of the kingdom of heaven? What does this background imply about the characteristics of the kingdom?

5. List some of the truths that Jesus taught about the kingdom through his parables.

6. How does Daniel's vision of the Son of Man help us to understand Jesus' role as messianic King? What are the three fundamental characteristics of Daniel's Son of Man?

7. How should readers respond to Matthew's portrayal of Jesus as the Davidic King?

Chapter 7: Matthew's Development of the New Abraham Theme

1. What evidence suggests that Jesus' title *Son of Abraham* serves a function similar to the title *Son of David*?

2. Why is it unlikely that the title *Son of Abraham* merely identifies Jesus as a true Jew?

3. How does the Gospel of Matthew teach that God has rejected all Israelites who have rejected Jesus?

4. How does Jesus' selection of the disciples demonstrate his intention to found a new Israel?

5. What is the Old Testament background for the term *church*?

6. What are some examples of how Matthew transfers promises given to Old Testament Israel to the New Testament church?

Chapter 8: The Theological Significance of the New Abraham Theme

1. How is the election of the new Israel similar to the election of the old Israel?

2. How does Matthew show that the new Israel will consist of both Jews and Gentiles?

3. What important aspects of the mission of Old Testament Israel must be fulfilled by the new Israel?

4. What are some ways in which Matthew emphasizes the holiness of the new Israel?

5. What are some ways in which he demonstrates the importance of propagating the gospel?

6. List several practical implications of Jesus' role as the new Abraham.

Chapter 9: Matthew's Development of the New Creator Theme: The Titles of Jesus

1. What Old Testament evidence suggests that the Son of Man is a divine figure?

2. How did the translators of the Septuagint, the author of the Similitudes of Enoch, and Rabbi Aqiba view the Son of Man?

3. What is the significance of Jesus' description of himself as personified Wisdom?

4. What evidence suggests that Matthew uses *Lord* as a title of deity when referring to Jesus?

5. Does the title *Son of God* merely describe Jesus as the Messiah or also express Jesus' deity? Explain.

6. Why do many scholars believe that the title *Immanuel* is key to Matthew's view of Jesus even though the title appears only once in his gospel?

Chapter 10: Matthew's Development of the New Creator Theme: Other Descriptions of Jesus

1. What is the significance of Jesus' claim that he is greater than the temple?

2. How does Jesus' conception by a virgin imply his deity?

3. What are some examples of *Yahweh* texts that Matthew applies to Jesus?

4. How do specific miracles such as the cleansing of the leper, the stilling of the storm, and walking on the water demonstrate Jesus' deity?

5. On several occasions in Matthew, Jesus speaks as one would expect only God to speak. Give examples.

Chapter 11: The Theological Significance of the New Creator Theme

1. Why does the title of this chapter refer to Jesus specifically as the new Creator rather than simply as God?

2. How does Matthew show that Jesus, as God, came to perform the miracle of new creation?

3. What is the theological significance of the form in which the Holy Spirit appeared at Jesus' baptism?

4. What references to "new creation" appear in the New Testament outside of Matthew's gospel? How does Paul's teaching on new creation fit with Jesus' teaching and Matthew's theology? Who likely inspired Paul's doctrine of new creation?

5. What should be the reader's practical response to Jesus' identity as God?

Select Resources on
Matthew's Theology

Allison, Dale C., Jr. *The New Moses: A Matthean Typology*. Minneapolis: Fortress, 1993.

———. *Studies in Matthew: Interpretation Past and Present*. Grand Rapids: Baker, 2005.

Aune, David. *The Gospel of Matthew in Current Study*. Grand Rapids: Eerdmans, 2001.

Beaton, Richard. *Isaiah's Christ in Matthew's Gospel*. Society for New Testament Studies Monograph Series 123. Cambridge: Cambridge University Press, 2002.

Blomberg, Craig. *Matthew*. New American Commentary. Nashville: Broadman, 1992.

Broadus, John A. *Commentary on the Gospel of Matthew*. American Commentary on the New Testament. Philadelphia: American Baptist Publication Society, 1886.

Bruner, Frederick Dale. *The Christbook: Matthew 1–12*. Rev. ed. Grand Rapids: Eerdmans, 2007.

———. *The Churchbook: Matthew 13–28*. Rev. ed. Grand Rapids: Eerdmans, 2007.

Carson, D. A. *God with Us: Themes from Matthew*. Eugene, OR: Wipf & Stock, 1995.

Carter, Warren. *Matthew: Storyteller, Interpreter, Evangelist*. 2nd ed. Peabody, MA: Hendrickson, 2004.

Davies, W. D., and Dale Allison Jr. *Matthew*. 3 vols. International Critical Commentary. Edinburgh: T & T Clark, 1988–1997.

Evans, Craig A. *Matthew*. New Cambridge Bible Commentary. New York: Cambridge University Press, 2012.

France, R. T. *The Gospel of Matthew*. New International Commentary on the New Testament. Grand Rapids: Eerdmans, 2007.

———. *Jesus and the Old Testament: His Application of Old Testament Passages to Himself and His Mission*. Vancouver: Regent College Publishing, 1998.

———. *Matthew: Evangelist and Teacher*. New Testament Profiles. Downers Grove, IL: InterVarsity Press, 1989.

Garland, David E. *Reading Matthew: A Literary and Theological Commentary*. Macon, GA: Smyth and Helwys, 2001.

Gibbs, Jeffrey A. *Matthew 1:1–11:1*. Concordia Commentary. St. Louis: Concordia, 2006.

Hagner, Donald A. *Matthew*. 2 vols. Word Biblical Commentary. Dallas: Word, 1993–95.

Hill, David. *The Gospel of Matthew*. New Century Bible. London: Oliphants, 1972.

Keener, Craig. *A Commentary on the Gospel of Matthew*. Grand Rapids: Eerdmans, 1999.

Kingsbury, Jack D. *Matthew as Story*. 2nd ed. Philadelphia: Fortress, 1988.

———. *Matthew: Structure, Christology, Kingdom*. Philadelphia: Fortress, 1975.

Kupp, David D. *Matthew's Emmanuel: Divine Presence and God's People in the First Gospel*. Society for New Testament Studies Monograph Series 90. Cambridge: Cambridge University Press, 1996.

Luz, Ulrich. *Matthew*. 3 vols. Hermeneia. Minneapolis: Augsburg Fortress, 2001–7.

———. *The Theology of the Gospel of Matthew*. New Testament Theology. Cambridge: Cambridge University Press, 1995.

Meier, John P. *The Vision of Matthew: Christ, Church, and Morality in the First Gospel*. Eugene, OR: Wipf & Stock, 1991.

Morris, Leon. *Matthew*. Pillar New Testament Commentary. Grand Rapids: Eerdmans, 1992.

Orton, David E. *The Understanding Scribe: Matthew and the Apocalyptic Ideal*. Sheffield, UK: JSOT Press, 1989.

Osborne, Grant R. *Matthew*. Zondervan Exegetical Commentary on the New Testament. Grand Rapids: Zondervan, 2010.

Powell, Mark Alan. *God with Us: A Pastoral Theology of Matthew's Gospel.* Minneapolis: Fortress, 1995.

Quarles, Charles L. *Sermon on the Mount: Restoring Christ's Message to the Modern Church.* NAC Studies in Bible and Theology. Nashville: B&H Academic, 2011.

Simonetti, Manlio, ed. *Matthew.* 2 vols. Ancient Christian Commentary on Scripture. Downers Grove, IL: InterVarsity Press, 2001–2.

Stanton, Graham N. *A Gospel for a New People: Studies in Matthew.* Edinburgh: T & T Clark, 1992.

Turner, David L. *Matthew.* Baker Exegetical Commentary on the New Testament. Grand Rapids: Baker, 2008.

Wilkins, Michael J. *Matthew.* NIV Application Commentary. Grand Rapids: Zondervan, 2004.

Index of Scripture

209

211

212

Index of Subjects and Names

scribe, 25–27, 30, 36, 193
Septuagint, 37, 41, 44, 50, 63–65,
        92, 108, 136–37, 142–44, 159,
        164, 168, 170, 178–79, 200
Shepherd, Michael B., 80
Sim, D. C., 184
Simonetti, Manlio, 174, 205
Smith, Billy K., 114
Smith, Gary V., 152, 161, 173
Son of Man, 17, 23, 87–94, 109,
        117–18, 134–38, 141, 145,
        163, 171, 183, 198–200
Stalker, D. G. M., 61
Streeter, B. H., 10
Suffering Servant, 16,
        60–64, 192, 197

Talmud, 14–15, 23, 38, 43, 62,
        80, 113, 117, 121–22, 135,
        137, 173, 178, 181
Targum, 61, 80, 120–21, 181

Tasker, R. V. G., 117
the Twelve, 8, 107–9, 183
Turner, David L., 74, 77,
        101–2, 156, 170, 205

Vermes, Geza, 184
vertical reading, 23
von Rad, Gerhard, 61

Wallace, Daniel, 38, 75, 116, 158
Wesley, Charles, 189
Wildberger, Hans, 152, 161
Wilkins, Michael J., 30, 74, 179, 205
wisdom, ii, xiii, 17, 22, 123,
        133, 138–41, 200
Witherington, Ben, 160
worship, xi, xiii, 2, 23, 35, 92,
        122, 128, 135, 138, 149,
        170, 185–89, 193

Zehnle, R. F., 62